MEMORIES

A COLLECTION OF AUTOBIOGRAPHICAL SHORT STORIES

Ruth VanDyke

LeRue Books
Reno, Nevada

Copyright ©2023 by Ruth VanDyke

All rights reserved.

No part of this book may be reproduced in any form or by any electronic or mechanical means, including information storage and retrieval systems, without permission in writing from the publisher, except by reviewers, who may quote brief passages in a review.

ISBN: 978-1-938814-41-9

Library of Congress Number: 2023912047

Photos from the author's collection.

Cover design by LeRue Press with images provided by author.

Printed in the United States

For information, or additional copies, contact: LeRue Press, 280 Greg Street, Suite 10, Reno, NV 89502. www.LrpNv.com

DEDICATION
To Larry

So many years have come and gone.
We've stuck together through right and wrong.

We've laughed and cried, we've loved and lied,
A bond so strong can't be denied.

And now the years go quickly past,
We have to make the good times last.

We'll see the world, enjoy the days,
Fill our lives with joy and praise.

So much to see, so much to do…
I'm thankful to spend my life with you.

ACKNOWLEDGEMENT

Special thanks and credit to my dedicated editor Sheriann Lee. Without her help and constant encouragement these stories would have never been shared. Sheri is my niece and was born on my birthday. She has been my diligent sidekick and devoted confidant for sixty-five years.

TABLE OF CONTENTS

Backyard Memories 1
Elementary School 5
The Lake 11
My Hero 15
Snow 19
A Letter to Myself At Twelve Years of Age 21
Grandpa Keane 27
A Girl's Best Friend 31
A Very Special Thanksgiving 37
My First Born 39
Sixteen Hundred Miles 43
Serendipity 47
Strangler in the Night..51
My First Car 55
Three Strikes You're Out 59
Discrimination 63
#MeToo 65
Never Look Back 69
An Unforgettable Thanksgiving 75
The Longest Part-Time Job 79
Not On My Watch! 83
Worst Date Ever 85
A Miraculous Transformation..89
Halloween Memories 93
Mother Nature's Wrath 97
The Best Compliment Ever 99
Craters of the Moon 105
The Unspoken Power of Music 109
And Then Along Came King 113
Making a Difference 119
Sam the Man 123
A Tribute to St. Jude's Children's Hospital 125
Trip of a Lifetime 129
The "Marbleous" Years 133

A Christmas Angel	137
My Way With Words	139
Mary Frances	143
My Last Wedding	147
The Pie (A Funny Food Folly)	151
My Favorite Entertainer	155
The Gift	159
Terrifying Turbulence	163
Never Too Old To Learn a New Sport	167
Return of the State Patrol	171
Donna Marie	175
My Overactive Olfactory Nerve	181
A Forever Home	185
The Mother Road	189
Ethical Will to Donald George	195
Ship's Quips	197
My Best Friend	201
Jeremiah Joseph	205
A Favorite Place	209
Returning to New Orleans	215
Teaching Moments	219
Bathtub Tales	223
Flowers	225
The Changing Times	227
The Inevitability of Change	231
Pandemic 2020	233
Atomic Strong	251
My Happy Place	253
Pet Peeves	257
April Fools' Day	261
2020 Revisited	265
Obituary	269

MEMORIES

A COLLECTION OF
AUTOBIOGRAPHICAL SHORT STORIES

BACK YARD MEMORIES

    I have to think of my 'back yard' as the whole area of the city where I grew up. Thumbing through an 1864 to 1974 commemorative book of Butte, Montana, and the 1975 "Butte's Memory Book," I was catapulted back to the 1940s.

    On the east side of town, from the earliest settlement days, there was an area known as the 'cabbage patch.' As a child I could only imagine the reason being because the early pioneers grew cabbage there. Pictures from the 1800s show little wooden shacks with weary looking, bedraggled women sitting on the rickety porches. My back yard! I have a dear friend from Butte who still calls me "the original Cabbage Patch Kid."

    Sometime in the late 1930s the city cleared out the cabbage patch to build a low-income housing project. I was two years old when we moved into 704 Silver Bow Homes. The units were built in two sections, each section having nine rows, and each row containing ten apartments. They were two story units and quite modern for that time. Between the two sections of buildings there was a playground which in those days would have been any child's dream. There were monkey bars, or 'the climbing castle' as we called it, a long row of teeter-totters and two sets of swings. Each apartment had a small fenced yard, but I don't remember

Jerry, Me and Sis

any of them having a lawn or a garden. From the time I was about eight years old my mother and I would plant sweet-peas in the spring and tie them up on the wrought-iron railings which surrounded the back porch. I can't recall ever playing in that yard. Why would we with such a well-equipped playground at our disposal? Kids of all ages played all day, every day on that playground. When the street lights came on at dusk it was our signal that it was time to go home.

My earliest memory of the playground is of a frigid winter morning when I was only four or five years old. My brother (who was eight years older than me) told me to put my tongue on the steel bar of the teeter-totter. What a cruel thing to do. The older kids all laughed as I ran home screaming in fear that I had left part of my tongue behind. In spite of that cruel trick my brother did watch out for me. He carried me home bleeding when I fell from the very top of the monkey bars and split my lip open. He also rescued me after I was clipped by the milk truck while crossing Arizona Avenue, the main street on the west side of the housing project, which was supposed to be off limits to us kids. Six months after that incident, a German Shepard dog jumped out of a car window and bit me on the butt as I was running down that same street. My brother appeared out of nowhere, again to rescue me from where I was not supposed to be. He had told me at some time before that day that a female dog was a bitch. He was shocked, but amused to hear me cry, "That bastard" as the dog's owner pulled him off of me. I guess I had gotten my 'B' words confused.

On the east side of the housing project there was an area where the residents could parallel park their cars. In the 1940s not too many people, especially those in our economic class, owned an automobile. There may have been a dozen cars that parked there regularly. To this day I can't imagine why my little friend, Dorothy, and I would do such a thing, but we methodically went from car to car removing the caps off of all the tire valves and we threw them down the street drain. I really believe that the older kids must have put us up to it. That was the first time I ever remember being in trouble. I was punished by having to stay in the back yard and not being allowed to play with "Doffy" for a few days. She stood on the outside of the fence and cried, "I'm so soowy, Boofie." I told my mother that Doffy didn't talk very well, she called me "Boofie."

We lived in Silver Bow Homes until I was thirteen years of age and as I reminisce about my younger days I can almost smell the sweet-peas and hear the calls of "olly, olly, oxen free," echoing from the playground on a cool fall evening. Fond memories of what I remember as my back yard.

Elementary School

"But I don't want to play on the girls' playground. I want to shoot marbles with the boys!"

Growing up in Butte, Montana, known as "The Richest Hill on Earth," in the 1940s and 50s was in itself an adventure. Of course I didn't realize or appreciate that fact in my younger years. It never crossed my mind that someday my claim to fame would be growing up with my mischievous, rebellious cousin Bobby, who was later known as Evel Knievel. My uncle Gene (my mother's youngest brother) was married to his mother, Ann.

I wasn't able to start school at the age of six because I had rheumatic fever and was bedridden. So, my elementary schooling began with what they called in those days a 'bed-side' teacher. It seems that I was already a step ahead of her, having learned all of the basics from my three older siblings. Our age difference (they were seven to eleven years older) made being the baby a real advantage. One of my earliest recollections is hearing my mother warn them, "Don't talk to the baby 'til she's had her coffee." A dainty flowered china tea cup and saucer with one sugar cube and a half a cup of evaporated milk was the order of the day. That warning still holds true today. "No talkie before coffee," minus the sugar and milk. I have graduated to heavy cream!

The day came when I finally had to attend real school. I was not at all happy about it. I was anxious and fearful. The school was an old dilapidated building which was built in the late 1800s. It smelled of mold and stale urine. A narrow winding stairway led to the musky basement where the stinky bathrooms and the auditorium were located. I had myself, and by third grade all of the other kids, convinced that the basement was haunted. I spent eight long years trying to avoid it.

My first day of school, entering the gloomy classroom full of strange, scary little people in the middle of the school year, had to be the worst nightmare of any child's life. My heart pounded even a little harder when Father Taylor – The Reverend Edmond Taylor – stormed into the classroom to meet the new girl. He was a gargantuan, ruddy faced Irishman whose voice was so forceful that I knew it would scare off the devil himself. My knees were trembling and my palms were clammy as I tried to squeak out, "Good morning, Father." His brogue was so heavy that I wasn't quite sure what he was saying to me, which made me even more nervous. Father Taylor left my first grade classroom that day with all of the children standing and hailing him with, "Good day, Father." All but one very frightened, shaking little redhead in the front row.

When I later told my mother about this scary encounter she laughed and dug out her 1923 eighth grade graduation picture to show me. There in the front row was a young, handsome Irish priest, Father Taylor. She assured me that his English was now much improved from the day that she met him. She was in the fourth grade – a shy, quiet girl. Father Taylor would go to each of the classrooms to question the students on their catechism lessons. Mother either didn't know the answer or could not quite understand what he was saying, so she just stood there looking at him quizzically. The catechism books were heavy, leather bound text books. He hastily raised the book and came down sharply on the back of her head, causing her to stumble into her desk. Obviously no one had warned Father Taylor about my mother's feisty, four-foot-eleven

Sacred Heart 1923

-inch, redheaded mother. Grandma's visit to the rectory that day was the object of gossip throughout the parish for many years to come. Father Taylor would cross the street to avoid facing her from that day forward.

Another memorable encounter for my mother with Father Taylor was for her prenuptial counseling. He asked her if she believed in 'de voice.' "Oh, yes Father," she replied. He haughtily repeated the question, and smiling, she again shook her head positively and said, "Yes, I believe in the voice." Exasperated he huffed out of the room leaving her perplexed as to why he would be so upset. Of course he couldn't counsel a young Catholic bride who believed in divorce.

When it came time for recess on that daunting first day, I was surprised to find out that the boys' playground was on one side of the school yard and the girls' playground on the other side. I was happy that I had brought my marbles with me. Most of the boys had nice leather marble bags but some of them had cloth ones made from flour sacks. I had just an old, darned sock. I was so proud of my aggies and colorful corkscrews and most of all my shiny blue and yellow cats-eye shooter. I secretly hoped that these fellows played for 'keeps.' "What do you mean Sister, that I have to play on the girls' playground? What do girls play? I can play hop-scotch and jacks at home alone any day." There is a Norman Rockwell painting of a young girl with red pig-tails in a cotton frock and dull brown oxfords shooting marbles with the boys. My mother insisted that Rockwell must have used me as a model for that picture.

I thought that Father Taylor's eyes were scary until I saw this person (I wasn't really even sure of her gender at that point) glaring down at me, resolved to send me to play with the girls. Questioning her gender didn't seem unusual to me. My tiny, spirited Welsh grandmother had a gentleman friend she fondly called her 'boarder,' who lived with her. We children adored him. My older sisters and brother called him "Grandpa Daley" until I learned to talk and translated it to 'Tappa Daley.' From then on he was Tappa Daley to everyone. One of my earliest memories is of him teaching me to tie my shoes. He would tell me stories about when he was a little girl and he had me convinced that I was going to grow up to be a strong young man. Thus, the gender confusion. My mother assured me at four or five years of age that I was, and always would be a girl. It was about that same time that I came to realize that Tappa Daley was more than Grandma's boarder since they shared the same bedroom. I was nine years old when Tappa Daley passed away and I felt guilty telling Sister Mary Theresa that I had to miss school to attend my *grandpa's* funeral. It's difficult to lie to a nun, but it seemed easier than trying to explain to her who Tappa Daley really was.

By the time I reached the sixth grade the nuns had given up

Sacred Heart 1954

trying to keep me off of the boys' playground. I could at that time out-run the whole track team, even the eighth graders, probably the total number of six runners. Tappa Daley would have been so proud of me! The nuns did at this time however, forbid me to play football when they realized that I was being tackled more often than necessary.

In my eighth grade graduation picture, as in my mother's, there he is 'The Man,' Father Taylor, who during my most impressionable years taught me not only the importance of education, but how to savor every amusing, laughable, priceless moment of our lives, and never, ever to give into anything contrary to our beliefs. He embedded in me the fear of God and the love of mankind.

Leaving grammar school, I resigned myself to the fact that I would never be able to be the quarterback on the football team. I decided that I might as well settle for cheerleader or homecoming queen. But I never gave up my love of marbles. I shot with the big boys in a marble tournament in Las Vegas in 1997.

THE LAKE

Summer, 1946. The anticipation of a summer vacation at Meadow Lake was almost more than I could contain at six years of age. An old rented cabin secluded from the city, fishing, swimming, boating and most exciting of all, our cousin Bobby coming from California to join us as he had done every summer for the past few years.

My brother Jerry and Bobby were close in age. Jerry was twelve and Bobby fourteen that summer. Bobby's mother, Ruth, had died when Bobby was just nine years old, shortly after his sister Margaret Ann was born. Their father Bob relocated with the children to California after Ruth's death and eventually remarried. We were all aware that Bobby was our Grandpa Keane's favorite grandchild, probably due to the fact that he had lost his mother, Grandpa's only daughter.

My recollections of Bobby are filled with joy and laughter. He was always smiling, and would swoop me off my feet singing to me and my sister, Mary Frances, who was his age, "I'm a Big Girl Now." To this day I remember every word of that song. He and my brother were the best of buddies and we all loved the stories that he told about life in California.

Bobby had been diagnosed with Aortic Dissection (the disease that took actor John Ritter's life). He was cautioned not to exert himself and told to take it easy swimming. The boys loved to take the little aluminum row boat out on the lake to fish and they were very familiar with the lake. The previous summer Bobby had rowed all the way across the lake and back to take Jerry to the hospital in Ennis to get a fish hook removed from his head.

On a pleasant, sunshiny Saturday, the day before we were scheduled to head home, the boys set out for their last adventure on the lake. The water was calm, crystal clear and a beautiful azure blue. A few hours had passed and the sky began to cloud. It looked like a storm was brewing. "I hope those boys get back before it starts to rain," my mom said in a worried tone. My dad assured her that they were responsible, knew the lake well and would be fine. The clouds came in swiftly and shadowed the sun. The lightening illuminated the sky and the thunder shook the shore. The lake resembled an angry ocean.

Jerry accounted later that as the wind picked up speed the water got rougher and rougher. Trying to turn back to get to shore Bobby dropped one of the oars. There was a man in a motor boat near them and they called to him to please retrieve their oar. He heard them and could easily have reached the oar but he took off, heading the other way. They were about a mile and a half from the lodge and Bobby just kept rowing with one arm. Jerry said that if they could have gotten the boat turned around there was a possibility that they could have ridden out the storm. As the winds got higher Bobby told Jerry, "Strip down so we can swim if we have to."

About a quarter of a mile from the shore a huge wave swept over the boat and washed them out of it. Bobby started swimming, telling Jerry to hang on to the boat, that he would go for help. Jerry recounted that the last time he saw Bobby his left arm was over his head in a stroking position. He knew that Bobby could swim as far as the shoreline, and seeing the boat still afloat he swam to it and held on. After what seemed to him like hours he was able to pull himself back into the boat. He sat in the middle of the boat seat which was capable of holding four people. Later one of the rescuers who was searching for them said that through his binoculars he thought that he sighted three cans floating across the lake. What he actually had seen was Jerry in the middle of the boat with an air tank on either side of him.

Many years later I questioned my brother about his thoughts while floating alone in that boat. He told me that because he was so thirsty and had been told not to drink the lake water all he could think of was, "If all the land were apple pie and all the sea was ink, and all the trees were bread and cheese, what would we have to drink?"

Everyone at the lodge had set out to search for them. My mother spent seven hours sitting on the shore. I don't remember her moving or talking to anyone, just crying and praying. Mary Frances and I were sent to the cabin. Sometime during the night I heard a very strange commotion. I jumped from my bed to find my sister convulsing. She was having the first of a lifetime of epileptic seizures. I raced out of the cabin screaming for help. I scurried up the hill to the office. I was hysterical and still not fully aware of the tragedy continuing on the lake.

"Where is my mother?" I cried. "Where is my brother?" The manager hastened to get to my sister as a sweet older lady tried to calm me down. I was terrified and confused. I thought that my sister was dying.

When they finally found the boat at daybreak, someone hurried back to tell my mother. All that the man knew was that there was only one boy in the boat. No, he didn't know which one. My mother confided to me years later that she prayed that it was Jerry in the boat, but she didn't know how she could ever face the guilt of being responsible for the loss of Bobby. At the hospital Jerry told a newspaper reporter that he was sure that Bobby was safe and hiding on the other side of the lake because he was afraid that he would be in trouble for having left him.

They recovered Bobby's body five days later with his left arm still over his head in a stroking position. Bob senior wouldn't speak to or even look at Jerry at the funeral, or ever for that matter. Jerry couldn't even cry at the funeral he was so ridden with remorse. When he got home he went to his room and cried and cried all alone for what he later said seemed like hours.

It had been seventy years since the accident, on the sixth day of July, 2016, when my brother recounted it to me. He said at that time that he remembered it as clearly as if it were yesterday.

Bob returned to Los Angeles and proceeded to immediately get rid of Bobby's model planes, wall posters and every possession. He cleaned out Bobby's room and told his little sister, Maggy, who was only six years old, that Bobby had gone to camp and was never coming back and that she was never to mention his name again. Bobby had been the only stable thing in her young life. How could he be gone? She learned the truth when she saw a newspaper clipping of the accident several years later. Maggy was sent away to boarding school. She entered the convent when she was seventeen years of age in order to get her education. She, my brother and I met many years later when she was teaching at Seattle University in 1969.

When my brother was eighty-three, in October of 2016, we discussed our next trip to the lake. He requested it to be his final resting place.

POST SCRIPT: Jeremiah Joseph Keane, Sr. passed away on March 2, 2018. His remains were scattered at Meadow Lake in Ennis, Montana, on July 1, 2018.

Rest in peace my beloved brother.

MY HERO

I barely knew my biological father. He was in the Merchant Marines during the Second World War. I don't even remember him living at home. I do, however, have fond memories of the wonderful presents that he would send... beautiful silk pajamas, musical ebony jewelry boxes and delicate china tea sets from the Orient, fur muffs, beaded purses and handmade Indian dolls from Alaska. How I wish I had kept it all.

John Francis Keane was handsome, charming, very well-read and worldly. My mother once said that when he was good he was very, very good and when he was bad, he was 'horse shit'! Those were her exact words. The bad times of course had to do with his disabling disease – alcoholism. My mother refused to submit herself or her children to his drunken abuse, so their marriage was over before I ever got to know him. When he would come to town over the years he would take me to the circus or out for a banana split. I didn't know him, but I knew that I didn't like him.

I can't pinpoint the date when my hero came into my life, I only know that just before my seventh birthday, in April of 1947, my mother married the kindest, most loving, soft-spoken, funniest, and humble man that God ever created. Of course I didn't appreciate all of those virtues at that time. He wanted to get married on April Fool's Day, but my mother wouldn't agree to that.

George had never been married and didn't have children.

George and me 1947

He would tease my mother sometimes, telling her that he only married her for her kids. He adored my mother. He said that when he was a young man and she was working at the movie theater he would go there just to see her, not the movie. She didn't even know that he existed at that time.

George was a simple man and a good provider. He worked in the underground copper mines. When he moved into our home we were living in a low cost housing development on the wrong side of the tracks, where the *'ticky-tacky-houses'* were all in a row, just like the song says. We lived within walking distance of the Eagles Club which is where he and my mother had met. Although he wasn't a drinker, he would stop there for a few beers after work once in a while. One evening he was a little late getting home and Mother was beginning to get nervous. Just after dark a knock came to our front door. It was the young girl from the housing unit just behind ours. "Mrs. Goles, I think your husband is in my mother's bed," she uttered looking totally embarrassed. All of the apartments had exactly the same lay-out and he had walked in their front door, proceeded directly up the stairs, stumbled into the bedroom on the right side of the hall and toppled onto the bed. One beer too many! Luckily the lady of the house was at work at the time and her teen-aged daughters were quite amused by the incident. My mother was mortified and tried to talk my brother, who was laughing hysterically, into going to get him. "He's *your* husband, *you* go get him," was his quick answer. She did, and of course she made him go apologize the next day. We never did let him live that one down.

My mother, who never drank, made it clear that she had no intentions of putting up with another drunk. The only other time we ever saw him tipsy was after a wedding reception. He sat down at the kitchen table and asked for a glass of milk. Mother poured him a tall glass of milk. He took it from her hand, put his head back and proceeded to pour the whole glass of milk over his shoulder. He handed the glass back to her and slurred, "Boy that was good. Can I have another one?" My brother and I were in stitches laughing, but Mother was beyond perturbed. When my brother told him about it the next day he sheepishly apologized. "No problem, just like old home week," my brother quipped. That was the end of his drinking days except for once a year when he and Mother attended the Eagles State Convention. We never saw him drink at home again.

At the convention the following year my mother, thinking that he had had enough to drink, took him to their hotel room. At that time the old hotels had real keys and you could actually lock the door from the inside or outside. Mother locked him in and went back to the dance. About an hour later she heard someone say, "Well Hi, George, where have you been?" She went back to check the room and the door was still locked and she knew that he didn't have a key... hmmm. The next morning, she heard one of the housekeepers telling someone, "The little guy in that room raised such a fit last night and told me that if I didn't let him out of the room he would climb through the transom so I had to unlock the door."

George purchased a new house for my mother on the west side of town the year that I was in the eighth grade. Shortly thereafter he bought his first car. It was a green 1949 Hudson Hornet. He was so proud of that car. One of our first road trips was to Boulder, Montana, about an hour and a half from Butte. On the way home we got a flat tire. He didn't know if we had a spare tire, didn't know how to change one anyway, he confessed. So in white shorts and a white blouse in the middle of nowhere I learned how to change a tire. He was so proud of me! Some years later when I told that story someone replied, "He must have been a white collar executive not to know how to change a tire." "No," I smiled, "he was a miner."

George would come home from the mine and bathe every night before dinner. One night he fell asleep on the couch after dinner and I proceeded to paint his toenails bright red. He got up from the couch and went directly to bed, never looking down. He got up in the morning, dressed in the dark and went to work. When he went in to bathe that evening we heard him screaming from the bathroom, "What if there had been an accident in the mine and I was taken to the hospital?" he howled. We had another good laugh.

Although George had a great sense of humor, he did not appreciate vulgarity or dirty jokes. My oldest sister, my mother and I were canning peaches one evening while he was in the living room watching the evening news. As Mother peeled a peach it slipped out of her hand flying across the table. "That was slipperier than a wet tit," she quipped. He vaulted out of his recliner into the kitchen scolding her, "Is that any way to talk in front of your daughters?" Even in his later years he refused to be amused by my kids' 'whoopy cushion.' He called it *uncouth*.

One day while visiting when we lived in Hawaii he was sitting on the lanai having coffee and reading the newspaper and in a quizzical tone of voice he called out to my mother, "Mary, where is your yet? My what?" Mother questioned. He repeated the question, this time asking, "Where is a woman's *yet?*" Mother gave me a wondering glance, "Do you know what he is talking about?" she asked me. "I have no idea," I replied. Holding the newspaper up to show us the article he was reading, he said, "It says right here that this man shot his wife and the bullet is in her *YET.*" (still in her)

It didn't matter what I did growing up it was always the best in my dad's eyes. I was the best singer in the choir, I was the best dancer, the best student. I grew up confident of everything I ever did only because of his never ending encouragement and approval. I remind my husband often that I know that I am the best driver ever because my daddy told me so. His heart was broken when I married young and left home. He had hoped for so much more for me.

At sixty-nine years of age, he began to have horrific headaches and Mother noticed that he was walking awkwardly. He was diagnosed with a brain tumor. Surgery left him paralyzed on one side. He had always been a smoker and since his condition was terminal I was able to talk the doctor into letting me take cigarettes into his hospital room. This was, of course, in the 1970s. He was allowed to smoke as long as I stayed with him. I wanted to spend every minute he had left with him.

In the movie "Looking for Mr. Goodbar," Diane Keaton is shown standing over her father's coffin when he opens his eyes and winks at her. My mother said that I stood at George's coffin and stared for forty minutes while the rest of the family went to lunch. I just knew in my heart that I would get a wink. He would want to give me a morsel of consolation, just to let me know that I would be OK without him.

The man who drove the hearse to the cemetery kept peering into the rear-view mirror at me and my siblings as we laughed and joked and told all of these stories and more. We requested that he take the long route as Pa told us he wanted to get his money's worth on his last ride. I didn't shed a tear after he passed until Father's Day that year when I cried all day.

This amazing man gave us all such joy in life. I smile whenever I hear the song words "We had joy, we had fun, we had seasons in the sun." I have yet to meet a man who could hold a candle to him. He always was and always will be MY HERO.

SNOW

Authors note: This short story is fiction. It is the only fiction story that I have ever written. Maybe someday I will continue it into a romance novel.

I awoke to the eerie sound of silence. I was hesitant to move, not wanting to disturb the peaceful sensation that I was experiencing. Why does it feel like the whole world has stopped moving? If you listen carefully the silence is beautiful. It must be snowing. Did you know that fresh snow absorbs sound? That is why it is so quiet.

I hopped out of bed, ran to the window and opened the blinds to see the earth blanketed by glistening, freshly fallen snow. That was not exactly what I was looking forward to on this particular morning. I had planned to take the bus into town to attend a job fair. Growing up in central Idaho I was used to dealing with harsh winter weather, I just wasn't expecting it this soon. "Oh, well, bundle up warm and get going," I mumbled to myself. "I hope that the damned bus is on time today."

The snow was still falling when I reached the bus stop. I realized half-way there that I was feeling extremely happy and singing to myself, "Let it snow, let it snow, let it snow." There were four other people waiting for the bus and when it stopped everyone seemed to be in a hurry to be the first to board. I just hung back with a young gentleman who had appeared just as the bus pulled up. He motioned for me to go ahead of him and as I stepped up the heel on my new stylish boot caught the edge of the step and I fell backward, right into his arms. Luckily he didn't lose his balance or we would have both been lying in the snow. I was so embarrassed, but he just smiled shyly and helped me onto the bus. The bus driver was visibly irritated by the delay I had caused. He opened his mouth to say something but thinking better of it he just grunted. Amused by his disapproving reaction, the young man took a seat directly across from me, smiled and winked. *Is that butterflies in my stomach, or should I have taken time to eat breakfast?* I looked away, straightened my coat and wished that this twenty-minute bus ride was over.

Realizing that the roads were slippery and the snow was still falling, now even a little more heavily, I wondered if the bus wasn't moving a bit too fast for the conditions. I noticed that some of the other passengers were getting antsy. In a split second the bus was sliding sideways into the ditch. Panic erupted as people were thrown from their seats. Luckily the bus didn't roll, it just glided into a huge snow bank. No one was hurt, just badly shaken. The grouchy driver was moving from person to person checking to make sure that no one was injured. He was trying to comfort everyone with a sense of calm to minimize the panic. I realized that the handsome stranger who I had been trying to ignore had taken my arm and was holding me up. "Oh, thank you, I'm OK," I said pulling away from him. He held his hand out and introduced himself as Mark. "Pleased to meet you, Mark. I'm Joan."

We were about two and a half miles from the next bus stop and there was very little traffic in the area. There were, of course, no cell phones in 1950 so this was a matter of wait or walk. Within minutes a passing car stopped and told the driver that they would go for help. We had no choice but to sit in the cold and wait for another bus to rescue us. Funny how people who hadn't even looked at each other when they got on the bus were now conversing like they were long lost friends. "I'm going to be late for work," several lamented. I wasn't at all upset about missing the job fair. "So, where are you headed young lady?" the chivalrous fellow inquired. I told him, and to be polite I asked, "Are you from around here? I've never seen you on the bus before." His smile and those amazing blue eyes took my breath away. "I'm just visiting my buddy's family in Sandpoint. I was born and reared in Arizona. This is the first time I have ever seen snow and I'm lovin' it. Come on, let's get off of the bus and enjoy this winter wonderland." *Is he crazy?* Was my first thought, but I quickly decided that if we were going to be here for a while I might as well enjoy his company.

We walked for a few minutes, making small talk. He told me that he and his buddy, Jimmy had just completed Marine Corp boot camp in San Diego and received orders to Korea when their leave time was up in a week. It was 1950 and General Douglas MacArthur, the commander of all allied forces, had been ordering US troops to Korea since June. "The Forgotten War" it was dubbed, the conflict that set the stage for decades of tension between North Korea, South Korea and the United States. President Truman referred to it as a "police action" as the United States never formally declared war.

I was skipping a few feet ahead of Mark when I felt a sudden *whop.* A huge snowball hit the side of my arm, and I was engulfed in a spray of soft, fluffy snow. As quickly as I could turn around I scooped up as much snow as I could and chased him toward a slopping hill a few feet ahead. He fell and rolled down the hill with me right behind him. We were both laughing with glee as he caught me at the bottom of the hill. I decided this was the perfect time to show this Arizona boy how to make a snow angel. At the top of the hill the cantankerous bus driver was hollering and motioning to us to get back as the new bus had arrived. We were wet, rosy-cheeked and still laughing as we boarded the bus.

When we got into town, Jimmy was waiting for Mark and they insisted that I go to a nearby diner with them to have hot chocolate and dry out. Well, my day was already botched so why not? I was actually enjoying Mark's company. We laughed as he told stories of growing up in the desolate little town of Wellton, Arizona, just east of Yuma, and his childhood dreams to see the world. They insisted on buying me lunch and the afternoon seemed to just fly by. "I must catch the next bus home. My folks will be expecting me and if they heard about the bus going off the road they may be worried." "No, no, you don't have to take the bus, I'll drive you home," Jimmy insisted. I knew that my parents would be upset if I showed up in a car with two strangers, but what the heck, I was really enjoying their company and hadn't even given a thought as to their trustworthiness.

It was already dusk when we arrived at my house and I decided to invite them in. My mother's first words as she eyed my new friends were, "Where have you been? I was just beginning to worry." My dad had taken it upon himself to shake hands with the guys and welcome them. That is not what I had expected. Dad was impressed with the fact that they were Marines and that they had taken care of his stranded daughter. Mother, always the perfect hostess, invited them to stay for dinner, much to my surprise. They accepted the offer and we enjoyed a glorious evening. When it began to snow again Jimmy decided that he had better get his dad's car back to Sandpoint. We said our goodbyes at the door. Mark held my hand and said that he wished he had met me sooner. He asked for my address. I jotted it down for him and as they walked toward the car my heart did a little skip, knowing that I would probably never see him again.

I was wrong. I was attending junior college in our little town and working evenings at the library. When I walked into the library after school the next day I wasn't paying any attention to who was there. As I walked behind the counter I saw a beautiful pair of blue eyes peeking at me over a book. Mark had gone to my house and my mom told him where he could find me. When he tried to talk to me I kept shushing him so he asked me for a piece of paper and a pencil. I was so not prepared for the note that he handed me. "Joan, you will probably think that I am crazy and maybe even tell me to leave, but I have to let you know that from the moment I saw you at the bus stop I have not been able to get you off of my mind. I'll be leaving Saturday not knowing when or if ever I will return. When you rolled down the hill and into my arms yesterday I didn't want to ever let you go. I just wanted to hold you. Please say that you will write to me while I am away. I am not asking for a commitment; I realize that you hardly know me. I just want to leave here knowing that I might have hope or a reason for returning." I read the note and when I looked up, teary-eyed, he was gone. When I closed the library I was hoping that Mark would be waiting for me. The snow had started falling and the street lights cast an eerie glow. Again I started humming, "Let it snow, let it snow, let it snow."

Saturday morning rolled around and my heart was heavy because Mark hadn't called or come by the house. "Oh, well," I told myself, "it was all just a fairy tale dream and my prince was just some lonely Marine headed off to war. I will pray every day for his safe return." ……..to be continued (maybe).

A LETTER TO MYSELF AT TWELVE YEARS OF AGE

My Dearest Ruth Agnes,

Wow, the years have quickly flown by and here you are – a young lady already! No longer that chubby, happy baby or that mischievous, adorable toddler. You have blossomed into a graceful, winsome preteen. Oh, I understand how you dislike that ravishing red hair and how you cry about your ugly freckles. They are only ugly to you, dear. And no, that Golden Peacock Bleach Cream will not make them disappear, so please do me a favor and stop pestering your mom for a dollar to buy it.

I hope that you will always appreciate the loving home in which you are blessed to grow up, and the unending encouragement you receive daily from your mother and the very best step-dad that any girl could ever dream of having. He is always so proud of everything you do. Well, most of the time! I don't know that he appreciated you painting his toe nails bright red while he was asleep on the couch. Luckily on another occasion he found the pink foam rollers that you put in his hair while he was napping. He later smiled relating those stories.

I know that you enjoy school, and that is a good thing. I might suggest, while you are at an age to accept suggestions, that you take your education seriously. Just because things seem easy for you now does not mean that you shouldn't apply yourself in a more earnest manner. Trust me, the day will come when you will be regretful if you do not take the opportunity to make the most of every chance you have to further your education.

With your teen-age years in the near future, you will be faced with many challenges. Always remember that you were born a leader, you never have to put yourself in a position where you feel that you have to 'follow the crowd.' The decisions that you make and the path that you follow in these formative years will determine the outcome of your entire life. Be very cautious when choosing your friends. Always remember your mother admonishing you, "show me your friends and I'll tell you who you are."

You will likely face many disappointments in life, the first and most devastating being told that you have to be over five-foot-six to dance with the Radio City Music Hall Rockettes. It won't take you long, however, to realize that stage life is actually just a dream, and that you would be happier and much more fulfilled teaching children to dance. Disappointment is nothing more than feeling let down when things don't go the way you would like. Knowing you, the girl that you are now, I think that you will always be strong enough to overcome any setbacks you might encounter. Be confident and trust your own judgments.

Brace yourself for the fact that not everyone in the world is going to adore you. It is a cold place out there in the grown-up universe and you will encounter many cruel, uncaring human beings. I can assure you that your heart will probably be broken more than once. Learn early on to *"pick yourself up, brush yourself off, and start all over again."*

Make it a priority in your life to always be dependable, honest, steadfast and, most of all, caring. There will be, I am sure, many who will look to you for guidance, count on you to be there for them and trust in your judgment.

Me at 12

Treasure your friendships, keeping in mind that strangers are only friends that you haven't met yet. If you see someone without a smile give him yours. And that smile… please don't ever lose that sincere, trusting grin, that contagious laugh, that snicker, that smirk. It is all a part of what makes you you. Don't ever let anyone take that away from you.

Knowing the importance of family, I am sure that when you have a family of your own you will treasure every minute seeing each of your children take their first steps, cut their first tooth, start school, learn to make their own decisions, to flourish. I know, I know… you hate kids and you never want to be responsible for anyone but yourself, let alone becoming a mother. Well, my dear, the day may come when if that is your calling, you will have to make up your mind to do your very best to earn the title "Mother of the Year" or "Best Mom Ever." I know you can do it. Motherhood is without a doubt, one of the greatest joys in life but also subject to heartache beyond comprehension.

Do you remember the assignment that you recently had asking you to list three unexpressed desires in your life? Your response was three things that you wanted to see – Cuba, the Kentucky Derby, and Niagara Falls. Those are pretty far-fetched wishes, but I hope that your travels in life will allow you to fulfill all of your hopes and dreams. May you travel the world.

As you grow older I pray that you will look back on your life without regret. I hope that you will learn in your golden years to be able to laugh at yourself, to reminisce fondly about the good ol' days, to forgive, and to pass on as well as you can, a legacy that your future descendants will carry with pride.

Life is so good… Live it to the max!

Sincerely,

Your Future Self

GRANDPA KEANE

My first recollection of being aware of my love for food comes from fond memories of the smell of my paternal Grandpa Keane's bakery. Joseph Keane was born in 1877 in East Meath, Meath County, Ireland. The family migrated to the United States in 1884. Joseph was one of fifteen children who grew up in Hell's Kitchen in New York City.

Prejudice and discrimination followed the Irish immigrants to America in the 1880s, especially those who adhered to the Catholic religion. Grandpa's eldest brother, Patrick, was able to get a job as a cook when they arrived in New York. Grandpa and some of his other brothers went to work in a bakery. In time, being a natural born politician, Grandpa became the president of the first Baker's Union in New York State. After serving several years in that office he was run out of (or as he liked to tell it "politely asked to leave") the state due to union and political uprisings.

He met and married his beautiful Julia while he was living in New York. My father, John Francis Keane, was born in New York City in December of 1903. There were three more children born to Joseph and Julia; Joseph Jr., Victor, and Agnes Ruth. Victor died as a toddler in a horrific accident. Grandpa tossed him in the air and his head hit the low hanging chandelier crushing his skull, causing a brain hemorrhage which led to his demise. The family never spoke of the incident. I learned of it only as an adult. Grandpa never got over it, he carried his guilt to his grave. Agnes Ruth died in her twenties after giving birth to my cousin Margaret Ann who was born just three weeks before me. I was named after her.

Joseph moved his young family west to Montana in the early 1920s and opened his first bakery business in the basement of the Rialto Theater in Butte, Montana. In 1923 he opened the new Royal Bakery. My father and my uncle Joe both worked in the bakery, as did my brother until he went into the Navy in the 1950s. After his military service he worked as a baker also. My very first job was in my grandpa's bakery when I was in high school. Grandpa used to tease me about eating up all of the profits. Oh, how I loved those vanilla wafers. He would be honored to know that the recipe, in his own handwriting, is on the cover of my autobiographical cookbook, "Memories with Recipes."

My father was in the Merchant Marines during the Second World War, so he was away most of the time. Grandpa took it upon himself to look after my mother and sister and brother. Mother helped out at the bakery, wrapping bread. Grandpa saw to it that the family always had plenty to eat. "Do the children need shoes?" he would question her periodically.

I barely remember my grandmother, Julia. One of my fondest memories of her is when she gave me a green velvet dress with an ecru lace peter-pan collar and dainty pearl buttons. My mother made me wear it to the hospital the day that Grandma Julia passed away. I was only about six years old and I was left in the room alone with her when she was dying. I refused to ever wear that dress again and to this day I can't stand the feel of velvet.

On Friday nights when I was still in grammar school Grandpa would take me out to the racetrack to watch the greyhound dog races. Oh, how I loved going to 'the dogs' as he called it. We would stop first at the county hospital, which he and everyone in town called "the poor farm," to visit his brother Patrick. Uncle Pat would give me a quarter every week to bet on the dogs. Grandpa would let me pick my own dogs and cheer with me when I won and warn me of the dangers of gambling when I lost. Before I was born Grandpa had saved up for a year to take the train to Churchill Downs to attend the Kentucky Derby, his life-time dream. He had planned on betting a hundred dollars on his favorite horse but when he got there he decided that he could only afford to bet fifty dollars. Good call, his horse came in second to the last. It was a sad train ride back to Montana. Fifty dollars was a lot of money in the 1930s.

Grandpa traveled back to New York almost every year. Most of his siblings and their families still lived there. On each trip he would bring my cousin Joanne and me gifts from Macy's. When we were in high school, having a new Jantzen sweater from Macy's in New York was the highlight of the year. I wore those sweaters well into my thirties.

Grandpa was always concerned about us getting a proper education. I would never have done as well as I did in school had it not been for my Sunday morning breakfasts and pop quizzes with Grandpa. He would take me and Joanne out to breakfast and question us on geography, history and current events and fill our heads with politics that we really didn't understand. I had better know my times tables and how to spell hippopotamus by the time I was in the fourth grade. On one occasion Grandpa inquired as to what I would like to be when I grew up. I very seriously and proudly told him that I hoped to be a burlesque dancer someday. He told me to just never forget that I was Irish, Catholic, and a Democrat, stressing that Democrat came first. How does a nine-year-old know what a Democrat is?

Grandpa was a brilliant, self-educated man who loved to read. His hope was that we would pursue the formal education that he never had the chance to attain. His heart was broken when I chose to get married instead of attending college. He was the one, however, who walked me down the aisle. I will always remember him singing to me the morning of my wedding, *"Happy the bride, the sun shines on today. What a beautiful wedding it will be, what a wonderful day for you and me..."*

One of my most treasured mementos is a letter that I received from my grandpa in October of 1961. It read in part: "Your letter indicates that you are happy which, at least to my thinking, is the most important thing in life. You are very proud of your boys, which is all to the good, and as I told you once before, it is up to you and Pat, by example and training that in the years to come you will both be just as proud of them, even more so than now. May God help both of you to do your part."

Grandpa passed away one year later, on Halloween, October 31st, 1962, at eighty-five years of age. I credit him, and am thankful every day for my love of reading and horse racing, my Irish pride, Christian faith, and my staunch Democratic beliefs.

A GIRL'S BEST FRIEND

My aunt Doris was legally blind. She and her younger sister, Gertie, were both born with what was at that time (in 1916) called 'underdeveloped eyes.' I am sure there is an updated medical term for the condition. She attended a school for the blind from an early age where she learned to make the most of what vision she had. She could read large print at a close range and she could see well enough to lead a normal life. Doris was a petite, attractive young lady with dark hair and magnetic dark brown eyes. The pupils of her eyes were larger than normal due to her condition and extremely sensitive to light. She and my uncle Dan were married in May of 1941. In spite of her vision challenge she raised three happy, healthy children. She and Uncle Dan both lived to be 89 years of age.

Doris learned to sew and became an expert seamstress even though she could not distinguish color. My mother and I would go shopping with her and her daughter, Mary Kay, who was four years younger than me. We would match the thread colors to the fabric for her. I became so intrigued with her sewing ability that by the age of twelve all I wanted to do was to learn to sew.

In the 1950s one of the big fashion rages was the Pendleton wool plaid jackets. Doris could duplicate that pattern to look exactly like the factory made jackets. She made most of her children's clothes, as well as her own without ever using a printed pattern. After much coaxing she agreed to teach me to sew. Most of the time I just watched her sew and picked up what I could of her techniques. My first actual attempt to sew was one of the wool jackets that she had cut out for me. I loved the feel of the sewing machine and the fabric magically slipping through my fingers. The more I sewed the more I was convinced that I had to have my own sewing machine. "No, we cannot afford to buy a sewing machine," was my mother's quick response to my plea. "Aunt Doris will let you use her sewing machine." I pouted and told her that if I could have a sewing machine I would *never, ever* ask for anything else for as long as I lived. I was such a dramatic kid!

Back in those days there were door-to-door salesmen who sold everything from vacuum cleaners to vegetable seeds. One day, by chance, a Singer sewing machine salesman came to our door. Again I pleaded and begged for a sewing machine, but again the answer was, "We cannot afford it." Well, this particular salesman did not want to take '*no*' for an answer, so he came up with a great solution. "I will let you have this White Rotary machine for thirty-five dollars." It was an old treadle machine that had been converted to electric. "No, we do not have thirty-five dollars," Mother snapped back. His persistence paid off when they agreed to two dollars down, and two dollars a week until it was paid off. So, every Wednesday afternoon Hank would show up to collect the two dollars while never giving up trying to convince my mom to upgrade to a new Singer Sewing Machine.

The 'never asking for anything else' didn't last long. Now that I had my sewing machine I needed pink polka-dotted Swiss material to make curtains and a dressing table skirt for my bedroom. All I ever wanted to do was sew. My friends would be out playing, riding bikes or going to the movies while I was sewing. My witty mother would taunt me, singing, "The sewing machine, the sewing machine, a girl's best friend. If I didn't have a sewing machine, I wouldn't have a friend." I don't know if that was really a song or if she had just made it up, but I loved hearing it and I would hum along happily as I sewed.

My sophomore year in high school we were required to take Home Economics. Sister Rose Gertrude reminded me of Santa Claus with her chubby, rosy cheeks and hearty laugh. She took me aside the first day of school to ask me if I would stay after class to show her how to thread a sewing machine. She had heard from the previous class that I had made the three tiered skirts that several of the girls were flaunting. I felt honored to help her and kind of smug to know that I knew more about sewing than the teacher.

How could I fail in Home Economics? I had never in my entire school life had a 'D' grade. D was for devastated! The fact that I had thrown my apron project across the table because Sister wanted me to pin the pattern to the fabric, should have nothing to do with my sewing ability. I was so taken back by this grade that I pranced right to the office and told the principle, Sister Mary Seraphine, that I might have deserved a D grade in conduct or citizenship, but not in sewing. The grade didn't get changed, and my friends were all quite amused by the incident.

I made my majorette uniform for our twirling corps and when my best friend found out how much money I had saved by making it, she asked me to make hers. This was just the start of my first business venture. I was soon making costumes for the local dance recitals and school plays and the uniforms for our Irish dance troupe.

My long-distance boyfriend, who was in the Navy, returned home on leave unexpectedly in August of 1957. He vowed that he would not return to Oklahoma without me. My family was not happy, but after a lot of crying and pleading and pledging our unending love, my mother gave in and agreed to sign the consent which was necessary to get a marriage license, as I was underage. We quickly planned a wedding and had to drive to Helena to obtain a dispensation from the Catholic Diocese to be married in the church without the required prior notice.

With one week until the wedding day and no money how was I to have a wedding dress? My mother had a long white lace formal dress that she had worn for her drill team events. I eyed it carefully and decided that I could indeed transform it into a beautiful wedding gown. I cut it to street length, removed the sleeves, which became long finger-less gloves, tailored it to fit perfectly and used the excess that I had cut off the bottom to cover my wide-brimmed Easter hat. Perfect. My sewing machine, my 'best friend' had saved the day!

When I left home the first thing I packed was my sewing machine. My new husband was overjoyed when I told him that I could tailor his Navy uniforms. It didn't take long after settling in our new apartment before his entire Navy division was requesting my tailoring services. I was busy sewing every day and thrilled that I was actually getting paid well for my work.

Just before Christmas, when I learned that I was pregnant, I was anxious to make maternity clothes. I dragged my hubby to the local department store to show him the prices and then went to the fabric shop. Four outfits for the price of one. You sure couldn't beat that. He was so impressed that he decided to surprise me for our first Christmas by buying me the Singer sewing machine that I had longingly wanted for so many years. I don't like surprises and I was less than thrilled when I learned that he had traded my old White Rotary sewing machine for the newest model Singer Slant-O-Matic, with all the bells and whistles. Instead of thanking him I cried and told him to take it back. He said that he wouldn't return it, and even if he did he couldn't get my old one back. I finally thanked him for it and decided that the best thing I could do was to get to know my *'new'* friend.

When we were transferred to Puerto Rico in 1959 I was delighted to find a whole company of sailors just waiting for a tailor. One young fellow was being discharged from the Navy and heading home to get married. We were taking him to the airport in San Juan for an early departure, so we invited him to spend the night before his flight with us. He had a duffle bag full of dirty clothes and my husband told him that I wouldn't mind doing his laundry. I was OK with that. I just happened to have my sewing machine set up on the dining room table and I spotted some pink lace that I was using on the costumes I was making for a dance recital. I don't even remember the fellow's name, but I have often wondered what his fiancé thought when he unpacked his duffle bag and the fragrance of lavender sachet preceded his lace trimmed boxer shorts. I didn't even tell my husband what I had done until after the plane had taken off.

I continued to make most of my clothes over the years and a few things for the kids. When my marriage ended after sixteen years, my new sewing machine got a little reprieve. I didn't touch it for several years. When I married Larry in 1979 I was still calling my 1958 Singer my *new* sewing machine. I wasn't doing much sewing though. I made my daughter's junior prom dress and I tailored a wedding dress for a friend. I just didn't enjoy sewing anymore. How I could ever have enjoyed sewing was beyond me. Sewing made my neck stiff, my eyes tired, my hands hurt, and the stress of trying to make everything perfect gave me a horrible headache. I vowed that I would never sew again. Larry was amazed at my sewing ability and realizing how old my *new* machine was he decided that it would be a great idea to get me a brand new one. Thank God that Sears didn't take trade-ins. He gifted me with a nice new Kenmore sewing machine which eventually ended up in a garage sale.

In 2007, or there about, I took my fifty-some year old '*best friend*' into the local Singer Sewing Machine Shop for a tune-up. The service man had a good laugh when I called it my '*new*' sewing machine and he informed me that it would probably cost more to overhaul it than it would to buy a new one. The new machines are made in China or someplace other than the USA, and the bodies are plastic. I informed him that I didn't care what it would cost, I wanted it to be just like brand new. And so it is. It is now retired to a closet and is called on only once in a while when someone asks me to hem their new jeans or to stitch a seam. Larry says that he now understands why I still call it my '*new*' sewing machine… because it never gets used. I call it my *best friend* because it's been with me for my entire adult life.

A VERY SPECIAL THANKSGIVING

If you grew up in an average, middle-class American home more than likely you celebrated Thanksgiving the same way that my family did. Relatives came from near and far to gather together, perhaps for the first time in a year. The ladies would all congregate in the kitchen preparing the holiday feast while the gentlemen relaxed in front of the TV watching football. Before the days of television, they may have instigated a hot poker game or, weather permitting, a tag football game outside on the front lawn. The jokes about family squabbles or Uncle Charlie, after a few beers or shots of schnapps, loudly airing someone's dirty laundry were not always fabricated stories. More often than not someone ended up with hurt feelings, a bruised ego or maybe even a black eye. Oh, the good old days. The perfect holiday celebration.

The food was always fabulous. Even though my mom was not what some would consider a great cook, she always managed to prepare a superb feast for Thanksgiving. Her gravy was the best of any I have ever tasted. Everyone agreed that they had never had better gravy. We would have a luscious fruit salad that she prepared only once a year. Her candied sweet potatoes, mashed potatoes and dressing were topped only by the delicious pumpkin and mince meat pies.

I had no interest in what was going on in the kitchen. Cleaning up after dinner was my job. I didn't ever learn to cook. Little did I know that someday I might have to feed a family. That was the farthest thing from my mind when I married and moved away from home in the summer of 1957. When I told my new husband that I didn't know how to cook he assured me that it was not a problem, we could eat Dinty Moore Beef Stew and soup. What I forgot to mention was the fact that I didn't even know how to use a can opener.

When November rolled around the first year we were married I was beginning to feel a little homesick, longing to be with my family for the holidays. I was reminiscing about my mom's turkey gravy, and in a moment of enlightenment I decided that I could probably cook a wonderful, memorable Thanksgiving dinner. So, we bought a little turkey and all the trimmings and I carefully planned out the menu. I was excited to embark on my first big cooking venture. I called my mom, babbling my plan, unable to contain my enthusiasm. She was, of course, encouraging but I seemed to sense a bit of amusement in her voice. "Good luck, honey. I'll be anxious to hear how it goes."

"Oh no, we don't have a roasting pan and sure as heck can't afford to buy one after all that we spent on the food," I lamented. Pat, always the problem solver, smiled as he assured me, "That bird is small enough to cook in the large frying pan." I stuffed the bird just as I had remembered my mother doing and was quite proud of myself for following the dressing recipe to a tee. The oven was heated and I was right on schedule with the potatoes, yams, cauliflower and fresh cranberry sauce. The aroma coming from the kitchen was divine. I was flaunting a satisfied smile and taking on the air of a gourmet chef. I could hardly wait to brag to my mother.

Time to take the bird out of the oven. No one ever told me, nor had I figured it out myself, that handles on frying pans are not oven proof. Being very cautious and using my new, up until now unused pot holders, I gingerly lifted the pan from the oven rack. I heard Pat, who was standing behind me cautiously warning, "Be careful, don't burn yourself." In a split second I was holding a hot pan handle and the pan was on the floor. The bird bounced and was sliding down the slanted kitchen floor toward the hallway. I have no words to describe my devastation. I was sitting on the kitchen floor crying while Pat was trying hard not to laugh. "It's okay, we can wash the turkey. It's still edible," he calmly exclaimed, trying to console me.

As I gazed unbelieving through my tears at the greasy mess on the floor I sobbed, "But there goes my gravy." Not a Thanksgiving goes by that I don't smile recalling my very memorable, very special, gravy-less first Thanksgiving dinner.

MY FIRST BORN

On July 1st, 1958, I brought into this world a whopping, eight-pound fifteen-ounce bundle of joy. I was much too young to be taking on the responsibility of another human being. I was just a child myself, barely eighteen. I had never been around babies and I remember asking my husband, "What will we do with a baby?" "We will love him," was his calm answer. He was as happy and proud that he was going to be a dad as I was scared and apprehensive. For nine long months he claimed that he wanted a daughter, but after Patrick was born he admitted to me that he only said that because he knew how desperately I wanted a boy.

After twenty-three long hours of labor and finally hearing someone say, "It's a boy," I was anxious to meet my son. Every new mother envisions a beautiful baby. I could hardly contain my shock and horror when I saw this screaming, bloody, red mass of humanity with huge swollen testicles and a head that looked like it had a built-in dunce cap. "Dear God, please let him be normal," I prayed to myself. "Why is his face so purple and squished?" I didn't know that the forceps they had to use to deliver him had bruised his tender flesh. The doctor assured me that the bones in his little pointed head were soft and she could mold it into a normal shape. At that point they sedated me. When I came to my mother was holding my hand and reassuring me that the baby was OK and that I was going to live.

Doctor Neilson was a humongous, tough looking German woman who showed absolutely no pity during my lengthy labor, but her face was soft and warm, almost loving, as she placed my "not-so-beautiful" baby in my arms. "He is perfect," she whispered to me. That was all I needed to hear. The bonding began.

Patrick was a bright baby who learned quickly and could melt the coldest of hearts with one slight grin. When he was a year old his father was transferred to San Juan, Puerto Rico. We lived in a quaint little village, Fajardo, where Patrick learned to speak Spanish at an early age. "Habla Español, Mama," he would coax me. It was a delight to see this young toe-headed boy chit-chatting with the old Puerto Rican men in the town square. They would converse and laugh and I had absolutely no idea what they were saying. How they loved him!

He grew tall and strong and excelled in everything he attempted, especially sports. By the time he was thirteen years of age he was six-foot three-inches tall and wore a size thirteen shoe. This of course was a plus for basketball, but his first love was baseball. He played in Little League and made it all the way to the all-star team as a pitcher. At nineteen he was chosen to try out for the major league scouts. He was the youngest in the group and he had the highest rating. I was so proud of him, but to my disappointment he was not recruited and he never did get the opportunity to pursue a career in baseball.

He graduated from high school, not with high honors but with acceptable average grades. He was handsome, well-spoken and very mild mannered, quite the ladies' man. His plan was to join the Air Force but when his step-mom offered to pay for him to go to beauty school he decided to give it a try. He had been the family's personal barber for some time and all of his buddies were sporting the new 'Glen Campbell' look thanks to his barbering talent.

The girls in the beauty school class were all infatuated with this clean-cut, good looking new guy, but he had eyes for only one. Rose was a stunning, quiet girl of Dutch and Hispanic descent. Her alluring brown eyes twinkled and her smile turned heads and brightened any room she entered. Within a year she and Patrick were married and blessed me with my first grandchild at just thirty-eight years of age. Nicole was a delightful, bright, blue eyed baby and once I got over the shock of being a grandma she was the light of my life. Although Patrick enjoyed hair-dressing and was extremely good at it, he wasn't earning a satisfactory living for his new family and he had no insurance coverage. He decided it was time to get a *real* job.

Fast forward eight years. New job, new wife and a new baby boy. Bryan Lee was born on Mother's Day in 1985. Patrick was elated; he now had a son and a fishing partner! Nicole, who was then seven years old, informed me that she didn't like the idea of not being the only grandchild.

Every mother knows that there is no hurt in the world as painful as seeing your child suffer. The day that I received the phone call that Bryan was in the hospital my perfect world became a muddled, blurry nightmare. What is neuroblastoma? It is a rare childhood cancer. My three-year-old grandson, a healthy, happy toddler and my son's pride and joy had been diagnosed with this devastating disease. We lived through hell for eleven months of treatments, an experimental drug never before tried on humans, so much heartache, so many tears. We buried Bryan on Memorial Day 1988.

Patrick knew that he had to get on with life. "I need a change, Mother," he confided in me. He moved to Idaho and took on the challenge of building his own log house with the trees on the property that he bought there. He enjoyed the fishing and was soon looking forward to a new baby girl. The pain of the loss of Bryan persisted and was soon being numbed by alcohol. He was what they refer to in Alcoholics Anonymous a functioning alcoholic. No one ever saw him inebriated but he was drinking on a daily basis. He never missed work. His co-workers all looked up to him. One of his greatest joys was teaching the younger fellows that he worked with how to fish.

Alcohol – cirrhosis, synonymous? Thirty years of abuse had taken its toll and it was too late for a transplant. "I love life, Mother," were the words he spoke as I held him close. I had to be strong. I promised my husband that I would not let Patrick see me cry. The tears did roll down my cheeks as I watched the priest give him the last rites and kissed him good-bye.

In 'The Prophet,' the poet, Kahlil Gibran, writes: "Your children are not your children. They are the sons and daughters of life's longing for itself. They come through you but not from you, and though they are with you yet they belong not to you."

Along the shores of the Skykomish River, Douglas firs and hemlocks soar into the sky from a forest floor lush green in underbrush and woodland flowers. The sound of the rippling river erases any evidence of a world beyond this place. On the shore a lone man awaits the next big bite, caught up in the satisfaction of knowing this is where he belongs. As he goes through the motions of many trips before, he smiles. With a happy and fulfilled heart, he makes his final cast. The thrill of the catch. He pulls back and with a gentle hand releases. This is his moment, his home, his serenity. Reunited with his son he will be a part of this peace and tranquility for all eternity.

SIXTEEN HUNDRED MILES

Sixteen hundred miles, forty-two dollars and a 1955 Oldsmobile 88. When gas was nineteen cents a gallon and we were young and fearless, planning a trip from Oklahoma to Montana did not seem out of the question. My husband had a fifteen-day leave from the Navy and we had a six-week old baby who we were anxious to introduce to our families back home. Pat had the gas mileage figured out to the dollar and if we drove straight through we could make it to Montana in twenty-four hours. That of course would also save on motel costs. In 1958 disposable diapers were very rarely used and quite expensive. We agreed to try them out for convenience sake, but that didn't leave enough extra cash for a diaper bag. Pat insisted that his duffle bag would work just fine. A car seat? Back then the car seats hung over the middle of the front seat and didn't even have a seat belt. It certainly wouldn't accommodate a new born. I cringe now when I think of riding with a baby on my lap or laying him on the back seat with only a pillow roll to protect him from falling off of the seat if we had to stop suddenly.

Baby Patrick seemed to enjoy the motion of the car and was sleeping better than he did at home. We snacked all day on our packed lunch and bottled water and decided that we would stop in Denver for dinner. After devouring our sixty-cent hamburgers and having the baby's bottle warmed, we continued on. Pat assured me that he would be able to drive all night and that we were almost half way there already.

Just a short distance out of Laramie, Wyoming, on highway 80, I asked Pat if we could pull off of the road so that I could change and feed the baby and he could maybe take a short nap. It was nearing midnight. The moon was full, the sky was clear and the stars seemed to be dancing in tune with the gentle summer breeze. We exited the highway onto a state road which I later learned was State Highway 30, leading to Medicine Bow National Forest.

As I was feeding the baby, we were enjoying the calm July night and discussing our plans for the future. All of a sudden bright headlights lit up the interior of the car. I thought that it might be a highway patrolman checking to see why a car was parked in this remote area. Pat quickly hopped out of the driver's side of the car. I just held my baby close as I felt the anxiety creeping up the back of my neck. I looked out the window and saw a man walking toward my side of the car. He wasn't wearing a uniform, he was dressed in a bright Hawaiian print shirt. Pat jumped back into the car and started the engine, but he couldn't back out because we were blocked in by the stranger's car. He recklessly turned the steering wheel to the left, gunned the engine and broke a trail right through the brush, leading not to the freeway but onto the deserted County State Road 30. The speedometer rose to one hundred miles an hour and the mystery car that had stopped behind us was right on our tail. We didn't know what make or model the car was but I had noticed as we hastily pulled out that it had the rearing stallion of the Wyoming license plate on the front. I was crying and begging Pat to slow down. "You are going to kill us," I shrieked. "Would you rather die in a car crash or be raped and murdered?" was his somber reply. I held my breath and held my baby close and prayed, and for six or seven miles the race was on. The headlights behind us suddenly dimmed as the car seemed to be slowing down and in just minutes the car was out of sight. We continued to speed on into Medicine Bow. We were both terrified, but the baby had slept through the whole ordeal. We soon saw the lights of a dingy little motel and Pat slowed down and announced that we were not driving any further. We woke the proprietor who after hearing about our grisly episode quickly got us settled into a 'not-so upscale' seven-dollar and fifty-cent room. As we collapsed, shaken with images of *what-could-have-been* flashing through our minds, the baby decided that it was awake time as the car was no longer moving. I rocked him back to sleep, which was actually soothing to me. Pat slept for several hours and awoke at day break anxious to get back on the road.

    We backed out of the motel parking lot and the car would not go into drive. Pat jiggled the gear shift and nothing happened. "What the hell," he groaned. Not being mechanically inclined he knew as little as I did about cars. The motel manager, seeing our dilemma, appeared out of nowhere to see if he could help. It turned out that he didn't know much about cars either. He did offer to call the local mechanic for us. We waited about an hour for the guy to show up and when he did he informed us after checking the car that he would have to have it towed to the shop as the transmission was completely stripped (whatever that meant). So there we were, in what seemed like the middle of nowhere, almost broke and no car. All I could think of was the movie "Bad Day at Black Rock," and I dubbed it "Bad Day at Medicine Bow," which is how we referred to the experience from that day forward.

After checking the car, the repair man told us that the transmission would have to be replaced and it would cost about three hundred dollars. Oh my God! That was more than Pat's monthly income. They would also have to order the transmission from the factory so it wouldn't be available for a week to ten days.

We made a collect call from the repair shop to Pat's dad in Butte and luckily got ahold of him. He didn't own a car so he couldn't come to get us, but he told us that if we could get to a train station he would arrange to have our train fare paid to get to Butte. We would have to leave the car in Medicine Bow and beg, borrow or steal the money to pick it up to get back to Pat's duty station in Oklahoma by the time his leave was up. The shop owner's wife offered to take us to Rawlins to the train depot where our tickets were waiting when we arrived. We had to stuff everything that we had brought with us into the duffle bag which Pat hauled over his shoulder and I carried the baby.

It was a dreadfully long and trying train ride and took up two days of the time we had planned to spend with our families. The train attendants were friendly and helpful. They mixed the baby's formula for me and disposed of the ill-fitted disposable diapers. By that time, we were all in dire need of a bath. It was disheartening to even think about having to make the same trip back in order to pick up the car. We would have to borrow the money from Pat's dad, who would probably have to borrow it from the bank, to pay for the car.

Our visit was enjoyable, but far too short and it was time to head back. As we boarded the train, duffle bag and baby in tow, Sarge (Pat's dad) handed me a huge pickle jar full of change… nickels, dimes and quarters that he had been saving for the baby. Thank goodness for that, as it was what we had to use for food on the train and gas when we picked up the car. We made it safely back to Oklahoma the day before Pat had to check in.

This trip has always been a reminder to me that no matter how badly things seem to be at the time, there is usually a positive outcome. It was, for sure, an adventure to remember – our "Bad Day at Medicine Bow!"

SERENDIPITY

I think that it is safe to say that everyone has at some time in their life experienced an unexplained event or happening that at the time seemed unbelievable. When the same thing occurs over and over again you begin to wonder if there is some meaning or message to be learned. People come and go in our lives, many of them when you live to be a ripe old age. We tend to forget people easily if they have no special place in our life. I fondly and vividly remember most of my school mates. I have attended all but one of my high school class reunions over the past sixty years. Many of these people stand out more than others in my mind, some for positive reasons and some for reasons that I would rather forget.

My grammar school days were the happiest times of my childhood. I loved school. I hated summer vacation. In the 1940s in Butte, Montana, there were no school buses, everyone had to walk to school. I smile now thinking of the people who joke, "I walked to school in waist high snow, uphill all the way there and back." We did, and sometimes it really *was* forty below zero! That is the coldest I remember it being. We had no 'snow' days or school closings. By God, you were there every day. Getting there was actually half of the fun.

Teasing, as it is perceived in today's society, did not seem to be an issue in our day. Maybe it should have been. Kids are cruel and there is always the little 'under-dog' who is often picked on. Such was the case in my day of one Bill Brookins. Bill was a chubby kid with ruddy cheeks who always had a sheepish grin on his face. He was the last to be picked for any team and was laughed at in class for his nonsensical answers to the teacher's questions. He wasn't a dummy at all, even though some of the kids called him stupid. He always had good grades and was irritatingly helpful to every teacher, but his social skills were obviously lacking.

I did not like Bill, but oftentimes found myself empathizing with his difficulty at making friends or being accepted. He despised me, taunting me with, "red-head, pee the bed," or calling me 'freckles.' We lived in the same block, so walking to school meant that I would encounter him every morning. Some days I would walk two blocks out of the way to avoid him. One particular day it was snowing and I didn't want to take the long route so I blatantly walked right past him. When I got in front of him he threw a snow ball which hit me in the back. I turned around, doubled up my fist and aimed for his fat tummy. He grabbed my hand and slid it down the heavy zipper of his puffy jacket. It ripped the skin off of the top of my hand. Oh my, you would have thought he had cut my hand off the way it bled. I screamed, turned around and ran for home. I was cold and sobbing and covered in blood when my mother met me at the front door. "My goodness, what happened?" she shrieked. "I got my hand caught in Bill Brookins' zipper," was my feeble reply. Mother laughed later, repeating my answer to the family.

  I did not want to go to school that day with my hand all bandaged. I hated being late and I did not want to see Bill Brookins' ugly face. I knew that he would laugh and tease me. He did. This was in the fourth grade and just one (probably the worst) of my many undesirable encounters with him over the years. Eighth grade graduation day could not come soon enough for me. I would be going to an all-girls high school and was relieved to know that I would never have to deal with Bill again.

  In the summer of 1954 I was looking forward to taking the train to Reno to vacation with my uncle and aunt. The Sunday after I arrived in Reno my aunt took me to mass at St. Thomas Cathedral. I doubt that she was a church goer, I think she did it just for me. I was impressed with the church and the choir. I walked out feeling exuberant about my summer adventure. Then I heard a strangely familiar voice behind me, "Ruthie Keane, what are you doing here?" There he stood in front of me grinning from ear to ear, my worst nightmare, Bill Brookins. He too was on vacation with his family. I didn't let this brief meeting spoil my vacation, but I prayed that I would never see his face again. Our paths never did cross during our high school years. Thank God!

  Fast forward to May of 1958. My husband was in the Navy, attending Oklahoma University in Norman, Oklahoma. I was driving our classy 1955 Oldsmobile 88 down the main street of town. My pregnant belly rubbed the steering wheel, even with the seat back as far as it would go for me to be able to reach the gas pedal. As I came to a stop at the red light, I glanced at the car next to me to see a youthful, rotund face smiling at me. "Hi, Ruthie." Not possible, this could not really be happening.

"Pull over," the driver, none other than Bill Brookins, requested. So I did. This reunion was more amicable than any of our past encounters. We laughed at the coincidence of meeting again so far from home. He had joined the Navy right out of high school and planned on making it his career. "Good to see you... until we meet again," was his parting statement. As I shared our chance meeting at the next class reunion, the question everyone asked was, "Wonder where Bill is now?" No one had ever heard from him and nobody seemed to know his family or how to contact him.

In 1964 my husband was transferred to Norfolk, Virginia. Shopping in a local, busy supermarket with my three boys, the youngest just a baby, I heard someone calling my name. Without even turning around I realized that the voice was someone from my past. Yup, behind me was a mature, handsome sailor with that same baby-faced grin and impish blue eyes smiling at me. We hugged and laughed and he greeted each of the boys personally as if he knew them. This third coincidental meeting, which neither time nor distance seemed to interfere with, was such a joy. We exchanged phone numbers and I gave him my address and we promised to keep in touch. Life tends to get busy and we just never seemed to find or take time to communicate. The years passed. At every class reunion his name came up, that irritating, aggravating, mischievous, outcast Bill Brookins.

I don't know where he is today or if he is even alive. I haven't tried to find him, I just keep waiting for the day when we will share our next serendipitous meeting.

STRANGLER IN THE NIGHT

"Doo-be-doo-be doo." Every time I hear "ol' blue eyes" crooning this tune I smile and recall a time long, long ago when life was not as fast paced or uncertain as it is today. It was, however, a difficult time for our country. We were in the midst of the Vietnam War, referred to today in South Vietnam as the 'American War.' It has also been known as the only war America ever lost when the Republic of South Vietnam was taken over by the North Vietnamese. It still today remains a very controversial topic. The United States largest military presence in the war was from 1965 to 1968. At that time, I was living in Philadelphia. My husband was in the Navy, serving on a nuclear submarine which was on a three-month rotation schedule. My anti-war belief became a huge barrier to our relationship. "Stifle it," he would tell me. "You cannot voice your disparagement over the war while living in military quarters." Really? Well, when he was home I was very careful to keep my feelings under wraps, but the months that I spent alone with my children allowed me to vent to whomever was willing to listen to me.

Never before in history had the media had such access to cover a war, or for that matter all of the anti-war demonstrations which were going on in our country at that time, not to mention the Civil Rights Movement which was intensifying daily. The images of the fighting not only in Vietnam but in our own neighborhoods haunted my mind night and day. My nephew who was in the Army had been sent to Vietnam and I prayed daily that he would be safe. I could not comprehend our troops, young sons, fathers, and brothers dying for what in my mind would never be a victory for anyone. The South Vietnamese didn't even want us there. To make it even more unbearable for me, all of the casualties of the war who were from the East Coast were being sent to the Naval Hospital in South Philadelphia which was right across the street from our housing. The Naval Hospital is where I took my children for their doctor appointments. I could also get their haircuts there for fifty cents. I had enjoyed walking across the street with the kids until it became common to see young men in wheel chairs, some missing limbs. This was such a visual reminder to me of what I didn't ever want to have to face. I would leave the hospital some days so emotionally upset, even in tears. One day a young doctor had to come to my aid as I was irrationally trying to push my baby's stroller through a revolving door. I just wanted to get out of there. It got harder and harder for me to go back with each trip.

Returning home from one of my dreaded trips to the hospital one day I saw new neighbors moving in next door. I decided to be neighborly and take them some homemade oatmeal cookies. People from New Jersey are not always of a friendly nature, or so I had heard. When these folks acted less than thrilled with my attempted hospitality and offer to help them I just high-tailed it back home. The next day the lady of the house came to my door to thank me and apologize for her curt behavior. She introduced herself to me as Tina. She was Italian, with bleached blond hair, ample cleavage and a much friendlier attitude than I had experienced the day before. I liked her immediately and even more so when I realized that I could voice my opinion of world affairs to her without being repressed. She agreed with me about the war. She respected my thoughts and opinions. She was well spoken and appeared to be educated and she laughed easily. I admired her. She had no children, but was quite comfortable around mine. While both of our husbands were deployed we became friends. She told me wonderful stories of a life that I envied. I had, up until then, only experienced raising kids, cooking, Walt Disney movies and Captain Kangaroo. She spoke of the excitement of the night life and dancing to live music at the clubs. I was enthralled with it all.

Tina had a brother, Gino, who was as handsome as she was beautiful. She told me that he worked in the garment district in New York City. Once a month he would drive a big panel truck down to Philly. It was filled with clothing racks of beautiful expensive men's and women's clothing. He would allow us to go through it and pick whatever we wanted for five dollars per garment. This should have given anyone a clue that it was probably not a legitimate business that Gino was running. Being limited in funds, I would pick out only two or three things at a time. Now I understood why Tina always looked like a fashion model.

One day Gino showed up with a brand new twenty-one-inch console color television set. In 1965 these sold for four or five hundred dollars. All of the tags and manuals were with it. He told me that I could buy it for a hundred dollars. This was a one-time only offer he added. Oh, my husband would be so thrilled with a new color TV when he got back from his tour of duty. I reluctantly went to the credit union and withdrew the hundred dollars from our meager savings account.

Pat returned home to a contemporary dressed wife and a brand new upscale TV set. Was he happy? Oh, no, he was a little bit smarter than his gullible wife. He had Gino all figured out. He was impressed with Tina, however.

One evening Tina came to the house to ask if I would like to go to bingo with her at her family's parish church, just over the Ben Franklin Bridge in Camden, New Jersey. She said that she knew I never got to go out and with my husband home now to watch the kids it would be a good break for me. He agreed with her. I hadn't been anywhere without my kids in years so I was excitedly looking forward to my night out. As I was getting ready to go, Pat was watching the local news and he told me, in kind of a joking way, to be careful because there was a serial killer in New Jersey who had strangled three young women and they were all redheads. I laughed and told him not to worry, I would be safe with Tina, and we would after all be at a church.

Bingo was fun. There were three of us – one of Tina's cousins met us there. We didn't win but we had a great time. When we left the church Tina suggested that we should go over to Gino's friend's night club. I was all for it; this was my first night out. There were, of course, no cell phones at that time but I wasn't worried about calling my husband, he had told me to have a good time.

This sheltered girl from Montana had never seen such a luxurious place. There was black leather upholstery, stainless steel paneling, and hanging lights everywhere. It was like walking into a 1930s movie scene. The girls had teased me earlier in the evening about the serial killer, so when we walked into the club and heard Frank Sinatra crooning, "Strangers in the Night," they changed the words to "Strangler in the Night" to serenade me. It felt good to be part of the grown-up world. We laughed a lot.

A very handsome, well-dressed man escorted us to a corner booth and took our order. Never having ordered a drink, I just said, "White wine, please." Tina recognized one of Gino's friends when he nodded and smiled at her. He approached our table and she introduced us to him. By now I was beginning to feel uncomfortable and out of place, and I just wanted to go home. I was relieved when he got up and left the table, but he returned after talking to two other pristine groomed gentlemen at the bar. He came directly toward me and I felt my heart do a little skip. "Ma'am, I don't want you to think that I am being forward, I just have a favor to ask. Would you get up and pretend that you are with me and walk with me to the door?" Tina kicked me so hard under the table that I must have jumped a foot. "No," was my shaky answer. *Oh my God! Is this the strangler? What am I doing here?* I thought. He walked back up to the bar and he and the two men he had talked to headed to the door. Wow, was I glad to see them leave. "I'm ready to go, Tina. I have to get home."

We didn't hear the shots, but before we finished our drinks and made it to the door the police had the place shut down and surrounded. It wasn't the serial killer they were looking for; it was someone who had just shot three men as they were leaving the club.

When I finally arrived home my sleepy hubby inquired, "Did you have a good time? I guess the strangler didn't get you… ha, ha." In the morning I told him that I would never again leave the house at night without him. The local news that day was not about the serial killer, the Vietnam War or the civil rights demonstrations, but about the New Jersey Italian Mafia murders.

Tina and I remained friends, but I never dealt with Gino again and I have to smile whenever I hear Frank Sinatra singing "Strangers in the Night."

MY FIRST CAR

I learned to drive at fourteen years of age in my brother's 1944 Plymouth coupe, standard shift of course. When I was in high school my dad purchased a sleek green 1949 Hudson Hornet and I was allowed to drive it back and forth to the dump now and then and occasionally five blocks to church on Sunday mornings. I didn't get my driver's license, however, until I was eighteen years old. I longed for the day that I would have my very own car. When I got married in 1957 my husband had a classy tomato red and white 1955 Oldsmobile 88. I did get to drive it, but still it wasn't *my* car. As our family grew we graduated to a station wagon – several station wagons – over the years. I didn't have a car of my own until I was over thirty years old.

In 1967 we moved to Bremerton, Washington, and I went to work at the Sears service department. Deciding that I would need something to drive to work, my husband purchased an old beat-up Dodge pickup truck. It was faded pink, dilapidated, scratched and dented and it sounded like a freight train chugging down the tracks. The muffler had a hole in it and the clutch was in need of repair. Even though I thought I knew how to drive a stick shift, I would pop the clutch and jerk up the road like a lame lobster in wet sand. The guys that I worked with labeled me 'Clutch' and would all be snickering when I walked into the shop following a loud back-fire as I turned off the engine. One of my favorite of the thirteen men I worked with was a Hispanic man named Juan. "Here comes Clutch in her Dutch (Dodge) truck," he would chime, laughing.

One morning a customer, overhearing the teasing, asked me if I would be interested in buying his parent's car, a 1964 Ford Thunderbird. They were no longer able to drive and he was trying to sell it. Wow, my dream car. I took his number and told him that I would call him that evening. That car was all I could think about the whole day. "How much do they want for it?" my husband questioned me when I told him about it. "Eight hundred dollars." "Well, I guess we could go take a look at it."

"Sure, you can come over and check it out tomorrow morning," the friendly voice on the other end of the line told me when I called.

As we drove up to the address he had given me I saw the shiny, black car of my dreams in the front yard. It looked brand new, as if it had just come off of the showroom floor. It was love at first sight. I was near hysteria with joy as I jumped out of the car. It seemed just too good to be true. My husband casually shook hands with the young man who came out of the house as I was swooning over the red leather interior, the classy console and the factory paper protectors on the floor of the back seat which had obviously never been occupied. My husband looked it over and while he was looking under the hood and checking the tires I was making a mental note of the fact that he didn't know any more about cars than I did. He dared not say no. I had already made up my mind that this was going to be my car.

He seemed almost anxious to pay the man, which surprised me. I drove away smiling and singing, my head in the clouds. I didn't give a thought as to why he was so agreeable about buying the car. It was my very own car, the title in my name. I had no idea that he was planning to leave me and wanted to be sure that I had my own transportation.

How I loved driving that car! It was quite a change from the station wagon and the old "Dutch" truck. The engine purred, it ran smoothly and within five months I had three speeding tickets and a warning notice from the DMV to prove its speed. One day I turned on the windshield wipers (an important necessity in Washington) and the radio quit playing. Soon after that incident the dashboard lights would not come on unless the radio was turned on and the automatic windows would only work if I turned off the radio. What's going on? I didn't know a mechanic so I ended up having to take the car to the local Ford dealer. "You have an electrical problem. Some of the wires were shorted and luckily nothing sparked or you could possibly have had a fire. I *think* we have it taken care of." For as long as I drove that car there was always an electrical glitch. I had it checked by two other people who were also stumped. It continued to run however, and I drove it until I remarried and moved to Missouri.

The man I married, John, had a best friend, Lee. They were both in the Navy and both confirmed bachelors. Lee was quite a character. He carried a huge plastic coffee mug and you could never be sure what was in it. Sometimes it was coffee, sometimes juice, but more often than not it was alcohol related – beer, rum and coke, maybe even straight vodka. He had an impish grin and a quick laugh. He was the kind of guy that you couldn't help but love. He and John were both near retirement from the Navy. John and I got married shortly after he retired and we planned to move to his home in Missouri. I agreed to let Lee rent my house until time for his retirement the following year. I knew that he would take good care of it as he was a 'spit and polish' military man. He wanted to buy my T-Bird also, but I just wasn't ready to part with it even though I wasn't planning to drive it to Missouri. Once we relocated and were settled in John bought me a brand new car. "Why don't you let Lee have your T-Bird? It's just sitting there and I can't see you bringing it down here now," he suggested. I reluctantly agreed and sent the title and keys to Lee and called and told him, "Happy Birthday." When Lee retired I sold my house and I wish that I could say 'lived happily ever after,' but not all fairy tales end that way.

  I have owned and driven many cars over the years, usually because they were affordable and dependable, not necessarily because I loved them. I had just accepted the fact that there would never be another dream car in my life.

  In the mid-1980s I received a phone call from my old buddy, Lee. He and my brother had remained friends over the years. "Hey, girl, so you're livin' back in Washington. How'd ya like to come to New Mexico and claim this damned car of yours? It's been sittin' in my brother's yard for years and he wants it out of here. I remember how attached you were to it and I thought that you might like to have it back. Damned thing doesn't run; no one ever did figure out the electrical problem. It needs a lot of work, but it's yours if you'll come get it." At that time in our life Larry and I were struggling to pay off our property. I was working two jobs and the time and expense of hauling an old car fifteen hundred miles just didn't seem feasible. I refused Lee's offer. I neglected to get his address or even his phone number. I have tried in recent years to find him, but to no avail.

  So now, every year at Reno's Hot August Nights car show, I seem to make it a point to hunt down every 1964 Thunderbird in the show and find someone who will listen to my sad story and cry with me. What I wouldn't give to have my very own first dream car today.

THREE STRIKES YOU'RE OUT

Who me? In trouble with the law? I'll have you know that I have been an honest, upstanding citizen all of my life. Well, we're not including minor traffic violations are we? Everyone gets a ticket now and then, don't they?

In 1972 I purchased a 1964 Ford Thunderbird for eight hundred dollars. Oh, it was a beauty, black with red leather interior. It belonged to an older couple, and it had less than thirty thousand miles on it. The back seat still had the factory paper mats on the floor. Driving it was quite a change from driving a station wagon. It didn't take me long to discover how fast it could go. When I got my first speeding ticket, I quickly learned that tears don't get you very far in a traffic stop. Within a month I was stopped again and received my second ticket. I decided that I had better slow down, just about the same time that I got a warning letter from the Washington State Patrol informing me that a third ticket in a six-month period could possibly cost me my driving privileges.

The summer of that year my mom and dad came to visit from Montana. My dad had just purchased a new Buick. He asked me if I would like to drive from my house in Bremerton to my brother's in Seattle since he was not use to the traffic and didn't know directions. I was thrilled. I had never driven a brand new car. It was a Sunday morning, so there wasn't much traffic. Just before we got into Seattle, I looked in the rear-view mirror and saw flashing lights approaching very quickly. As I took my foot off of the gas, I glanced at the speedometer and realized that it was somewhere past the ninety mile an hour mark. Oh, oh. "This is it," I thought. "Three times, I'm out." When the State Trooper started toward the car, my sister, who was in the back seat, blurted out, "Here comes 'mokey the bear." He was dark skinned and dressed in a uniform that did look exactly like Smokey the Bear. As he approached my window I could not stop laughing, and my dad was punching me, "Shut up, shut up!" "You're in a big hurry this morning, ma'am," Smokey said. "I see you're from Montana." "Oh, yeah," I thought, he knows there is no speed limit in Montana. I won't get a ticket. Then of course he asked for my drivers license and I had to hand him my Washington license. He wrote out a ticket and politely warned me to slow down. When we left my brother's house that evening I couldn't find my shoes and when someone asked what they looked like, my nephew, Dan, said, "They're the ones with the lead in the right foot." I don't remember how much the ticket was but my dad insisted on paying it. I was surprised that I didn't get another notice or warning, and I promised myself then that I was going to slow down.

  Several months later, at Christmas time in fact, one of my co-workers, Jeanne, invited me to her house after work to share a bit of Christmas cheer. My children were with their dad until Christmas Eve, so I had no reason to hurry home. I had accepted a dinner date with a fellow I had met at a Christmas party the previous week-end. He did not want to go to Jeanne's house with me, so he told me to take his car, drop him off at a tavern that was on the way to her place, and just pick him up in a couple of hours. Sounded like a good plan, as I didn't want to go to a tavern with him anyway. I was not a drinker, but Jeanne told me that she was sure I would love her husband's hot buttered rum. She was right. It was delicious. My co-workers, who were the only friends I had at that time, were all there. Everyone was laughing and having a great time and after a couple of Jim's hot buttered rums the time just seemed to get away from me. When I realized that it was almost 2:00 AM and John was waiting for me to pick him up, I panicked and left in a big hurry. I have never done well with direction and was not aware that I was driving in the opposite way of the tavern, nor was I aware of how fast I was going until the flashing lights behind me caught my attention. I fumbled for my drivers license as the State Trooper approached the car. "Where are you headed, ma'am?" "Home," I answered lamely. "And just where is home?" he questioned. "Bremerton." I was actually headed toward Silverdale. His next question was, "Have you been drinking?" "Well, I had a couple of hot buttered rums, but that's all." He then ordered me to get out of the car and had me walk the line and touch my nose. I guess I passed the field test and he didn't make me do a breathalyzer, just told me to get in the car, turn around and drive very carefully straight home. I was really nervous when I realized that he was following me, and I was concentrating hard on driving 'sober.' As I passed the tavern where I was supposed to meet John I saw that the lights were all out and there were no cars in the parking lot. Oh, dear, poor John.

Just minutes before I got to my house I realized that I was feeling kind of sick. I pulled into my driveway and saw the patrol car pull up to the curb. "Oh, my God," I thought, "I have to get into the house, I'm about to throw up." I got as far as the front door and had my key in the lock when I felt hands on my shoulders. As the patrolman spun me around, I spewed vomit all over the front of him. I was so mortified and at that moment was more sober than I had ever been in my life. As he was backing away, I heard myself apologizing and offering him money to have his uniform cleaned.

My next door neighbor, George, was the Kitsap County Deputy Sheriff and I was anxious to tell him the next morning what had happened. "Did you possibly get his name?" he questioned me. I remembered looking at his name tag at some point, and when I answered "Johnson," George shook his head and with an uncomfortable swallow mumbled, "That son-of-a-bitch." It seems that I had been too naive (or maybe drunk) to realize that he had a purpose in mind when he followed me home. Clenching his jaw, George explained to me that patrolman Johnson had a reputation for trading favors with female offenders. I was upset, but couldn't keep from laughing. "Hope he learned a lesson." Had I been given a ticket it would have been my fourth offense in a year. I prayed that I would never again encounter Mr. Johnson and vowed that I would never get behind the wheel of a car after 'just a couple' of drinks.

Oh, what about John? The bartender took him home and he was at my front door to get his car bright and early the next morning.

It was several years later before I ever got another ticket, but have twice since gotten two speeding tickets within months of each other. With the point system that they use in Nevada now, it seems that just as soon as I get my points deleted, my right foot gets heavy again. It's been several years since I've had a ticket and true to my vow I have never, ever gotten behind the wheel after having even one drink.

DISCRIMINATION

"Mom, what is a Haole?" my son Patrick bellowed as he came through the door after his first day of school in Hawaii. I wasn't familiar with that slang term, but his younger brother Don laughed telling him, "It just means that you're a white boy, white boy."

Patrick had been enrolled in Damien Catholic High School, which was predominantly Asian and Polynesian students. He, being tall, thin and very blond, obviously stood out like a petunia in a pumpkin patch. Luckily he was out-going, self-assured and not easily intimidated or I am sure he would have felt that he was being bullied.

Being military brats, my kids had never experienced any kind of discrimination prior to this. Now my son was relating to me in detail how he had a better understanding of how the blacks in the south must have felt during the segregation demonstrations of the 1960s. He had best friends who were black and Hispanic but he had never considered them any different from himself, nor had they. This was not the case with the elite Asian population that he was dealing with now. These young men had been brought up to believe that they were far superior which tended to make outsiders to their culture feel like the underdog. Patrick took it in stride and his attitude of equality seemed to rub off, or at least mellow some of the boys, and he had soon made friends.

I had answered an advertisement to sell Avon. I thought it would be a great part-time job while the kids were in school. I was assigned a designated area which turned out to be one of the upper-class Japanese neighborhoods in Honolulu. I had not taken into consideration the encounter that my son had faced at school. I was a very fair complexioned redhead with a bright name tag that boasted of my Irish heritage, "O'Neill." When I was handed my assignment the other sales ladies snickered and rolled their eyes. I was totally unaware that *outsiders* were not seen very favorably in the closed culture community of Honolulu. "Ha," scoffed one lady. "You had better change that name tag to Yamamoto." They all giggled. My first reaction was a desire to just back out, quit before I had even started, but then I remembered Patrick's positive attitude and decided that if Rosa Parks could muster up the courage to take that front seat on the bus, I could sure as heck walk up on a porch and ring a doorbell. Ding-dong... Avon calling.

In just a matter of months I was not only accepted but embraced by my new clientele, proving to me that discrimination is not, nor should it be, a barrier to equality.

O'Neill family in Hawaii 1972

#METOO

The Cosby Show was a popular sitcom series which was televised from 1984 to 1992. Who didn't love Doctor Huxtable, the image of the ideal dad and family man? When the allegations of sexual misconduct against Bill Cosby were first made public in 2014 I was shocked, as were thousands of other fans of *The Cosby Show*. I questioned the fact that his accusers had not reported any of the incidents when they happened. Why would they not have told someone? As I pondered this question over and over I began experiencing opposing emotions. With a sinking feeling in my stomach I decided that it was time for me to face the fact that I too had neglected to do the right thing by not verbalizing a conflict that I had experienced once in my life.

I was 35 years old, and the mother of four when my husband of seventeen years asked me for a divorce. I pleaded with him to go to counseling with me but he refused and was remarried two days after our divorce was finalized. I was devastated to say the least. I had a good job but was not prepared, financially nor emotionally, to raise four children by myself. My boss, Don, realizing my overwrought state of mind suggested that I consider counseling. He referred me to his pastor, Jeff, who was a licensed marriage and family counselor and also a personal friend of his.

I reluctantly called to see if I could arrange an appointment to talk with Jeff. I was uncomfortable confiding to anyone about personal matters. I could not imagine how he could make me feel any better about myself or my situation, but I was willing to give counseling a try. His office was in his home and he agreed to see me the next day when I got off work.

I had worked for the service department at Sears for ten years. In the 1970s the company had a strict dress code. You were only allowed to wear a dress or suit in black, brown or navy blue. Slacks were not permitted, nor wereprint or flowered patterns or plaid. I had one plain sheath dress of each color and mid-heel pumps to match. I would occasionally add a piece of simple jewelry or a scarf. I kept my long hair straight back off of my face in a bun which was easy and looked neat and professional.

When I arrived at Jeff's office, after introducing himself and asking me to take a seat, his first words to me were, "You are a very attractive woman. Why do you present yourself as plain and cold?" *What?* I explained to him that I had just come from work and this was my work attire. I was feeling uncomfortable with the questions he was asking me about my marriage and my personal life. Being bitter and hurt by my husband's deceit, I made a derogatory statement about men in general. He informed me that the reason I felt so negative toward men was because I was jealous that I didn't have a penis. So help me God, those were his exact words. I was appalled. I could feel my cheeks burning and my hands tightening into fists. I just wanted to get up and run. I didn't hear another word that he said. When I left, feeling worse than I had when I got there, I felt an unshakable sense of something being wrong. Was I overreacting? Fighting to regain my composure, I agreed to see him the following week. I didn't want to recount the incident to Don the next day when he inquired as to how my session went, so when he asked I just smiled and said, "OK."

I debated all week whether or not to go back and was questioning myself about what he had said. It would, after all, probably be easier to be a man. And he called me *cold.* Who has ever met a cold redhead? I left work an hour early the day of my appointment to go home and change clothes. I donned a black mini-skirt, a silk ruffled blouse, black hose and high heeled shoes and brushed my long red hair into the famous 'Veronica Lake' over the eye flowing style. *Cold?* Hell, I looked hot! Jeff's mouth dropped when I walked into the room. "Now, that's more like it." He grinned, glaring at me in a way that made me want to fade into the background to avoid his sleazy glare. I hadn't intended my dressing up to appear as a come-on, but maybe I had overdone it a bit.

After inquiring about my week at work, Jeff began the session by relating to me a story about a woman who worked in a German prisoner of war camp during the Second World War. The captors would give a prisoner beer and after he had consumed a few glasses they would insert a glass rod into his penis and then use a mallet to crush the glass. This attractive woman would then be brought into the room to arouse him. The horror of the story, and the fact that he was telling me this, seemed to please him. He told me that I reminded him of that woman. "You enjoy building a man up and then seeing him suffer," he smugly replied. I felt my chest tighten and a quiver in my stomach. I sat frozen, my mind racing, not knowing how to reply or react to his allegation. "That is probably why your husband had an affair," he added. I could feel the tears welling up in my eyes. I thought that counseling was supposed to make me feel better. He recognized my distress and got up from his chair and walked toward me. I rose immediately, lifting my chin in an attempt to look confident, and headed for the door. He reached for me and calmly in almost a whisper said, "Let me comfort you." I did not want to be comforted, I just wanted to be out of there. He put his arm around me and when I stiffened, drawing back, he said, "You are going to have to learn to relax. I think we'll have to do some breathing sessions." I grabbed my purse and fled, slamming the door behind me.

On the drive home, thinking about what had just happened, I decided that I was more angry than upset. Why would he even think that it was acceptable to talk to me like that? Did he think that I was so vulnerable that I would fall into his arms? Having always been of a spiteful nature I was determined not to let this man break me. "I'll just show him," I thought out loud. When my boss questioned me the next day about how the counseling session went I was too embarrassed to tell him what had happened. This was after all his friend and pastor.

I kept my next appointment. I went directly from work in my *cold* persona. I had slipped the glass stirrer from a cocktail set and one of the kids little wooden mallets into my purse. I was seated in the office when Jeff arrived and when he inquired as to how my weekend was I placed the stirrer and the mallet on the desk, smiled and said, "Wonderful. How was yours?" I hadn't intended my prank to be a joke, but he laughed.

"We're going to do some breathing exercises today. Just relax and breathe deeply, filling first your stomach and then your lungs," he calmly instructed me. "Good, good, now exhale slowly through your mouth." We continued this breathing exercise for a few minutes and then he got up and stood behind me with his hand on my back. I was actually beginning to feel a little more relaxed. "Now I want you to get up and get on the floor so we can do some peaceful meditation." I don't know why I complied, but when I realized that he was standing over me I knew that I had to get out of there, and fast. He had become aware of my anxiety and attempted to hold me down. As I bolted to my feet I knocked him sideways to the floor. Spinning around and gasping for air, I vaulted out of the door, hoping that no one would witness my desperate escape.

Replaying what had happened in agonizing detail on my way home, I became overwhelmed with anxiety. I was fearful that if I told anyone what had happened they would blame me or pass judgment on me. I didn't want to tell Don that his friend was a pervert or a predator. I was saddened to think that his actions had taken place in his own home, with his wife in another room. Why was I feeling guilty? I decided right then that I had to just put the whole encounter behind me and never say anything to anyone about it.

So, who am I to ask, with all of the allegations coming out today, why the victims did not tell anyone when they were violated? Over the years I have regretted my poor decision not to seek counsel or report my experience. Perhaps it would have saved someone else from being a victim. The current #MeToo movement allows survivors to feel supported and to feel free to discuss issues surrounding harassment, assault and sexual bullying, to share their stories and to promote both social and legal changes that need to be addressed.

The #MeToo movement is thriving. No one should ever be afraid to speak out.

NEVER LOOK BACK

  I sometimes wonder if everyone has a timeline in their life that they don't like to talk about, or perhaps like to pretend didn't ever occur. Not necessarily a *bad* time, but rather an uncomfortable mistake or misjudgment. For years I never spoke about my second marriage or acknowledged that it ever even happened. Looking back now my silent years are memorable and laughable in many ways.
  After my divorce, being left with four children to raise alone, my whole life centered on my family. I was lucky to have a good job, and was able to work Mondays through Fridays, the same hours that the kids were in school. We stayed busy with little league, cub scouts, swimming lessons, bowling, band, and lots of home work. I taught CCD (Confraternity of Christian Doctrine) at the church on Sunday; our weeks were always full. My niece, Sheri, was living with us while attending Olympic College which was just a few blocks from our house. The kid's coaches, the scout leaders and my work colleagues were the only adults in my life. Sheri thought that I should have some kind of social life so when I received an invitation to attend a Christmas party that was being given by one of the little league coaches, she encouraged me to attend. The coach also happened to be a Navy officer living on the Naval Base. I did not want to go. Being an x-Navy wife and not knowing most of the people who would be there seemed intimidating to me. Sheri was persistent. As I started to get dressed I began to get a little excited about the prospect of a night out with adults. As soon as I walked out the door, however, I got cold feet, but it was too late. Sheri had locked me out and was not going to let me back in. "Please go, Aunt Ruth," she pleaded through the door.
  I was never shy meeting new people but when I arrived at the address on the invitation I was as nervous as someone on a first date. I rang the doorbell and was greeted by the host. He led me down a steep stairway to a sprawling recreation room full of talking, laughing people. I smiled and tried to be sociable as I was introduced to everyone. One

quiet, handsome, bearded man who met me at the bottom of the stairs was overly attentive and that made me uneasy. I tried to avoid him in the crowded room, but there he was, watching my every move. He later told me that when he saw me at the top of the steps he announced to everyone in the room that he was going to marry me. And marry me he did!

John Richmond Walton III was related to Sam Walton, the founder of Walmart. In 1974 Walmart was no more than a small retail store in Arkansas. John came from a humble background and a loving, close, religious family. He had joined the navy as a young man, married and had two sons. While he was on deployment in the Navy his wife left the young boys with his parents one day while she went shopping. She never returned. John's parents were awarded legal custody of the boys and raised them. John only saw them when he was home on leave, maybe once or twice a year. When I met John he was preparing to retire after a twenty-year Navy career. He planned to move back to Missouri where he owned a home and a large mechanic shop on the Eleven Point River in Thomasville. He was looking forward to getting to know his boys who by then were in high school. He professed his love for me and my kids and said that he did not want to go home without us. "Is this man crazy?" was my first reaction. Who in their right mind would marry a woman and take on three kids? My second son, Don, was living with his Dad at that time. John was wonderful with the kids and they really liked him. I was confused and scared. I knew that I didn't love him but I could envision a bright future and real security. I knew that if I refused his offer I would always wonder, 'what if?'

We were married by the Navy Chaplin at the base chapel. My brother gave me away and all of the kids were present. "Oh, my God, what have I done?" I asked myself almost immediately after the ceremony. My brother liked John. Everyone liked John. I realized at that moment that I didn't even know him. It turned out that his family didn't know him either.

The move to Missouri was exciting for the kids. Don chose to stay with his dad which was difficult for me but turned out to be best for both him and his dad at that time. My son, Patrick, was the same age as John's youngest son, Curtis, so he had no problem fitting right in at his new school. The two younger kids adapted well and loved the Walton family. The boys enjoyed living near the river where they fished and speared bull-frogs. Thomasville is a small town just east of West Plains. The house we lived in was originally a theater, where Porter Wagoner first introduced Dolly Parton. Across the street from the house was the country store and post office. One day a tourist walked into the store and asked my son, Raymond, who was hanging out there with his new friends, "Where's the post office?" "Right behind the potato chips, ma'am," he replied.

Every day was a new adventure. When my daughter came in the house to get her red coat in the middle of the summer I questioned her as to why she wanted her coat. She informed me that she was going to *olé* the neighbor's bull. The neighbor up the hill from us milked his cows twice a day and the local dairy came every morning to pick up the fresh milk. The first spring that I was there his cows got out of the fence and into a pasture of wild garlic. The dairy wouldn't take the milk. When I heard that he was going to dump it I asked him if he would let some settle and skim the cream off of the top for me. "Why?" he asked. I told him that I had the ingenious idea of churning it and making garlic butter. The neighbors were sure impressed when I distributed it throughout town.

I was enjoying country living. When John and his dad plowed the garden with a horse drawn plow I followed behind them, loving the smell of the fresh plowed dirt and the feel of it between my toes. John laughed when I asked for a pig for my birthday. "Most women want jewelry and furs," he said as he gifted me with Nelly. She was a beauty. When I told my dad about her, he chided me, "Nelly, Nelly with a pig skin belly, put an apple in her mouth and we'll all have pork and jelly." As Nelly grew bigger she got a little bit mean with the kids. I think maybe they teased her. I told my son, Raymond, not to go into the pen to feed her. It just so happened that I was in the yard hammering a gate onto a post one evening when I heard a piercing scream coming from the pig pen. Low and behold, there was Raymond half way over the fence with his right foot firmly engaged in Nelly's mouth. I raced to the fence, raised the hammer and came down firmly right between Nelly's eyes. She quickly released him and as he scurried over the fence she began staggering in a circle, finally dropping to the ground. I began screaming hysterically, "I killed Nelly, I killed Nelly." The neighbors came running across the yard, not knowing that Nelly was my pig. I guess they thought that I had killed one of my kids. By this time Nelly had recovered the blow enough to get up. I don't remember her ever going after one of the kids after that. Of course, they were all a little more cautious about going into the pen.

Upon learning how I loved my pig, one of the neighbors brought me a black and white Hampshire runt pig that the mother pig had rejected. I took it upon myself to feed it with a doll bottle every two hours. We named her Lil'Bit and kept her in a box in the kitchen. One day the local dentist's wife came to the house with my mother-in-law. When she saw the pig under the kitchen table she asked, "Isn't that a little unsanitary?" I replied with a smile, "Oh, the pig doesn't seem to mind." When Lil'Bit got big enough to put outside she refused to stay in the pig pen. She would dig her way under the fence, come to the back door and scratch at the screen to get in. She knew she was a house pet! We finally had to resort to putting an electric wire on the bottom of the fence. She learned quickly then that she had to stay there.

I also raised a big red Hampshire for another neighbor. We couldn't put him in the pen with the other pigs because he was lame and they picked on him, so he became our yard pet. The kids rode him and toted him around on a leash. The owner eventually came to take Big Red to the butcher. We didn't tell my daughter where he was going. The boys, being boys, waited to tell her when I served ground pork sausage.

So life was good, dreams can come true. So can nightmares. John had a drinking problem. I didn't know this before we were married, nor did his parents. He was never mean, never abusive, verbally or physically, just plain crazy when he drank. He bought me a beautiful new car. As I was washing it one day he confronted me saying, "I think you love that car more than you love me." Being quite flippant I replied, "You might just be right." He grabbed the keys and drove off. An hour or so passed and there was a knock at the door. "Mrs. Walton?" "Yes," I replied as my heart skipped a beat. "Your car is in the bottom of the river." "And John?" I questioned. "He's OK. We arrested him on a DUI." This was just the beginning of my year of hell.

One day I had my shoes sitting on the fireplace mantle and for no apparent reason John threw them into the fire. I bought him a denim jacket with real sheepskin lining, he threw it in the fire. He threw his sound system speakers in the fire. These actions were not in fits of rage, just random acts of crazy when he had been drinking. I was becoming more and more uncomfortable around him and concerned for my kids. I didn't want them exposed to his irrational behavior. I wasn't sleeping well at night and I knew that my only option was to leave. I should have known that it's impossible to try to reason with a drunk. I told him that I was planning to leave one evening when he had been drinking. He laughed and told me that I could never leave him. I guess to prove his point he went into the bedroom and returned with his gun. He started to cry and told me that he felt sorry for me. It was after eleven PM and the kids had been in bed for hours. I quickly woke them while he was ranting and raving and told them to get into the car immediately. If he was going to shoot me I wanted to be sure that the kids were out of the house. I grabbed my purse and ran to the car with my daughter in tow. I literally threw her in the back seat and slammed the door. Her nightgown was caught in the door and she was crying. I heard the bullets as I screeched out of the driveway. I drove ninety miles an hour to West Plains, about thirty miles away. I prayed that he wasn't following me. I went directly to the police station but of course there was no one there at midnight. I had no other option but to go to John's parents' house. I felt badly waking them. They were totally shocked at my story. "I don't know what's gotten into John. He was perfectly normal until he met you," was his mother's response. I guess I had been right – they really didn't know him. Mr. Walton took me back to Thomasville the next day to collect my personal belongings. I did not even look at John and we didn't speak. When I left I swore that I would never look back. I knew that I had not failed, but I still felt ashamed and embarrassed to face my family. I wanted to just erase the whole episode.

My mom and dad were visiting my sister in Fallon, Nevada, so I headed straight there. John knew where my sister lived and by chance he even had her phone number. I spent several days trying to explain to my family everything that had happened and tried to justify my leaving to myself. The Saturday evening after I arrived in Fallon my dad and I dropped my mom off at the local Catholic Church for mass. He and I decided to spend the hour at the local Nugget Casino. We picked her up at exactly 7:00 PM as directed. When we got back to my sister's house she informed me that John Walton had called her. She knew to tell him that I was not there. When I asked her where he had called from my heart skipped a beat when she said, "The Nugget." He had followed me to Nevada. I guess he gave up at that point. I never saw him again. I was relieved to get divorce papers in the mail when I returned to Washington. I read the divorce decree and tucked it carefully into a drawer. I never spoke of that marriage to anyone, ever. I wanted to believe that it had never happened.

Larry and I were married three years later. I did tell him my well-kept secret, just not all of the details. We had been married for four years when I received a phone call from a lawyer in Missouri stating that John wanted me to sign a quick-claim deed on some property that he was going to sell. I informed him that I was no longer married to John Walton. He came back with the news that since I had not shown up for the divorce hearing it had been deemed null and void. I was legally still

Mrs. Walton. Oh, oh! What's the punishment for bigamy? I asked him to send me the papers to sign and to please do whatever was necessary to finalize the divorce.

The nightmare was finally over but it was still years before I could talk about it. I had promised myself when I left that I would never look back. John has since passed and now I can look back and smile, remembering and sharing with my children stories of the good times we had in Missouri.

AN UNFORGETTABLE THANKSGIVING

Thanksgiving of 1975 stands out as one of my most amusing holidays ever. I was on pins and needles anticipating spending my first Thanksgiving with my new family in Missouri. John had bragged to his family for a whole year about what a great home maker and cook I was and now the time had come for me to prove myself worthy of his praise. We were to spend Thanksgiving day with the entire Walton family at John's sister's house in Branson, which was a two-hour drive from our home in Thomasville. Plans were made for us to arrive the day before Thanksgiving to give me time to make pumpkin pies and prepare my much-touted cranberry salad. John's mother had requested that I bake my Aunt Betty's acclaimed 'White Christmas Cake,' so I made it ahead of time to take with us.

I recall it being an especially pleasant drive that day. The kids and I were anxious to get to know the extended Walton family. I had not met John's sister, Laura. I had only talked to her on the phone, but I felt like I already knew her. She was friendly and outgoing. Her children were younger than mine but they were excited to meet their new cousins. What a glorious celebration this would be.

John's parents had arrived at Laura's earlier in the day. When we drove up, they opened the front door to greet us and Buffy, their overly rambunctious, some kind of terrier dog, bolted out of the door making a mad dash to the car. As I opened the back door to retrieve my beautiful 'White Christmas Cake' Buffy jumped, right paw first, full weight, on top of the cake. Luckily it was covered, first with plastic wrap and then foil. I was in tears thinking that the cake was surely ruined. Buffy's paw print was neatly embedded in the frosting, looking surprisingly as though it was an intended decoration. The cake was still edible. Everyone had a good laugh, which seemed to set the mood of the first meeting off on a positive note.

Laura was a gracious hostess and everyone made it a point to make us feel welcome. After a delicious spaghetti dinner, the men retired to the den, and Laura and I continued to chat as we washed the dishes and cleaned-up the kitchen. Our plan was for me to make the pies and prepare the cranberries for the salad that evening. The recipe for the cranberry salad calls for the berries to be crushed and sweetened with sugar to set overnight. Not having a food processor, I always chopped the berries in my blender. Laura got out her blender for me and told me the kitchen was all mine. I washed the berries, put them in the blender, hit the 'on' button and '*Kaboom*'! In a split second there were berries all over the wall, the counter and the ceiling. I had neglected to put the lid on the blender. I was beside myself. I didn't know whether to laugh or cry. Well, so much for the cranberry salad. Hearing my gasp of disbelief and shock, Laura with the guys close behind her, rushed into the kitchen to find me stammering, so embarrassed that I wanted to run and hide. Their wide-eyed amusement and uncontrollable laughter seemed to outweigh my inability to even speak. I turned away to try to regain my composure, but found myself covering my mouth and biting my lip to hide my smile. It was funny.

After cleaning up the mess and listening to everyone replaying the humorous event, it was time to make the pies. Oh, good, a chance to redeem myself. Using my mother's never-fail crust recipe, I set about to make two pumpkin pies. Laura stayed in the kitchen with me, she said to learn to make pie crust but I always wondered if it was to make sure I didn't destroy her kitchen again.

The oven was preheated, the crust and filling were made and the pies were ready to be baked. With one pie in hand, I reached to open the oven door with the other hand and in an instant the pie was upside-down on the hot oven door and all over the floor. No, this couldn't really be happening. This mishap was not quite as laughable as the first, especially for me. I quickly turned my head to hide my tears. Laura tried to console me as we waited for the oven to cool down so we could clean up the mess. It was well after 11:00 PM before I was able to bake the second pie which, thank God, turned out perfect.

I managed to stay out of the kitchen Thanksgiving day, figuring I had done enough damage the night before. Dinner went off without a hitch, minus the cranberry salad and with just one pumpkin pie and a beautiful dog paw embossed 'White Christmas Cake.'

After leaving Missouri in 1977 I lost contact with the Walton family. Every Thanksgiving I laugh, remembering my earnest attempt to impress them. It is highly unlikely that they have ever forgotten me or my preposterous comedy of errors. Another memorable Thanksgiving.

THE LONGEST PART-TIME JOB

In 1976, after a failed marriage, I returned to Washington State in order for my two youngest children, who were teenagers at the time, to be able to continue school in the place they considered home. I promised them that this would be our last move after years of military life and new schools every few years. I had worked in the service department for Sears for eleven years in three different states and I was quite sure that I would be able to transfer locations again.

We settled in a quaint little logging community on Highway 2, about a half an hour east of Everett. Gold Bar seemed like the perfect place for the kids to thrive. They adapted well and soon had new friends and were anxious to start school in nearby Sultan. Now it was time for me to get back to work. The nearest service department hiring for Sears was in South Seattle, at least an hour away and up to three hours in prime traffic time. My brother thought that it would be a great idea for us to move to Seattle to be near him and his family, but I had promised the kids that we were not going to move again and a promise is a promise.

I was hoping that there would be some kind of retail or grocery store clerk jobs available in the area. I could handle that. I loved working with the public. One of my new neighbors invited me to go to lunch with her the day the kids started school. Her friends owned a restaurant in Sultan. When we arrived and were seated, the owners of the restaurant came to our table and Lisa introduced me and promptly told them that I was looking for a job. "Oh, we are in the process of adding a bar and are looking for a bar manager. Do you know how to tend bar?" I hesitated to answer, but lamely replied, "Well, uh... my dad was a bartender, and I helped him out once at a wedding." I had no idea on earth how to mix a drink but I figured that I could open a beer, and that's what loggers drink, right?

By the end of lunch, I had agreed to take the job until I could find something permanent. They offered me three dollars and fifty cents an hour, plus tips. Construction on the bar was still taking place, but they asked if I could start the next day so that I could order the glassware and contact the vendors for supplies and write up the liquor order. These would be just some of my duties as the new bar manager. I had no idea what I was getting into. "Oh well, it's only a part-time job, I can handle it," I muttered to myself as we left the restaurant.

Within a week the owners, Bob and LeMoine, had me feeling like one of the family. I checked out "OLD MR. BOSTON'S BARTENDERS GUIDE" and learned the difference between a high-ball glass and a brandy snifter. I wanted to go to the other local bar in town to see what kind of liquor they served but I wouldn't dream of walking into a bar alone. I had no one to escort me, so I just roamed the aisles of the local liquor store and scoped out what I thought it would take to stock a bar. I also learned that vodka and orange juice is not a 'screw ball.'

The bar was in the back of the restaurant and all of the local people were anxious for the grand opening. I was not only the bar manager but also the only bartender. My first customer questioned me, "What is your bar whiskey?" "Ten High," I replied feeling quite smug about my choice of spirits. "Oh no, I want a good blended whiskey." I smiled as I put a shot of the Ten High in the blender, blended it and served it to him. The poor guy almost fell off the bar stool laughing. No one had ever told me the difference between a bourbon and a blended whiskey. That was just the beginning of my long bartending career. The bets were on – I wouldn't last three weeks.

When Bob and LeMoine sold the Chuck Wagon a year later, the couple who owned the Sportsman's Inn asked me if I would be interested in managing their bar. Wow! By that time, I knew a little more about the bar business and I also knew almost everyone in town. It is common knowledge that a bartender has to be a counselor, a priest, an advisor, part mom and part cop. In my case I also became the local logger's banker. This came about quite by accident one day when a down-and-out logger came to me crying because he had been offered a job but didn't have forty dollars for the cork boots that were required to work in the woods. I took the check that I had just written for my utility bill out of the envelope, cashed it and gave him forty dollars. Much to my dismay as soon as he left the bar smiling, his sister, who worked in the restaurant, came into the bar and said, "I sure hope you didn't give Gary money. You'll never get it back." But come Friday, Gary returned and handed me fifty dollars. When I tried to give him ten dollars back he refused it saying that it was my tip for helping him out. I thanked him and put the ten dollars in an envelope with his name on it and put it in a drawer in my office. By the end of that year I had a boot-box full of envelopes with seven or eight different names, all of whom were borrowing their own money from me. They would borrow ten or twenty dollars during the week and pay me back, sometimes even double on payday. I just kept the extra money in their envelope. I was also getting twenty per cent of any money that I collected on returned checks from my boss. I had my own little bank business going on.

One of the many things that I learned from tending bar is that you should never judge people. I also quickly caught on that a smart bartender knows absolutely nothing about anyone. If someone asked me who their brother left the bar with, I'd say, "Oh, do you have a brother?" I was happily single at this time but I wore a wedding ring as every man's second question after "What's your name?" was, "Are you married?" My answer was always the same, "What difference does it make? You are." That would shut them up fast.

One day my niece said to me, "Aunt Ruth, someday someone will walk through those doors right into your life." "Oh, no," was my quick response. "There will never be anyone in my life who drinks." I meant it. That Friday night one of the bartenders didn't show up for work and my boss called me in to work. Oh, oh, a busy bar on Friday night. I wasn't sure if I could handle that. My dad, who was not happy about me working in a bar, would jokingly tease me, "You're not a slow bartender, you're not a fast bartender, you're a half-fast bartender." Well, this night would be my test.

I was doing pretty well keeping up with the crowd. There was only one vacant bar stool, way at the far end of the bar. In walked a lone stranger. I set out a coaster, hardly even glancing at this dude and said, "What would you like?" "You," came the aggravating reply. Oh boy, here we go again. "What can I get you to drink?" When he answered "Double orange juice on the rocks" his voice and words took me so by surprise that I was forced to actually look at him. He had a nice smile and piercing blue eyes. I tried the rest of the evening to ignore him but he kept calling me back, questioning me and then questioning all of the customers about me. Although he was getting on my nerves I was at least impressed that he wasn't drinking. It took two years for us to become best of friends. His kids and mine were the same ages and they spent weekends together which meant that he and I were also spending time together. That time ended up being more than forty years.

After eleven years at my 'part-time' bartending job I went to work for Rite-Aid Drug Stores. In the year 2000, when my husband retired, I transferred from Washington to Nevada and worked for the company until I retired in 2003. Meantime however, I happened to stop in a little bar in Fernley, Nevada, on my way to Reno one day to use the restroom (my days of not walking into a bar alone long past). When I walked into the Silver Spur Saloon I became overwhelmed with nostalgia. The rustic wooden rafters, the mirrors, the atmosphere, even the smell and the people took me back to my first bar job. It was as if I had been swept back in time. Little did I know on that day that my stop would lead to another fourteen-year part-time job. Twenty-five years total is quite a long time for *'just a part-time job.'*

NOT ON MY WATCH!

When I moved from Missouri back to Washington my children's father offered to let me and our two youngest children move into his house rent free until I could get a place to live. The free rent was a good reason for me to consider staying in the town of Sultan, which is about forty miles northeast of Seattle. I felt that the schools would be better for the kids than in the big city also, so I decided that I would take the part-time job that was offered to me even though I had no bartending experience.

Things were going well for me. I was making a better hourly wage than I ever had, plus tips. Being a small logging community everyone knew everyone and it wasn't long before I became friends with the town planner, the local auto mechanic, the deputy sheriff and any number of the loggers. I was introduced to a couple who just happened to have a house for rent in Gold Bar, a little town just a few miles east of Sultan. They agreed to rent it to me for exactly what I was receiving for child support, three hundred dollars a month. I could easily live now on my meager wages and the kids wouldn't have to change schools. Things were looking up!

One of my regular customers was an old retired logger with the strangest name, Oather. He had three sons, who also frequented the bar. His son, John, approached me one day informing me that his dad had been diagnosed with early signs of dementia and the doctor said that he should not be drinking alcohol. John and his brothers came up with the idea that they could put 'near beer' in Budweiser bottles for me to serve to him. "We can't just cut off his beer," he declared. I went along with the plan and for a couple of weeks everything went smoothly.

One lackadaisical Sunday afternoon several of the loggers were sitting around enjoying their beer and shooting the breeze when in walked Oather. "Gimme a beer," he rudely demanded. By his slurred speech and sweeping arm gestures I could tell that he had been drinking. "How 'bout if I buy you a cup of coffee?" I smilingly suggested. "No, I want a Budweiser." I again refused and was surprised when, without a word or a fuss, he turned around and sauntered out. The loggers and I continued our small talk and joking, and in a very short matter of time I looked up to see Oather staggering in, headed straight toward the bar. I walked to the end of the bar and as I approached him he pulled out a gun. He held it right at my rib cage and slurred, "Now, are you going to give me a beer?" I have been told that when shock sets in your first mental response is to save yourself. My leg muscles tightened, but I knew that I couldn't run. I felt rooted to the spot. I focused my eyes directly on his, and placed my left hand firmly on his shoulder. I shook the index finger of my right hand in his face. My words came out strong and unshaken, "Give me the gun, Oather." "I have a permit to carry a gun," he retorted.

"You do not have a permit to shoot me, now give me the gun," was my strangely calm response. No one in the bar moved; you could have heard a pin drop. The customers later told me that they knew if one of them had attempted to approach him the gun may have gone off. Out of nowhere, his son John appeared, grabbing him from behind and retrieving the gun. As he led him out of the bar I began shaking uncontrollably with images of 'what could have been' flashing through my mind. My knees literally turned to jello and although I wasn't able to speak I could hear myself whimpering in a voice choked with tears. Someone came quickly to hold me up. When I finally calmed down I tried to use humor to lighten the moment. John returned within the hour to inquire if I intended to file a report or press charges. I declined, but made it very clear that I didn't ever want to see Oather in the bar again. My request was honored and he never again showed his face in the bar. He passed away just a few months later. Looking back now I realize that he wasn't an *old* man at all. He died at 65 years of age.

Perhaps that incident would have been the end of a bartending career for someone, but I brushed it off and continued in the business for many years without ever having another life-threatening incident. It does, however, go down in the books as the most terrifying event in my life.

Rest in Peace, Oather.

WORST DATE EVER

"First date"… "Last date"… "Worst date?" I didn't ever really date in my younger years. Oh, I did go to the junior prom, so I guess that could be considered a date, although it was more of an arranged event with a guy who was certainly *not* my boyfriend. If I remember correctly we didn't even go out to eat before or after the dance. My dance card was filled, but not one dance was with my escort. He politely dropped me off at the curb when he took me home, didn't even walk me to the door let alone try to steal a goodnight, or 'thank you for a good time' kiss. Oh, well, I didn't like him anyway. I actually had a huge crush on the guy we double-dated with who was my best friend's escort.

I met my husband-to-be when he was home on leave from the Navy the summer of 1957. I didn't have a boyfriend and had not dated at all. He offered to give me and my girlfriend, Maureen, a ride home from the Friday night drag races. I didn't even want to get into the car with him. He came to my house to see me several times after that, but didn't ever ask me out. When his leave was over I agreed to write to him, and so began our long distance romance. When he returned home later in the year we were married. So much for me and the "dating game."

My next 20 years were spent raising kids and struggling to survive, no time for socializing. After a second failed marriage, the farthest thing from my mind was getting involved with another man. I took a job tending bar in a little logging community in Washington. Most of the loggers became my friends and my personal life was never discussed. They all respected the fact that I wasn't interested in going out for a drink after work. A bar was the last place I would want to go. Nobody ever offered to take me roller-skating or out for pizza. So dating was definitely out of the question.

One of the loggers was quite unlike the rough and rugged others. They would stomp into the bar after work in their grubby work clothes, smelling of cedar and sweat. Orville was quiet and reserved and never came into the bar directly from work. He would always be freshly showered and dressed like a gentleman. He loved the woods and took great pride in his job as a 'choker setter,' the person who puts a short noose of wire rope around a log and attaches it to the skidding or yarding equipment. The younger, less experienced 'woodsmen' as he liked to call them, all looked up to him and would listen intently to his stories and readily take his advice. I was fascinated learning about this industry, so I too was intrigued by his knowledge of and dedication to his job. After a couple of beers, he spoke so softly that you had to get very close to hear him. Because he was so quiet and soft-spoken, I was taken by surprise when he asked me if I would like to take a Sunday drive up to the top of one of the local logging areas, Haystack Mountain. "Wow that would be great, I'll pack a picnic lunch." This was actually sounding like a date!

My nephew, Dennis, who was a paraplegic, his wife, Margaret, and their two children, ages five and seven, had recently moved to the area. I was so excited telling Dennis about my Sunday date. "Oh, I would love to go to the top of that hill," he exclaimed. "I hear that you can see both the Cascade and the Olympic mountain ranges from there." Realizing what a treat that would be for him, I made up my mind to ask Orville if we could take Dennis along. Of course he agreed to it. The next thing I knew the kids were all a buzz about it. How could we leave them behind?

Sunday morning rolled around and I prepared a very large picnic lunch. Sandwiches, chips, apples, bananas, and chocolate chip cookies, freshly baked the night before. I filled the cooler with sodas and water, and smiled, knowing what a treat this would be for Dennis and his family. Just before noon, Orville's big four-wheel drive pickup truck pulled into the driveway. I wheeled Dennis out, followed by Margaret. Their two kids and my two youngest jumped into the back of the truck and Margaret and Dennis climbed into the front with Orville. I threw the wheel chair into the back, and after loading the lunch box and cooler neatly between the kids I realized that there was no room for me. I stepped away waiving. "Have a great time."

Margaret later related the adventure as "nail biting," as Orville swerved and swayed along the rickety gravel forest service road up twenty-seven hundred feet to the lookout at the summit. He was busy pointing out the logging sights and the magnificent views as the kids were being thrown around in the back of the truck. They enjoyed their picnic lunch while I was enjoying a nice, quiet peaceful Sunday afternoon alone.

Orville, several years later, described that day to my husband as the *worst date* he had ever had. "And you can bet I never asked her out again," he added.

A MIRACULOUS TRANSFORMATION

"So, just who is this dude, Sheri?" I inquired when my niece called to tell me that she was planning to get married. "His name is Chuck. He is smart, well-read and so handsome." "And where did you meet him?" "Well, Aunt Ruth, I wasn't going to tell you this, but... I picked him up on Highway 92, on the approach to the San Mateo Bridge." My heart dropped and my head spun as I tried to contain my hysteria. "Oh my God, Sheri, why would you even consider picking up a hitchhiker? You could have been raped or murdered. He could have hi-jacked your car and kidnapped you. Whatever were you thinking?"

Sheri was an extremely reserved, well-educated young lady with a good Christian up-bringing. She had an excellent job as a key punch operator for a major corporation in San Francisco. She had always been quite choosy about who she made friends with up until this time.

"Well, it was late and raining and he looked lost and I could just tell by looking at him that he was harmless. When I asked him where he was going he said he was going to a party and invited me to go along. I refused and dropped him off, and when he asked me for my phone number I gave it to him. He called me the next morning to thank me for picking him up and asked if he could see me that day. I rearranged my work hours so that I could have lunch with him. I met him downtown for lunch and have been with him every day since."

"Oh, great! A two-week courtship and you are getting married. Not a good idea. For God's sake, Sheri, he's a commercial fisherman. I think that he is just looking for someone to take care of him. Please, please reconsider. You don't even know him."

My fear for her welfare turned into reality when a couple months later they came to Washington. Oh, he was handsome, well-spoken, and a charmer for sure. I could then understand how she was swept away. She seemed happy enough, doting over him and his every word. He spoke well of his mother, they had a close relationship, so I decided that he couldn't be all bad.

I was living in my ex-husband's house at the time with my two teenage children. I came home from work one evening and as soon as I opened the door the sweet smell of marijuana hit me right in the face. I had noticed Chuck's mood swings and was aware that he usually had a beer in his hand, but I was not prepared for this. It was the 1970s and marijuana possession was punishable with prison time. I would not, could not, have my children exposed to this behavior.

When I confronted Chuck and gave him a direct order to get out he brazenly informed me that it was not my house and I had no right to kick him out. I must confess that the scene that followed was not a pleasant one. How many times have you heard the expression, "Don't mess with a red-head?" He was calling me much worse than a red-head as he flew out the front door. I was so upset that I didn't even remember Sheri being there, but I guess she left with him. When I talked to her later that night I told her, in no uncertain terms, that I never wanted to see Chuck's face again and that she was out of her mind and headed to hell with him if she didn't get out of this relationship. "I hate him," I screamed. "You deserve so much better." Too late, shortly thereafter she found out she was pregnant.

Sheri was staying at my house when Johnny was born. She came to Washington so that I could be with her when she had the baby. I left to go to Montana for Christmas, giving Sheri strict orders not to have that baby while I was gone. God love her, she was in labor for thirty-six hours, giving birth just hours after I returned. The doctor asked Chuck to leave when he came in smelling of booze.

Sheri returned to California, and a couple of years later she and Chuck had a beautiful baby girl, Jamie. I spoke with Sheri often, trying to avoid even Chuck's name. She knew how I felt about him, and never complained to me about her life. She would always ask me to please pray for Chuck. I believe sincerely in the power of prayer, but I knew in my heart that his life was headed nowhere but downhill. I prayed for her and the kids every day. She eventually confessed to me that she had lived four years of hell. Chuck was using hard drugs and drinking every day. She had become fearful for herself and the kids. What if he had an accident? She would be financially responsible. She finally filed for a legal separation trying to avoid divorce. She was fearful that due to the lifestyle he was living he may not live for long.

When Sheri called and told me that Chuck had quit drinking and doing drugs I just rolled my eyes, shrugged my shoulders and replied, "Yeah, sure... whatever." She had talked him into going to church with her one Sunday. Her faith was ever strong, and she was doing her best to raise her children according to her Christian beliefs. Whatever kind of miracle took place that day I may never understand. I do know, however, that it was a life-changing one.

Sheri called me a few months later to say that they wanted to come to Washington to visit me. I told her that she and the kids were welcome but to please not bring Chuck. "But, he wants to see you, Aunt Ruth." "Well I do not want to see him... ever!"

I was at my work place one afternoon shortly after my conversation with Sheri. I looked up to see a handsome, well-dressed young man walking toward me with a huge smile on his face. "Oh, no, it can't be," was my quick reaction. He would not dare approach me at work. Or maybe he would, knowing that I would not repeat my screaming rage from our last meeting in a public place.

Before he got even within arm's length of me, I looked deep into those captivating steel blue eyes and I suddenly felt a strange, warm, calming glow come over me. This was not the Chuck that I knew and hated, this was a soul bursting with a Christ-like love, holding his arms out to me, not speaking a word. Dear Lord, all of the years, all of our prayers and hopes, could this really be true? I fell into his arms, my unforgiving and hate turning to tears of joy. We laughed, we cried and I praised the Lord for giving me this peaceful feeling of love, forgiveness, and understanding.

As the years passed Chuck became a true advocate for his church and has never been ashamed or embarrassed to share his faith, spread the word of God and share his story of recovery. He and Sheri raised their children, along with many foster children over the years in a loving, Christian home. He has been a positive father image and a mentor to many people and is blessed to watch his grandchildren grow up. Now that we are all retired we spend as much time together as we can.

So, ask me if I believe in the power of prayer. Am I convinced that people can change? You bet I am!

HALLOWEEN MEMORIES

As a child I loved dressing up, so Halloween was one of my favorite days for as far back as I can remember. I also loved music, and at a very early age I began making up songs. I would sing silly little jingles that didn't make much sense about whatever happened to be going on around me. At about nine or ten years of age I composed my Halloween song, words and music. It *really* didn't make much sense, as living in Montana you didn't ever trick-or-treat in the *heat*. But, heck... it rhymed with *treat*. "Halloween, Halloween, my favorite holiday of all. When we go out to trick-or-treat, in the cold or in the heat, Halloween, let's have a ball." I smile now thinking of how this nonsensical ditty became somewhat of an anthem for me every Halloween. I even taught it to my kids when they were old enough to trick-or-treat. It did make a little more sense when we were living in Hawaii. We would sing it while making our popcorn balls. In those days you could give out homemade goodies when the kids came knocking on the door. Oh, how they loved those popcorn balls.

Growing up, our costumes were always something we could concoct at home. I don't ever remember having a store-bought costume. My mother could cleverly transform me into a pirate, a clown, a ghost, a hobo (which was always my favorite) or a gypsy. Some of the kids did have plastic face masks, but they were nothing compared to the commercial costumes they have today.

I could hardly wait for my kids to be old enough to trick-or-treat. When Patrick was three years old, I made a darling clown costume and painted his face. When I took him to the mirror to see himself, he became hysterical, screaming and kicking. I quickly washed the make-up off, calmed him down and decided that it probably was not a good idea to take him out among the ghosts and goblins.

At thirteen, Patrick was six feet tall and wearing a size thirteen shoe. For Halloween that year he decided that he wanted to be a mummy for the school Halloween party. I "slit-a-sheet, a sheet-I-slit" into strips and wrapped him carefully, doing each leg and his arms individually so that he could move. Only one eye, his mouth, and nostrils were visible on his head. It was an amazing costume. We hadn't considered the fact that he may have to use the bathroom, and I didn't think to wrap his legs so that his knees would bend. Oh, dear, he couldn't get into the car. Luckily we had a station wagon, so his brother Don and I slid him through the tail-gate door. My neighbor told me the next day that he was sure glad that he realized it was Halloween or he would have probably

Halloweens Past

called the police. The costume did win a prize and it didn't take him long to get unwrapped.

I have two favorite 'adult' memories of Halloweens past. Larry and I were married in the month of August in 1979. My two youngest children were fourteen and sixteen. On Halloween that year the kids were invited to a party so they were gone for the evening. When the trick-or-treating slowed down, about 9:00 PM, Larry announced that he was going to shower and relax and watch a movie. As soon as I heard him get in the shower I decided to play a trick on him to see if I could get a treat, or at least to minimize the 'bah, humbug' attitude that he had shown all evening about the trick-or-treating and Halloween in general. It obviously wasn't his favorite holiday. I went into the bedroom, quickly stripped and put on his long London Fog rain coat and one of his fedoras and ran out the side door. I waited until I heard him come out of the bathroom and then slipped around to the front door and rang the doorbell. I could hear him mumbling something about the fact that it was too damned late for kids to be out trick-or-treating. He hollered for me to answer the door. When I didn't respond he went to the door and when he opened it I did the surprise 'flash' and giggled, "Trick or *streak*." He was so shocked that he couldn't even speak for a minute. When he finally did regain his composure he was not at all amused. He was mortified! "Oh my God, get in here. What if the kids had come home?" I was laughing so hard, but for some reason he didn't think it was funny, which made it even funnier to me. I have always been modest, to the point of him calling me a prude at times. So, it's easy to see why my '*trick*' shocked the socks off him. This truly had to be his most memorable Halloween ever.

In the 1990s we hosted a marble show every October in Las Vegas. There were people from all over the United States and Canada who would gather every year for this event. One particular year the hotel planned a masquerade party over the Halloween weekend. We hadn't known about the event so were in a quandary as to what we could do for costumes. "I'm not dressing up stupid for any party," was my husband Scrooge's quick response. Alas, my friend Alan, seeing my disappointment, chimed in, "Come on, Ruth, we'll work out some costumes." Away we went to the nearest super market where, without even asking for my input, Alan purchased a huge Idaho baker potato, a lemon, and a ball of twine. When we arrived back at the hotel we went to the bar where Alan asked the bartender if he could use her ice pick. He carefully poked a hole through the potato, then the lemon, and ran twine long enough to go around our bodies through them. "Here, tie this around your waist," he instructed me handing me the lemon. He tied the potato around his waist and away we went to the party. "Now, they have to guess what we are, you can't tell them," Alan warned me. We did get some strange looks when we walked in, but it didn't take Larry long to figure out that Alan was a 'dictator.' No one ever did guess that I was a 'sour puss.' We didn't win a prize but we sure had a lot of laughs over it. I ended up the night teaching Larry and Alan my song…. "Halloween, Halloween, my favorite holiday of all!"

MOTHER NATURE'S WRATH

Growing up in rural Montana in the 1940s was, to say the least, living a protected life. We were not bombarded with news of the horrific and devastating events going on all over the world. We had no television blaring the news, or social media informing us of every major event as it happened. There wasn't even television reception where I lived until the mid-1950s. The daily newspaper was our only source of information. Every Saturday we went to the local movie theater where they would show news reels to accompany the featured movie, along with cartoons. I would gaze wide-eyed at the world news and at a very early age I became fearful of things that were foreign or unheard of in my little corner of the world. I vividly remember, at about four years of age, seeing a volcano erupting on the news. I became so traumatized that I had a nightmare of running from a stream of lava. I woke up screaming. My mother comforted me, telling me that we lived in God's country and didn't ever have to worry about such a natural disaster. "We are protected by the mountains all around us. No tornadoes, floods or volcanoes will ever be a threat to us," she assured me. Looking back now I smile, remembering how my mother could always calm my fears.

Moving to Oklahoma as a young bride was exciting for me. Seeing the weather reports on the local TV channel was not! When the neighbors pounded on the door to tell us that we had to go to the storm shelter at the Naval Base I just scoffed and told them that I didn't think that was necessary. No sooner had they headed to the shelter than a thunderous blast narrowly missed the apartment building that we were living in and wiped out several houses across the street from us. I had just experienced one of the most destructive tornadoes to ever hit that section of Oklahoma. This was my first encounter with the wrath of Mother Nature.

The summer of 1959 found me headed back to Montana to spend time with my family before moving to Puerto Rico to join my husband at his new Navy assignment. My son was just a year old and I was expecting my second child. I was so relieved to be back in the mountains that I loved and out of tornado country.

On August 17th, shortly after we had retired for the night, I heard a deep rumble. It was stronger and louder than any thunder I had ever heard. The crib in which my son was sleeping came flying across the room toward the hide-a-bed where I was, and the old wooden wagon-wheel chandelier swayed so hard that it hit the ceiling. The shaking continued for what felt like an hour, but it was in fact only minutes. This was the 7.2 magnitude earthquake that killed twenty-eight people who were camping at Hebgen Lake. The earth that crumbled from the mountain blocked the Madison River flow, which after three weeks created a lake more than one hundred and seventy feet deep, five miles long, and a third of a mile wide. Today the lake is known as Quake Lake. There is a monument there to honor the people who lost their lives while camping on that clear, still starry night. There were several aftershocks the next day, and I couldn't help but ponder that this made the tornado seem much less frightening.

Within a month of experiencing that horrific earthquake, I left Montana to reunite with my husband in Puerto Rico. Stepping off of the plane at O'Hare Airport in Chicago and seeing all of the lights and the size of the airport was probably the scariest moment of my life—that is until we landed in San Juan and there was no one there to meet me at the airport. I didn't know where to go and I couldn't find anyone who spoke English. By the time my husband finally found me, clutching the baby closely and silently crying in the cafeteria, he was in near hysterics. He had been delayed at the base because of a typhoon that had wiped out the island of Vieques, just off of the coast of Roosevelt Roads where he was stationed. He had no way to contact me to inform me of his delay. Wow! I had just missed experiencing my third natural disaster in three months, a tornado in Oklahoma, an earthquake in Montana, and now a tropical typhoon. I was beginning to believe that Mother Nature was out to get me! I comforted myself with the thought that at least I hadn't encountered my greatest childhood fear – a volcano.

I was living in Washington state two decades later, when on May 18th, 1980 I awoke to what sounded like a sonic boom. The dining room windows clattered as if to explode at any moment. Mount Saint Helens had erupted. Although the mountain was a hundred and seventeen miles from our front door we experienced not only the initial shock but also curtains of ash that covered the trees and created an eerie sense of darkness. It was reported to be the deadliest and most destructive volcano eruption in the history of the United States. Fifty-seven people perished that morning, including one Harry Randall Truman, the eighty-three-year-old owner and caretaker of the Spirit Lake Lodge. He had stubbornly refused to leave his home when told to evacuate days before the eruption.

Now, looking back on my life and recalling all of my travels, adventures and experiences, I can honestly say that defying the wrath of Mother Nature on several occasions has made me aware of the fact that lightening *can* strike twice in the same place. No one can predict when that next tornado, that earthquake, that typhoon or volcano will destroy the world as we know it today. I just hope that I do not ever have to live through my horrible dream, out-running a lava flow!

THE BEST COMPLIMENT EVER

"On my honor I will do my best to do my duty to God and country and to obey the scout laws. To help other people at all times. To keep myself physically strong, mentally awake, and morally straight." Imagine, if you can, trying to instill this motto into a group of rambunctious eight to ten-year-old boys. In the mid-1960s, as the mother of three boys, I became involved with the Cub Scouts. At the first pack meeting that I attended I had myself convinced that I could do a better job with these kids than some of the den mothers who were there. I volunteered to attend an upcoming training course, and left that evening feeling excited even though a little nervous about my new venture. My boys were beaming, hugging me and assuring me that we were going to have fun. I was thrilled that they were anxious for me to be involved in their scout program.

I was assigned to a den of seven boys who had been together for almost a year. They all knew each other, so I was the 'newcomer.' My first goal was to get to know each of the boys by name before our first meeting ended. I made up a name game, having each of them say a food that started with the first letter of their name. They were all amused calling Brandon 'banana,' Sean 'spaghetti,' Paul 'peaches'... and so on.

We made plans for a skit for the next pack meeting, everyone agreeing on a hand puppet show of the Beatles. They were all squealing and hooting and each one was singing their own lines from their favorite Beatles song. We settled on "She Loves You, Yeah, Yeah, Yeah!" I hadn't expected this much enthusiasm or energy from a group of boys. I made up my mind that our den would be the highlight of every pack meeting from that day forward.

One little fellow didn't seem as outgoing or as involved as the others. He stayed to himself and didn't interact with the other boys. Jimmy was an adorable child with chubby, rosy cheeks and bright hazel eyes that seemed to have a faraway glare. I singled him out by having him serve the treats and I noticed that the other boys were teasing him. I didn't make an issue of it but I talked to each boy individually as they left that day, reminding them of the scout laws which we had read at the beginning of the meeting, stressing being friendly, courteous, helpful and kind.

The following week I noticed that all of the boys were including Jimmy in the activities. Although he never seemed to quite fit in, he never missed a meeting and he was always the first to volunteer whenever I requested help. He seemed insecure and unsure of himself, but with a little coaxing he became the leader of our service project, learned to use a hammer and nails, took part in the soap box derby, participated in our skits and songs and even tried to learn to tap dance. I praised and encouraged him in everything that he did. It pleased me to see him become more confident and self-assured.

As each boy reached the age to advance to the Webelos scout rank I was sad to see them go, but especially so with Jimmy. I thought about him often over the years. My affiliation with the Boy Scouts lasted for over ten years. Just as one of my boys would advance there would be another one joining, so I was like the perpetual Den Mother. I was honored by the Boy Scouts of America as the first female scout leader instructor in the state of Washington.

Fast forward twenty years. I was shopping in an upscale bath and body shop at the Seattle Center. My husband and I were talking across the aisle when from behind me I heard a booming voice, "Mrs. O'Neill." I turned to see a well-dressed young man with familiar hazel eyes and a smile that could have melted the coldest heart. "I recognized your voice," he said as I was trying to figure out how he knew me. I glanced at the badge on his shirt. It read 'Manager – James.' "Remember me? I'm Jimmy." My heart did a quick flip as I recognized him and reached out to hug him. "Oh, Jimmy, I have thought about you often. How are you?" "I'm doing OK now, ma'am, but it's been a rough road. At my very worst times, and times have been pretty bad, I would think of you and the race and I'd just get up and start over. You are the only adult in my life who ever encouraged me to keep going. I have you to thank that I am alive and sober today." *The race... what race?* I was thinking to myself. "You read 'The Race' to us in scouts and gave us each a copy. I've kept mine all these years, and I read it often. I have always hoped that I would get to see you again someday to thank you for saving my life." By that time, we both had tears in our eyes.

When I arrived home I went directly to my cedar chest where all of my precious memorabilia from over the years was stored. There with all of my scout memoirs I found the well-worn copy of a poem that I had shared so many years before.

THE RACE

Quit! Give up! You're beaten! They shout and plead.
There's just too much against you now, this time you can't succeed.
And as I start to hang my head in front of failure's face,
My downward fall is broken by the memory of a race.
And hope refills my weakened will as I recall that scene.
For just the thought of that short race rejuvenates my being.
A children's race, young boys, young men; now I remember well.
Excitement, sure, but also fear; it wasn't hard to tell.
The whistle blew and off they went, young hearts and hopes of fire.
To win, to be the hero there, was each boy's desire.
And one boy in particular, his dad was in the crowd.
Was running near the lead and thought, "My dad will be so proud."
But as he speeded down the field across a shallow dip,
The little boy who thought to win, lost his step and slipped.
Trying hard to catch himself, his hands flew out to brace,
And mid the laughter of the crowd, he fell flat on his face.
So down he fell and with him hope, he couldn't win it now.
Embarrassed, sad, he only wished to disappear somehow.
But as he fell, his dad stood up and showed his anxious face,
Which to the boy so clearly said, "Get up and win that race!"
He quickly rose, no damage done... behind a bit that's all,
And ran with all his mind and might to make up for his fall.
So anxious to restore himself, to catch up and win
His mind went faster than his legs. He slipped and fell again.
He wished that he had quit before with only one disgrace,
I'm hopeless as a runner now, I shouldn't try to race."
But, in the laughing crowd he searched and found his father's face,
That steady look that said again, "Get up and win the race."
So, he jumped up to try again, ten yards behind the last.
If I'm to gain those yards, he thought I've got to run real fast.
Exceeding everything he had, he regained eight or ten,
But trying so hard to catch the lead, he slipped and fell again.
I've lost, so what's the use, he thought, I'll live with my disgrace,
But then he thought about his dad, who he'd soon have to face.
"Get up," an echo sounded low. "Get up and take your place."
"You were not meant for failure here, get up and win the race."

With borrowed will, "get up" it said, "you haven't lost at all.
For winning is no more than this; to rise each time you fall."
So up he rose to win once more and with a new commit,
He resolved that win or lose, at least he wouldn't quit.
So far behind the others now, the most he'd ever been.
Still he gave it all he had, and ran as though to win.
Three times he'd fallen stumbling, three times he'd rose again.
Too far behind to hope to win, he still ran to the end.
They cheered the winning runner as he crossed first place.
Head high and proud and happy; no falling; no disgrace.
But when the falling youngster crossed the line, last place,
The crowd gave him the greater cheer for finishing the race.
And even though he came in last, with head bowed low, unproud;
You would have thought he won the race, to listen to the crowd.
And to his dad he sadly said, "I didn't do so well."
"To me you won," his father said, "You rose each time you fell."
And now when things seem dark and hard and difficult to face,
The memory of that little boy helps me in my race.
For all of life is like that race, with ups and downs and all,
And all you have to do to win – is rise each time you fall.
"Quit!" "Give Up!" "You're beaten!" They still shout in my face.
But another voice within me says, "Get up and win the race!"

"THE RACE"   by Dr. D. H. "Dee" Groberg

So many times over the years I wondered if anything that I had ever said or done while working with the kids in scouts and little league and teaching CCD had made an impact on anyone's life. Hearing Jimmy's sincere "thank you" was the greatest compliment that I could have ever received.

CRATERS OF THE MOON

Is it possible that one wrong turn on a desolate road in southern Idaho could be a turning point or create a complete new outlook on one's life journey? So, why was I driving ninety miles an hour at three o'clock in the morning? It was a late August afternoon in 1981 when we drove out of Spanish Fork, Utah, after having participated in the Utah County Fair. We had loaded our disassembled booth into the back of the truck, braced against the back wall by bungee cords. Tired and hungry after working a five-day fair, we took time to eat a quick fast food hamburger and plot our course back to Seattle. We had to be at the airport in Seattle the next day to pick up my daughter who would be returning from California, so time was not exactly in our favor. "I can drive all night. I like to drive at night," I assured my husband. We made room in the back of the truck for him to set up a cozy bed. With the gas tank filled we headed out singing "On The Road Again." Almost nine hundred miles in thirteen hours shouldn't be a problem.

Straight up Highway 15 North to West Highway 84, would take us right into Twin Falls, Idaho. Larry drove to the next gas stop and then I took the helm and he climbed in the back of the truck for a nap. Happily singing along with the radio, I guess I got caught up in the moment and passed the turn off. About sixty miles up the road, when I saw a road sign which read, 'Butte – 205 miles,' I realized that I was still heading north on Highway 15. The gas gauge was creeping toward empty and I knew that I had to stop at the next gas station. I couldn't turn back and I really had to pee. As soon as I pulled into the gas station in Idaho Falls (I was supposed to be in Twin Falls,) Larry exited the back of the truck. I didn't want to tell him where we were but he figured it out as I made my way to the ladies room. When I returned he was questioning the attendant about how far out of the way I had driven and if we had to go all the way back to Highway 84 to head west. "Well, no sir, you could take the county road 20 through Craters of the Moon. It will get you back to Highway 84." By then it was well past midnight and Larry's agitation and frustration with me was quite obvious. "Please just get back in the back of the truck and try to calm down and rest," I pleaded, silently cursing under my breath. "I can make up for the lost time."

The moon was almost full and it cast an eerie glow through the low hanging clouds. As I pulled onto Highway 20, I realized that it was not going to be the smooth drive of the interstate or even comparable to some of the rough side roads I had encountered in Utah. Craters of the Moon is a vast ocean of lava flows (618 square miles to be exact) in the Snake River Plain area of south central Idaho. The farther I drove the creepier the atmosphere seemed. I began to sense that I was somewhere in the twilight zone.

Washington Irving in his "Adventures of Captain Bonneville" described this area as "a place where nothing meets the eye but a desolate and awful waste, where no grass grows nor water runs, and where nothing is to be seen but lava." Ahead of me, out of nowhere I saw what appeared to be hundreds of jack rabbits, huge rabbits, running from all directions. As I tried to dodge them the truck was jerking and swaying like a carnival ride. Larry started banging on the back window. "Just hit them, you can't miss them all, just keep driving." Oh, the horrible sound as the tires were thumping down the road. Whatever made me think that it would be any easier if I drove faster? Larry continued banging on the window, which was beginning to irritate me. The more he banged the heavier my foot seemed to meet the gas pedal. I was not about to stop and I finally signaled him a message with my middle finger. I was in tears and my heart was pounding. I kept telling myself to just breathe and calm down.

All of a sudden I saw headlights up ahead of me facing off of the road lighting up the weird, frightening landscape. I realized as I got closer that there were people in the middle of the road. "Oh, my God," I whimpered, grasping the steering wheel tightly. "Has someone broken down out here in the middle of nowhere?" As I got closer I could see that it was a group of intoxicated Native Americans, hootin' and hollerin'. I made the quick, desperate decision that I was not going to stop. Their vehicle was blocking half of the road. I sped up, hit the ditch and kept going. "What the hell? Stop, Stop!" Larry was screaming from the back. I just kept driving, praying that this nightmare would soon end. I was not about to stop until I reached civilization.

I made it safely to Twin Falls, unaware that in the back of the truck Larry was bleeding profusely from a huge gash in his head. The frame work from the booth had broken loose during my wild adventure.

He didn't say a word as he stepped out of the back of the truck. He didn't have to. He was covered with blood and both eyes were already starting to blacken. I was crying and then started to laugh uncontrollably. I guess that my hysteria overtook his anger and he found himself trying to comfort me. After calming me down and cleaning himself up he insisted that he would drive the rest of the way.

We made it to Seattle, with no time to spare, to meet my daughter's plane. Many years later I read a travel brochure about Craters of the Moon and it featured an article about the Apollo astronauts training there for their mission to the moon. I don't know how it looks during the day but I can always tell people that I had an 'out of this world' experience one dark night in Idaho.

Now, how would this experience present a turning point in my life? Well, it was the confirmation that I am totally 'directionally challenged.' From that day forward neither my husband nor any of my family would trust me to get them anywhere. The family joke remains, "Please don't let Mother drive."

THE UNSPOKEN POWER OF MUSIC

Music can soothe your soul, evoke memories, lift your spirits, brighten a dreary day, light up a room, create a smile or laughter, motivate swinging or swaying, or maybe even frighten you, which brings to mind a late Friday night at a deserted airport in Reno, Nevada, in the early 1980s.

My friend, Elsie, and I and an older gentleman friend had driven a beat-up old 1960 era motor home from Seattle to Reno to partake in a *'new product'* trade show. Ben was almost eighty years of age, but was still very active, sharp and eager to present the new "WE CARE AMERICA" self-defense products to the public. 'Personal and Home Protection' read the bright, eye-catching poster that adorned our booth. Mace was not legal, but the chemical used in the key-ring sized, thumb triggered aerosol devices that we were selling was approved as non-lethal, and guaranteed to spray up to three feet. The advertising brochure claimed that this product could subdue a two hundred pound plus predator. The home defense models were as large as an average bug spray can and could spray up to fifteen feet. There were door stop models that would activate the spray when a door was pushed open.

By the end of the first day of the show we had convinced most of the vendors that they should not be without these products and that their daughters, mothers, wives and sisters definitely needed to carry the pocket model with them at all times for protection. Sales were great!

Elsie's husband, Cliff, was flying into Reno the night that the show opened, and we were to pick him up at the airport. His scheduled flight was just after midnight. Ben chose to stay at the hotel, as this was way past his bedtime. Knowing that there were slot machines at the airport, Elsie and I decided to go early and invest a few nickels until time for Cliff's arrival.

The airport was unusually secluded as the only late flight scheduled for that night was the one from Seattle. You were allowed to go directly to the arrival gates back then, so at about eleven thirty we decided to wander upstairs to wait for the plane to land. It was so quiet and desolate that I began to feel uncomfortable. "I hope that you have your self-defense key ring with you," I said half-jokingly to Elsie. "Why? There's no one here to use it on," was her quick come back. Neither one of us had thought to arm ourselves with the product that we were promoting.

My uneasiness all of a sudden turned to absolute fear when I sensed that someone was following us. I was afraid to turn around. I grabbed Elsie's arm, "Stop. Someone is behind us." I whispered. When we stopped I heard what sounded like chains rattling and a strange voice, mumbling words that I could hardly understand. "Gotta' be damned... wanna' be damned"... By then my heart was pounding and my palms were clammy. "I'm going back to the ticket agent's desk." As I turned around ready to run, I came face to face with the largest, scariest human form I had ever encountered. He was dressed all in black. An ankle length black trench coat hung omnivorously over his mammoth structure and he had gigantic silver chains around his neck and dangling from his over-sized belt. His words became louder, "You can't run away forever." He seemed oblivious of my sheer panic. *Is this guy drunk or drugged or just crazy?* were the thoughts running through my mind. As we rushed past him he proceeded to turn around and continue to follow us, singing even louder as he danced and rattled behind us. "I'll be gone in the morning... in the bottom of the pit..."

When I finally frantically approached the ticket agent, almost in tears, she began to laugh. "Don't you know who that is?" she questioned me. "I don't care who it is, call security NOW!" I demanded. Realizing how upset I was, she quickly assured me that this menacing gargoyle was Meat Loaf, and he was not going to hurt us. "He is completely harmless. He is just waiting for the flight from Seattle."

I, not being a fan of hard rock music, was not aware of who Meat Loaf was, and I could not understand or relate to the words I was hearing, "No one's gonna stop me." By the time he sauntered up to the desk, still singing and rattling his chains, I had calmed down somewhat, and now that I knew we were not in any danger I became a little amused. "Bring out the dice," he loudly bellowed to the ticket agent. "We don't have any dice, sir," she calmly answered. "This is Reno, you have slot machines here, and you must have dice. I want to roll the dice with this lovely lady," he said pointing in my direction. "I'm going to roll her for a trip to wherever in the world she wants to go, and I'll make damned sure she wins." The only place I wanted to go at this point was anywhere that I could get away from this maniac. Security final showed up and accompanied me and Elsie to the arrival gate, with our new friend right behind us serenading us with "Like a Bat Out of Hell,", which I later learned was the fourth best-selling song on the music charts at that time.

When the trade show ended on Sunday, I vowed to never, ever leave home without my hand held self-protection device. I was, however, a little thankful that I hadn't had it with me that Friday night at the airport.

Returning to work the following Monday at the bar that I managed, the first thing that I did was check the jukebox, and sure enough there he was, "Two Out of Three Ain't Bad" and "It's All Coming Back to Me Now." Given that I could understand those words, I became Meat Loaf's biggest fan. Elsie was relating the story to anyone who would listen and referring to him as my '*boyfriend.*' She never did get his name right, though. She still, after all these years, calls him '*Meatball*'… And I still get goosebumps whenever I hear "Like a Bat Out of Hell."

.....AND THEN ALONG CAME KING

I've often heard it said that a dog can brighten your life, make you laugh and every day silently accept your tears without judgment, snuggle with you, forgive your faults and love you unconditionally. I grew up in a public housing project where animals were not allowed. Other than my Aunt's bull dog, and Boots, my grandma's cocker spaniel, who I saw only occasionally, I was never around animals. My mother always told of the horrified look on my face when someone handed me a kitten when I was three years of age. Shortly thereafter, I was bitten by a German Shepard as I was running down Arizona Avenue. The dog jumped out of the window of a parked car and very firmly attached himself to my rear end. I was petrified and screaming. My brother appeared out of nowhere about the same time that the dog's owner showed up. The dog, who seemed to me to be the biggest monster I could ever imagine, had bitten through my dress and left his teeth marks on my buttocks. I wasn't nearly as hurt as I was scared. My brother scooped me up as the dog was being rushed back to the car. Through my tears, I sobbed, "that bastard." My brother was shocked and then he began to laugh when he realized that I had just gotten the "B" words mixed up. From that day on I was terrified of dogs, especially German Shepherds. I grew up wondering how people could become so attached to their pets. I couldn't believe that someone would actually allow an animal on their bed.

My boys, at a very early age began pleading to have a dog. One day my son, Don, was late coming home from school and I was getting worried. I started out of the house to walk toward the school and low and behold, here comes Donny with a mangy old dog on the end of a rope. As he approached me, tugging on the poor dog, he pleaded, "Look Mom, he followed me home. Can we keep him?" We were living in Navy housing at that time and were not allowed to have pets. Their dad promised them that when we returned to Washington and bought our own home they could all have the pet of their choice. That is how we ended up with a white Persian kitten, with one blue eye and one green eye, a German Shepard, and Ralph, the alligator, who just happened to be my favorite pet. The kids took good care of their animals, which also included several hamsters. I very soon came to accept the fact that a cat or dog did, in fact, have a place on a child's bed.

When Larry and I got married in 1979, we bought five acres, five miles out of town and set up our home on the top of a hill. We had just gotten settled in when one afternoon Larry came home from work with a huge smile on his face, his eyes wide and glowing. He was almost breathless with excitement as he informed me that we would be going to meet our new dog that evening. "Dog… what dog?" I inquired, trying to comprehend what he was talking about. We had never discussed getting a dog. "Well, you know we really need a watch dog living out here in the country." He then related to me the *'rest of the story.'* His friend, Marvin, had a friend who was a police officer and worked with the canine unit. He had recently been divorced and was being transferred from the Seattle Police Department. He was not able to take his trained police dog with him. He had left the dog with his ex-wife and she had to move into an apartment where she was not allowed to keep the dog. "He's a beautiful dog and he really needs a home. This would be a perfect spot for him with five acres to roam. I told Marvin that we would go by and see the dog tonight, so they'll be expecting us." I could feel my body tense as I listened to him. "God gave me my kids, and I had to take care of them. Nobody can tell me that I have to take care of a damned dog!" "I'll take care of him, I promise," he retorted in an almost pathetic tone of voice. How could I say no?

When we arrived at Joyce's apartment, she greeted us with a smile and right behind her, not barking, but showing his teeth was the most beautiful dog I had ever seen. She assured us that he was harmless unless commanded otherwise, but I was very leery as she led us into the living room. The minute I sat down on the couch, King (I learned that was his name) proceeded to come toward me. I was so petrified, I grabbed Larry's arm and he became aware that I was shaking. King got between the coffee table and me, stared at me for a minute and then proceeded to lay right on my feet, where he stayed the whole time we were there. "Please don't let him bite me," I pleaded silently to God. I listened intently as Joyce told us all about King. He was four years old, of pure German breeding and had been trained as a police dog to attack on command. Now I was really scared. I finally agreed that we would take him home on a trial basis only. I could tell that Larry was thrilled, but I still had my doubts.

    The next day Larry put a leash on King's collar and led him around the whole perimeter of the property. He 'marked' each corner and seemed to know that this was his new home. He was now officially "King of the Hill." We realized after a week or so how protective this dog was of me.   He would make his way between me and Larry whenever he felt that Larry was getting too close to me. One day Larry came up behind me and grabbed me teasingly. King was in the laundry room, we were in the dining room with the kitchen being in between. King lunged, I don't think that he even hit the kitchen floor and before we knew what was happening he had Larry's forearm in his mouth. He didn't bite him but he sure gave us the message that no one was ever going to hurt me. King would run to the car to meet me every day when I arrived home from work. He followed me everywhere and it wasn't long before I fell in love with him. He was supposed to be a watch dog and protect our home, and he would do just that if I was home. If I was not there the UPS delivery man could get out of his truck and open the garage door to leave a parcel. If I was home, he would have to honk the horn for me to come and retrieve a package, as King wouldn't let him get out of the truck. Whenever we had company we would have to put him in the garage until our guests were safely in the house. One day my friend, Linda, called me to ask to borrow something. I was just leaving for work and I told her that I would leave whatever it was in the garage and she could pick it up at her convenience. Linda was familiar with King and he had never been aggressive toward her. She opened the garage door and went in to fetch what she was there for, but when she tried to leave King would not let her out of the garage. She finally resorted to getting a can of dog food out of the cupboard and feeding it to him. While he was happily gobbling up his treat, she quietly rushed out of the door and closed it. Phew, that was a close call!

    When King was six years old I brought home a fluffy black ball of fur, Cocoa, who was an Australian Shepard and Chow mix. Cocoa was playful, being a puppy, and King was such a serious old guy. It wasn't long before he was romping and playing with Cocoa and they became best friends. They discovered the swamp down the hill behind our property and the porcupines discovered them! Oh, what a disaster, and they didn't learn the first time to stay away. After a couple of emergency runs to the vet we learned how to remove the quills.

One morning I opened the back door and there on the deck was a bleeding, whimpering King. He was covered in blood and one of his eyes was out of the socket. We rushed him to the vet who after examining him came to the conclusion, by examining the tears on his body, that he had encountered a cougar. He was in surgery for what seemed like hours. They saved his eye and he recovered in time, perhaps a little less aggressive. He even quit visiting the porcupines.

Whenever we went on vacation or just away for a week-end we could have the neighbors watch Cocoa but we had to put King in the kennel just to be sure he wouldn't attack anyone. Everyone was afraid of him. "He is NOT a nice dog," my brother scowled after his first encounter with him. The girls at the kennel assured me, however, that he was just fine there. They would walk him every day. He was never threatening to any of them and did fine with the other animals. One year when we returned the attendant told me that King had fallen in love with a beautiful female German Shepard. She said that they ate together, slept together and were inseparable. King's new friend had saved an elderly lady from a house fire. She had to be put into a nursing home after her hospital stay and her family didn't want to keep the dog. I ended up taking the heroic dog to the vet, paying to have her spayed and the bill for her board at the kennel. When we got home King was happy as always to see Cocoa and completely ignored his new girlfriend. He and Cocoa wouldn't let her eat

with them, I would have to take her to the garage to feed her. I was hesitant, after all that I had spent on her, to mention to Larry that I didn't even like her. I ended up putting her picture and a "free to a good home" sign up at the vet's office and within a day she had a new home. King didn't even miss her, nor did I.

As King got older he developed arthritis and we could tell he was in pain. I didn't want to put him on steroids and Larry reminded me daily that we couldn't let him suffer. "Well, if the day ever comes that he has to be put down I don't even want to know about it," I told him adamantly. One day while I was in town, as I passed the local jewelry shop, I saw beautiful pictures in the window of the owner's dogs. His wife was a professional photographer. I went into the shop and asked if it would be possible to have a portrait taken of me and King, as he was getting old and I knew that I wouldn't have him forever. "Sure, why don't you come in Thursday when you get off work and we can do that." I rushed home so excited to tell Larry. His reaction was not what I had expected. "You have more pictures of that dog than you do of your kids," he said gruffly as he stormed out the back door." "What is his problem?" I wondered. When I came home from work the next day and King did not run to the car to meet me, I hurried into the house. "Where is my dog?" "You told me that you didn't want to know when the time came," Larry muttered with tears welling up in his eyes. "That is why I had to run out the back door yesterday. I just didn't have the heart to tell you."

Anyone who has lost a dear pet can understand my hurt. I was blessed to know the unconditional love of a dog and have my best friend for eight years. A year later we went to a friend's house, and there, over the mantle was a breathtaking portrait of her and her beloved German Shepard. I burst into tears and had everyone in the room crying when I related my story.

Who do you think will be first to greet me when I reach the golden gate?

MAKING A DIFFERENCE

In the early morning hours of June 28, 1969, the police raided the Stonewall Inn, a gay club in New York City. The riots that ensued served as a catalyst for the modern gay rights movement. It has been over fifty years since that incident occurred. The LBGTQ community today no longer has to hide out in slinky, undercover bars or avoid establishments that would, in the 1960s society, refuse service to anyone who appeared different or 'queer' as the word of those days described them. We now celebrate our Gay Pride with parades, flying flags, being free to worship with people who used to scorn anyone for being anything other than what the general population considered 'normal,' and living our life with someone we love without being ostracized.

In the 1970s I moved to a small logging community in western Washington State. Sultan could rightly be labeled a typical 'red-neck' town. Situated on the Skykomish River, most of the population consists of generations of loggers, fishermen, hunters, just the typical *good ol' boys*. At that time outsiders were not exactly welcomed with open arms. If the locals didn't know who you were or from where you came or why you were there, they suspiciously avoided getting acquainted. When I was hired to tend bar in one of the local hang-outs, bets were being made on just how long I would last.

One of the first people I met after starting my new job was a handsome, younger than me, gentleman who introduced himself as Ron. He was also new in town and had been hesitant about coming into the bar. Ron was a psychologist at the Fircrest Residential Rehabilitation Center in nearby Shoreline. Even though he didn't drink he liked to stop by the bar every afternoon on his way home from work to have a coke and visit. He appeared to dress right off of the cover of Gentleman's Quarterly. He had a great sense of humor and always had amusing stories to share with me. This was quite the opposite of the scroungy, rough, tough, foul mouthed loggers that I dealt with on a daily basis. Ron and I met every Friday morning for breakfast and to go 'junkin' as we called it. We would hit all of the garage sales, flea markets and thrift shops. We never, ever discussed our personal lives, just enjoyed each other's company.

When Larry and I got married in 1979 my mother was upset, she thought that I should have married Ron. "He just adores you. I see how he looks at you and you are so perfect together," she whined. "I love him too, Mother, but I am not his type, you know what I mean?" No, obviously she didn't and it was quite uncomfortable for me trying to explain it to her. Larry knew that Ron was the best friend I had, probably one of the best friends that I had ever had, and he was very accepting of our relationship. Ron was included in all of our holiday celebrations, parties and picnics. Ron loved to tell the story about Larry's dad introducing him to one of his friends one day. "This is my daughter-in-law and her queer boyfriend." We laughed about that for years.

One early spring afternoon a young lady walked into the bar. I immediately checked her ID, as she didn't look to be over twenty-one. Deb had just received a medical discharge from the Army due to a heart condition. To my surprise she was well over the legal age. She ordered a beer and struck up a conversation with Ron. Her family lived in town and she would be staying with them until she found a job and a place of her own. She was sharp witted, foul mouthed and a little rough around the edges, but I liked her. A couple of days later she came in and promptly asked me, "Is that guy, Ron, gay?" I really wanted to reply that I didn't think that was any of her business but I told her, "Yes, he is." "You're good friends with him, right?" "Yup, other than my husband he is my very best friend." "It doesn't bother you that he's gay?" she persisted. "Should it?" I questioned back.

Deb was spending a lot of time in the bar. She and one of the bartenders had become drinking buddies. Linda was married and had three teen-aged kids, who were in the same age range as my two youngest. She and her husband, Jack, had built a beautiful home on the hill overlooking the valley, just a mile from our house. Linda and I did catering together, played Bunco in a group and had a standing monthly 'out-to-lunch bunch' date with several other ladies. We became good friends. She was my shoulder to cry on when necessary and the one I laughed with most, my all-round good pal. She and Jack celebrated Thanksgiving brunch with us for several years. By the time I realized that her drinking had become a problem, I was also hearing rumors that she and Deb were involved in more than just a drinking relationship. I confronted Deb as soon as I got wind of the gossip and she tearfully confessed to me that she and Linda were, in fact, having an affair. Her family had rejected her when she told them that she was a lesbian. Linda had taken her under her wing to protect her and one thing eventually led to another. It is still hard for me to express my shock and my reaction to the situation. I couldn't even bring myself to talk to Linda about it. My kids were questioning me, "Is this true Mom?" Linda's husband was blaming everything that had happened on the drinking, which I was also feeling may have led to the situation. Deb was confiding in me, and Linda finally came to me filled with self-loathing, begging for my understanding. I was also the one who Jack turned to, his eyes appearing cold, devoid of all emotion asking over and over, "How could this be? Why, why?" I found myself right in the middle of what seemed to be something out of a second rate soap opera, not my real life.

The phone rang sometime after 2:00 AM. It was Deb's sister hysterically screaming, "She's dying, she's dying, please come quickly." Why hadn't she called 911 instead of me? Not thinking clearly enough to ask that question or to call it myself, I jumped in my car and raced to her house. Deb had obviously overdosed. We loaded her into my car and rushed to the emergency room. My husband's reaction to the incident was definitely not what I would have expected of him. "It would have been easier for everyone if you had just let her die." I spent most of the next few days trying to convince Deb that her life was worth living and that she could be who she was and live a useful, happy life. All the while I was torn over how all of this drama had effected everyone close to me.

Linda committed herself to a rehab facility and after completing her treatment she attended school to become an alcohol counselor. She went to work at one of the prominent alcohol treatment facilities in Seattle. She and Jack continued to live together and in time, and with counseling, they were able to mend their broken relationship to some extent. I remained Deb's confidant and went through another attempted suicide with her, acted as the go-between with her family and did all that I could to make her feel worthy of living a clean, sober, productive life. My last conversation with her was about her future. She was excited about a new job that she had started and her clean bill of health. Holding my hand, she repeated over and over how happy she was that I had stuck by her through all of the bad times, just as a mother would have. "You have made a difference in the meaning of my life," she confided. Our visit was cut short that day, as she had plans to take her nephews to the Mariners baseball game in Seattle. She looked self-assured and confident and sported a grin that seemed to convey her new found pride in being who she was. After the ball game Deb dropped the boys off at their home. Her sister told me that she looked tired and said that she was going to go home and take a nap. That evening I received a call informing me that she had died peacefully in her sleep of natural causes. The autopsy confirmed that it was a heart attack.

Linda took care of Jack until he passed away in 2004. She and I remain close, and even though she was recently diagnosed with early-onset Alzheimer's disease, which took the lives of two of her sisters, she remembers me and we still reminisce about the happy days we shared.

I recently came across a book that Linda had sent me for my birthday years ago. Her inscription read: "I can't begin to tell you how very much you have helped me through this difficult time of my life. Just knowing that I have a friend like you who really cares, I know I can make it."

My dear friend, Ron, passed away in 2001 from complications of AIDS.

SAM THE MAN

Life doesn't always take us on the path that we may have planned, but the old adage, "everything happens for a reason," comes to mind whenever I reflect on the places I have been and the people I have met.

Whoever says, "I want to be a bartender when I grow up"? It surely wasn't my idea of a vocation, but I must confess that the experiences I encountered in my new 'part-time' job were a challenge as well as an opportunity to learn how to deal with people. I met so many diverse people and made many dear, lifelong friends while working in the bar. One of my very first customers was a wiry, elfin little fellow who had only half of a nose and a perpetual twinkle in his eye. He was quick to inform me that he would take bets that I wouldn't last a week in the bar. Sam was in his eighties when I met him. He was a retired surveyor and had kept a journal for over fifty years. He could tell you the temperature and humidity for any day from 1927 to that present day. He walked about six blocks every day and would arrive at the bar at precisely 11:00 AM. He would order a beer and it became my routine to drain all of the prior day's empty liquor bottles contents into a shot glass for his daily cocktail. Can you imagine? Kahlua, peppermint schnapps, gin, rum... whatever happened to be left in the bottom of the bottles.

At exactly noon I would fetch Sam a bowl of soup from the kitchen. This was most likely his only meal of the day. I would turn on the TV so that he could watch the noon news. He didn't have television at home and he enjoyed seeing the live news. He was always up to date on current events. He was an avid reader and loved listening to ball games on his little portable radio. He said that it was just like being at the game, but without all of the people interruptions. Sam had never been married and the only relative that he had was a sister who lived in California. He had, however, been adopted by the whole community. He knew everyone and everyone knew and cherished him. I grew to love him almost as a dad. He let everyone in the bar know that no one had better ever offend me or they would have to answer to him. He wasn't too sure of Larry when we got married but they soon became best of buddies. Larry was always there when Sam needed anything done in the house or yard. Sam insisted on chopping his own fire wood. He would let Larry help him carry it inside, but he had to chop it himself.

In the summer when Sam would show up with a five-pound bag of sugar, I knew that his raspberries were ready for me to pick so that I could make his jam. His garden was his pride and joy and he was quick to share everything he harvested. We have never been able to find the variety of bean that he grew. It was something of a cross between a green bean and a wax bean. To this day we still search to find something even similar to what we refer to as a 'Sam bean.'

Sam was always quick with advice and I found myself confiding in him and sharing my daily problems. The best advice he ever gave me has ended up being my rule to live by, "When you don't know what to do, do nothing." I have passed these words of wisdom on to others on several occasions. "Wonders never cease," was his favorite expression.

I could have set my clock by Sam's arrival at the bar every day and the day that he didn't show up I became concerned and sent one of the local firemen to his house to check on him. Jack returned to inform me that he had found Sam peacefully at rest in his recliner. He had been listening to the baseball game on the radio with the plate of cookies that I had sent home with him half eaten on the table next to him. As sad as it was to lose him I was happy to know that he had passed, as Jack told me, with a smile on his face. I reminisce often about Sam and his common sense, prudence, and wit. Hardly a day goes by that I don't remind myself... "Wonders never cease."

A TRIBUTE TO ST. JUDE'S CHILDREN'S HOSPITAL

"Sing 'Cotton Peter Tail' for me ,Grandma." A sweet voice was making a song request over the sound of the "Silly Songs" cassette blaring loudly from the speakers of the truck. "Oh, the joys of being a grandmother," I thought to myself as I turned down the volume to serenade my two three-year-old grandkids. "Here comes Peter Cotton Tail," I sang in my best voice.

Bryan Lee O'Neill was born on Mother's Day 1985. What a beautiful, perfect baby boy, and what a joy for my son, Patrick, to finally have a fishing partner. His sister, Nicole, was six years old when he was born and was not at all thrilled about a new baby. "I don't like the idea of *not* being the only grandchild," she bluntly announced to me upon his arrival.

Four months after Bryan came into our lives, my daughter, Maureen, blessed us with a baby girl, Michelle. Cousins Bryan and Michelle were adorable together. Now, three years later, here I was with both of them singing and jabbering and laughing as I tried to fight back tears. We were on our way to Mary Bridge Children's Hospital in Tacoma, Washington.

One month, almost to the day after Bryan's second birthday he became listless, didn't want to eat and complained that his tummy hurt. He had recently had his annual baby check-up and everything had checked out fine. "Maybe he's cutting his two year molars," I lamely suggested to his mom. My son insisted that Patty make an appointment to take him back to the doctor the following Monday. On Sunday morning after refusing his breakfast, Bryan asked for a glass of milk. He drank it and within minutes he was spewing projectile vomit across the kitchen. "Get him to the emergency room immediately," was the response Patty received when she called Patrick at work. "I'll meet you there." At two o'clock that afternoon I received a frantic call from my son informing me that Bryan had been diagnosed with neuroblastoma, a cancer that most commonly affects children under five years of age.

Our trip on this dreary, rainy Seattle morning in March of 1988 was just one of many that we had made since that devastating call nine months earlier. The whole family had been trying hard to keep life as normal as possible, but with chemotherapy and all of the doctor visits and watching our little guy slowly growing weaker, it became more wearisome every day.

When we arrived at the hospital both of the kids gleefully jumped out of the truck, still singing silly songs, and danced their way to the door. Watching these two darling tow heads holding hands and skipping merrily up the corridor brought a smile to my face and made me momentarily imagine that in a perfect world Bryan was going to be just fine.

How he loved the nurses and they loved him. His eyes lit up when he saw Leah, who had been there for all of his treatments. He ran to the bookcase in the waiting room to pick out his favorite Winnie the Pooh book. Michelle was right behind him, mimicking every move he made. They had a little squabble over the book but of course Bryan won. Coaxing her to sit down next to him he began to '*read*' to her. He couldn't read at three years old but he talked extremely well, and he seemed to know every word of the story that I had read to him over and over while we were waiting for his treatments. "Okay, Bryan, let's go," Leah called out. He headed straight for the table without any fear or hesitation. By that time this was routine for him. I kept Michelle occupied while we waited and when his session was over he bravely climbed down from the table. Michelle, holding tightly to her stuffed animal, scurried across the room, jumped on the steps to the table and chimed with a huge grin, "my turn." As I hastened to retrieve her, I saw Leah turn away wiping tears from her eyes. I later learned that she had a little boy who was born on the same day as Bryan.

"A horse is a horse of course, of course." How did this little guy know when it was three o'clock every day? He would pull his bean bag chair up to the front of the TV and sing along as Mister Ed entertained him for a half an hour. His dog, a huge white husky named Yukon, was always by his side. One day I was giving Yukon more attention than Bryan thought necessary and he grudgingly stepped between us telling me, "Ignore him, Gramma, he's obnoxious." A pretty big word for a three-year old. His vocabulary was amazing, probably due in part to the fact that every day began with Sesame Street. After lunch, Bryan would sit by the window and wait for his visitor, a bluebird. It would visit almost daily perching on the tree that hung over the porch and Bryan would talk to it, even on the days that it didn't show up.

The doctors and all of the staff at Mary Bridge Children's Hospital were amazing. My son requested that I be with him the day that he was given the news that they wanted permission to try an experimental drug which could possibly save Bryan's life. Without it there was no hope. It was not successful and Bryan passed away in his dad's arms two weeks after his third birthday. The pediatric oncologist who had cared for him sat with us all night. I caused a horrible scene screaming that they could not tell me that there was nothing they could do. They *had* to do something. Doctor Kneburgy held me and consoled me right to the end. I was, and am, so grateful that I was there when our precious little fighter was delivered from his worldly pain.

Yukon greeted us at the door when we arrived home in the wee hours of the morning. He was happy to see us, tail wagging, until he realized that Bryan was not with us. He paced the floor and whined and finally laid down on Bryan's bed with me. The next day he was still looking for Bryan. I called the funeral home and asked if it would be possible for me to take Yukon in to see Bryan. They were very accommodating and told me to go to the back door in the late afternoon. Yukon ran right up to the coffin, jumped up with his huge front paws on the edge and just starred at Bryan for what seemed like a long time but was probably five minutes. He backed away and went straight to the car. He had said his good-byes and was tranquil from then on. He knew, he just knew.

Several years ago my husband and I were privileged to spend a day at St. Jude's Children's Hospital in Memphis, Tennessee. Thanks to all of the research they have done over the years, neuroblastoma is now a curable disease. Twenty-four kids had left the hospital cancer free the week that we were there.

There is a plaque on the wall of the Hipple Cancer Research Center in Kettering, Ohio, that reads: "This disease of cancer will be banished from life by calm, unhurrying, persistent men and women working in hospitals and laboratories and the motive that will conquer cancer will not be pity nor horror. It will be the curiosity to know how and why."

A dedication stone in the garden at St. Jude's Children's Hospital reads:

"Those We Have Held In Our Arms For A Little While, We Hold In Our Hearts Forever"

Thank you, Danny Thomas.

TRIP OF A LIFETIME

In 1948 Bing Crosby crooned, "Faraway places with strange sounding names, far away over the sea. Those faraway places with the strange sounding names are calling, calling me." At about this same time we were studying World Geography in school. Being somewhat of a dreamer, I always envisioned someday traveling to the exotic destinations we read about. The South Pacific, Italy, France, Greece, South America, Africa. I would read for hours and imagine the intrigue of traveling the world. "See the Pyramids Along the Nile," I would hum as I scoured the library for travel books.

Marrying a sailor gave me the chance to travel, but not enough to fulfill my aspiration of seeing the world. I was thrilled to live in Puerto Rico for three years and Hawaii for four, but still the wonder-lust and gypsy in my soul yearned to roam.

In the summer of 1986 I stopped at a booth in a flea-market in Washington, which appeared to be Christmas oriented. "Christmas in July?" I questioned the young lady who was working the booth. She explained to me that it was a home party plan company and she was working toward earning a trip to Hawaii. "Really?" I questioned her. She handed me a catalog and asked me if I would be interested in hosting a party for her. "Fifty-dollars-worth of free merchandise just for having a party," she quickly informed me. I wasn't interested in her offer but sure thought about how nice it would be to get to return to Hawaii. I quickly accepted her suggestion to sign up as a representative for the company, for which I would receive a $300.00 sample kit. I made it very clear, however, that I wasn't interested in doing parties but that I would take orders for 'catalog' or 'silent' parties. I signed the contract, walking away saying, "Now what the heck have I gotten myself into?" After showing the catalogs at work, I quickly booked six parties, took eight orders and had three people wanting to also join the sales force. By November of that year I had thirteen demonstrators signed under me, I was flying to St. Louis to train demonstrators for the company, and I had earned my trip to Hawaii with over fifty thousand dollars in group sales. I was still working my full time job.

Every year saw my group sales soar and every year I worked a little harder as the trips became more captivating. I could buy into the trip for my spouse for a thousand dollars, which I didn't have to pay up front, I could pay it off with the following year's first thousand-dollar commission. By the time I had earned my second trip, I had been promoted to supervisor for the company and was traveling to Florida and St. Louis every year for company training.

After the Hawaii trip came Greece, sailing the Greek Isles and Turkey. The following year the company trip was Brazil. I didn't think anything could surpass the thrill of seeing the original Girl from Ipanema strolling the beach, or standing at the foot of the Christ the Redeemer statue on the top of Sugar Loaf Mountain, but the best was yet to come. In the next four years we were able to take an Eastern Caribbean cruise, a Western Caribbean cruise and a Mexican cruise, followed by a trip that I had dreamed of for years – Italy. Touring Rome and the Vatican and seeing and eating in the small towns along the coast, was even more than I had ever dreamed possible. Being blessed by the Pope and eating pizza in Florence on my birthday were far beyond anything I had ever imagined. All of the trips were first class all the way. Could it possibly get any better than that?

In April, 1995, we embarked on yet another exciting adventure. We traveled from Seattle to New York, where we boarded an Egyptian Airline flight to Cairo. My husband's fear of flying couldn't keep us from this adventure. He had to be heavily sedated whenever we flew, and he woke up just as we landed in Cairo. Every long distance flight had been hard on him and it seemed to get worse with each one. The Semiramis Inter-Continental Hotel is probably the most elegant of all of the hotels we had ever stayed in. The welcome dinner and Egyptian Nights program was fabulous. The next day we toured the Egyptian Museum of Antiquities and the Great Pyramids of Giza, where we were able to venture through the catacombs. We walked to the Sphinx and were treated to lunch at the Mena House. This landmark hotel, which was built in 1869 as a royal lodge, rests in the shadow of the Great Pyramids and the Sphinx. It opened as a luxurious hotel in 1886, but during the first world war it was used as a hospital. Some of the original fixtures, fireplaces and doors are still in use, adding to the ambiance of the hotel. We were served a magnificent lunch, but I was too car sick from the bus ride to Gaza to eat. Riding a camel was a great adventure, that is until the man in charge of the rides refused to let me off of the stinky, spitting monster animal unless Larry would agree to pay him an additional twenty dollars. Larry just turned and walked away saying, "Well, just keep her then." I was, of course, hysterical by the time the guy decided to get me down. Quite an adventure! Larry did give him another ten bucks.

We toured The Khan Al-Khalili Bazaar, one of the largest bazaars in the Middle East, if not the world. It was built in 1382. Today the Khan is an immense conglomeration of shops and markets. It didn't take Larry long to learn that bargaining is the rule there.

From Cairo we flew to Aswan. Before boarding the Egyptian sailing ship, the 'Sonesta Sun Goddess' to sail the Nile, we were treated to a trip on a Felucca, a traditional Egyptian wooden boat with a canvas sail. We visited the Aga Khan Mausoleum, toured the Aswan High Dam, the Philae Temple and the Temple of Kom Ombo, with its towering pillars and fascinating hieroglyphics. We then set sail for Edfu. The Nile is a north-flowing river, so we were actually sailing up the river, not down. It is claimed to be the longest river in the world. The peace and quiet while sailing was almost eerie and I had to keep reminding myself that I was actually sailing up the Nile.

In Edfu we visited the Temple of Horus, which was built between 237 and 57 BC. It is one of the best preserved ancient monuments in Egypt. The original roof is still intact. I stood in total awe at the foot of the hundred and eighteen-foot-tall gateway, flanked on either side by granite statues of Hours in his falcon form. I was trying to take in all of the history and mystique of my surroundings.

In Luxor we visited the Valley of Kings and Queens where we explored the tombs of the Ramses dynasties and that of King Tut. The Temples of Luxor and Karnak were the last stop before flying back to Cairo. I was totally overwhelmed by all that we had seen in six days and I knew that I would probably never again in my lifetime have such an amazing and enlightening adventure.

Our farewell dinner, "1001 Nights," on our last night in Cairo was an experience that will always stand out as one of the most fantastic events of my life. Mr. Lloyd, who was the CEO of HOUSE OF LLOYD, the company that provided all of these amazing trips, had tents sent up in the desert, and transported us by horse and carriage to the foot of the pyramids where we were entertained by local musicians and dancers and served a nine course dinner. The party seemed to go on all night.

The next morning our flight out of Cairo returned us to reality with memories of what would always remain in my mind the TRIP OF A LIFETIME.

THE "MARBLEOUS" YEARS

"Have you lost your marbles?" I wish I had a dollar for every time my husband has been asked that question. In fact, in the 1990s his license plate frame read, "I've lost my marbles... I'll buy yours." After attending several marble shows in the Midwest, Larry decided to organize a marble club in the Seattle area. By 1994 the Sea-Tac Marble Collectors Club had grown to two hundred members. The annual Marble Meet that we sponsored in Seattle in March every year was drawing people from all over the United States and Canada. Within a couple of years, we were holding marble shows every year in Las Vegas, Santa Cruz and Denver.

Although the original concept of the shows was to enlighten and educate collectors about the history and collecting of marbles what turned out to be most rewarding, as Larry related in a magazine article in 2002, was the people we met and the friends we made along the way.

Oh, the people! Collectors are a very special breed and we came across everything from the eccentric to the fanatic from every walk of life. The members were of varied social statuses and economical ranges, from millionaires to poverty stricken. The one common bond was the love of marbles.

Folks came to the shows from all over the country. There were farmers from Indiana in their bib-overalls, chewing tobacco. A couple from Chicago, who scorned our beer drinking friends, but had daughters named Brandy, Chablis and Merlot. Tom Quinn was a stock broker from Connecticut whose poor wife, Pat, was not allowed to order her own food in a restaurant. She was content to eat whatever Tom ordered for her and she never complained. There were retired firemen from Colorado, foundry workers from Oregon, and a dentist from California. Bert Cohn was a millionaire from Boston. His father was a prominent stock holder of the Mattel toy company. Bert designed the Barbie Pink Corvette. He received royalties for every one that was ever sold. Dale was a common laborer from Portland, Oregon, who saved every payday for a year just to be able to take his Auntie to the Seattle Marble Show. When he and Bert were in a room together there was never any sign of inequality, they were just two of the guys talking marbles. When Dale's old beater car couldn't make it all the way to Seattle, it was one of the marble collectors who drove miles to rescue him and Auntie. The camaraderie which grew over the years made our group feel like family.

    Hal Sisson was a magistrate for the Queens Court in British Columbia and the author of three published novels. He also conceived, produced and starred in "Sorry 'Bout That," the longest running burlesque revue in Western Canada. When he retired from his law practice in 1984 he devoted his time not only to collecting marbles but also to competing in marble shooting contests. With his encouragement we instigated a marble tournament in conjunction with our shows. Seeing this distinguished gentleman on the floor with me and a carpet layer, a piano salesman, a car mechanic, a landscaper, a school principal and a marine biologist was all the proof we needed that we are all indeed created equal. Hal competed in the British and World Marble Shooting Championships in England in 2002. I treasure the last letter that I received from him shortly before he passed away.

    Raelyn was the wife of a lawyer in Portland and also an ordained minister. Her fabulous home was adorned with marbles from the banisters to the bathrooms and beyond. She loved entertaining the club members every summer with a huge picnic at her home. Having her attend the Las Vegas shows was a real asset as we hosted three weddings over the course of a few years. One of those weddings is especially memorable as the groom, for whatever reason, decided to hang his tuxedo on the ceiling fire extinguisher in the hallway of the hotel the night before the wedding. The hanger set off not only the fire alarm, but all of the hallway fire extinguishers on that floor. Harold and his bride took their vows the next day on the spiral staircase of the hotel lobby, she in her lovely wedding gown and he in slacks and a sports shirt.

    Eric Larson was a commercial artist in Portland, Oregon, and an avid marble collector. Over the years he had purchased several expensive marbles from Larry. He wanted only the best, most sought after marbles, and in mint condition. One evening we received a call from Eric. In an almost frantic voice he conveyed to Larry that he needed money. Would Larry please buy his marbles back? We would have to take an advance on our credit to do so, but we couldn't tell him no. He brought the marbles to us, thanking us over and over. We knew that there would be no problem selling them to get our money back. For some reason Larry chose to put them on a shelf in the closet, and there they stayed. Eric painted us a beautiful personal marble picture which hung on our wall for many years. Three or four years passed and Eric approached Larry at a marble show asking if he happen to still have a particular marble, a peppermint swirl with mica. "Sure do," Larry assured him. "Is it for sale?" Eric sheepishly inquired. "For *you* it is," came the reply. Over the course of a year, Eric had bought back every single marble. He couldn't believe that Larry had kept them all that time.

We had another artist in our group, Merlyn McCullough from Idaho. One of his paintings was a depiction of what Larry would look like at eighty years of age. It was titled simply, "Marble Man." He presented the original painting to Larry at our annual banquet in Seattle. A year or so later we were on our way back from a marble gathering in Idaho and when we stopped to get gas, the painting was stolen from the back seat of our car. Nothing else was taken. We were devastated and didn't even want to tell Merlyn, who shortly thereafter passed away. Several years later, long after our marble club days were over, I received a phone call from Raelyn, the minister in Portland, informing me that she had just found the original "Marble Man" painting at a garage sale. She mailed it to us in time for Larry's eightieth birthday.

  We met Alan Rammer in the early 1980s while attending a collectible show in Oregon. He was a marine biologist for the state of Washington. Alan truly missed his calling. He should have been a stand-up comedian. He kept all of us laughing with his antics and stories. He was our right hand man in the organizing and promoting of the club. He remains today one of our closest friends, more of a son I should say, always there to lend a hand or to make us laugh.

In 2000 one of the charter members of the marble club, Gerry Colman from Albuquerque, was on a waiting list for a liver transplant. Having a healthy, large liver and testing as a match, I volunteered to be a donor. Because I was over fifty years of age I wasn't eligible to donate. Gerry did get a transplant and over twenty years later is living an active life. He reminded us recently the he still has all of his marbles!

We were privileged to meet and work with some of the greatest contemporary glass artists in the business. David Salazar has a glass art studio in Santa Cruz, California, where he hosted an open house every year when we had our marble show there. We were able to watch the glass artists bringing to life mystical creations, and even got to try our hands at making marbles under David's close supervision. His glass work is sought after world-wide.

Oh, the stories go on and on, but like most good things in life there always comes an end. In any organization or venture you will find greedy people and wheeler-dealers who try to manipulate and swindle. It became apparent that there were some less than honest people infiltrating the collecting world. As the economy declined, there became a decrease of attendance at the shows and it was evident that people were now doing most of their buying and selling online. Why leave home when you can shop on eBay? So, the business side of our marble world met its demise. Over the years we have sold all but a few of our precious orbs, but we will always treasure the friendships and memories that we made in what we now refer to as "The Marbleous Years."

A CHRISTMAS ANGEL

Christmas is a time for remembrance, a time to reminisce, and to recall wonderful memories of the people who have touched our lives in ways that leave a forever imprint. Looking back over the years when our grandchildren were all still enthralled with Santa Claus and Rudolph and Grandma getting run over by a reindeer, there is a most memorable, incredible, life changing Christmas Eve that I replay in my mind every holiday season. The year was 1995. Our kids and grand-kids (numbering nine at that time) would all be gathering for Grandpa's annual Christmas Eve chili feed. Most of the kids loved the chili but for those who wouldn't eat it there was plenty more holiday fare to enjoy. We always saved some of the decorated sugar cookies that the kids had gathered to make with Grandma the week before for this special occasion. Every year there was an empty place at the table and in my heart, however, as one of our precious grandsons was no longer with us. Bryan Lee would be spending Christmas in heaven, as he had since 1988.

This story began in 1980 when my oldest son, Patrick, after a failed first marriage and the birth of his daughter, Nicole, in 1978, met and married a lovely, soft-spoken young lady. Melanie was very shy and quiet and we all loved her from the first time we met her. As many love stories go, this union lasted only a few years. Melanie never remarried. Patrick married again and in time had two more children. Bryan Lee was born in 1985. At two years of age he was diagnosed with neuroblastoma, a childhood cancer. After an eleven-month battle, he passed away in May of 1988 just two weeks after his third birthday. Hoping to heal and start a new life, Patrick and Patty moved to Idaho. They bought property and Patrick logged the land and built a cozy log home. They were blessed with a beautiful baby girl, Kasey Ann, who was born in 1990. Sadly, as often happens after the loss of a child, the marriage became intolerable, due in part to Patrick's alcoholism. He moved back to Washington, heavy hearted and sad to leave Kasey and the home that he had worked so hard to build.

In 1994, the same year that Patrick left Idaho, Melanie, his former wife, gave birth to a baby boy. She named him Jey-T, and confided to me years later that all she ever wanted was a tall, blond, handsome son who looked like Patrick.

While looking for work, Patrick stayed at his dad and stepmom's house. Unbeknownst to him Melanie lived just three doors down the street. The first time Patrick saw Jey-T it must have been love at first sight. He adored him. He would pack him in a back carrier to take him to the river fishing and spend most of his spare time with him.

Patrick and Melanie reunited in 1995 and that Christmas Eve the joy that Jey-T brought into our home and to our family was the best gift we could have ever received. I have always referred to that Christmas as my "Christmas Angel" year.

I like to believe that now every Christmas, Patrick and Bryan smile down from heaven on Jey-T and his beautiful family. His proud mom, Melanie, recently reminded me of the impact that Patrick had on Jey-T's life. "He is a kind, considerate, honest and of course handsome young man," she proudly bragged.

As Christmas draws near every year, my prayer is that my children and grandchildren will know and share the love and peace of the season and always remember the wonderful years that we had together, and that they will celebrate the true meaning of Christmas, the birth of our Savior, Jesus Christ.

MY WAY WITH WORDS

I recently heard it said that humor lives in the gap between the ridiculous and the real. Looking back on my life I realize that my family was gifted with an extraordinary ability to be able to laugh freely. Not everyone is born with the aptitude to laugh at oneself. In my case, I had to learn at a very early age that it is better to laugh at yourself than to be humiliated by others laughing at you.

Being the youngest of four children I learned to talk at an early age. By three years of age I could carry on a conversation with anyone. However, the words sometimes came out backward or the way that I understood them. My mother was perplexed when she heard me call my older siblings '*sonts.*' When it snowed and I ran to the window excitedly hollering, "Look at the *sone*, look at the *sone*, she realized that I had been calling them '*snots.*' I was constantly talking (imagine that) and my dad lovingly called me his little 'yak-yak' or 'jabber wacky.'

I loved going to church as a child. I think that it was because of the music. I longed to sing with the choir, and one Sunday I decided that it was my time to sing, so as the choir finished their last chorus I jumped up on the seat of the pew and in my loudest voice chimed, "Don't fence me in." I had never heard people laugh out loud in church before so I just joined in the laughter and continued singing. I was disappointed when my sister quickly whisked me out of the church. When we got out of the door two of the nuns who taught at the parish school approached us. I smiled and inquired, "Would you like to see my new *unna git* (underskirt) and *unna shit* (undershirt) that my sissy bought me?" My sister was mortified, trying to hush me but the women in the penguin suits walked off giggling.

My next memorable singing gig was joining in with the neighborhood kids who were practicing for a school program. "Jimmy crack corn," they harmonized. I sang right along, only my version was "Jimmy *crap* corn and I don't care." Again, I couldn't understand why they all laughed when I sang. It seemed to me that people were always laughing at me. A friend of my mother's handed me an orange one day. My mother asked me, "What do you say?" "Peel it," I replied as I handed the orange back. I wasn't being funny but they sure had a good laugh.

In grammar school, about fifth grade, I was chosen to be the emcee for the Christmas program. I proudly marched to the microphone and announced, "We will now have a piano Chebul by Billy solo." The audience roared. I couldn't imagine what was so funny about Billy Chebul playing the piano.

My family had gotten used to me talking backward. "My *ack bitches*" and "*Bass the putter*," but the kids in my eighth grade class were shocked when planning food assignments for the end of the year class picnic I inquired, "Who will volunteer to bring the *muckels* and *pisturd*?" I was baffled as to why everyone burst into fits of laughter.

For my sixteenth birthday my mother gave me a gold charm bracelet. I put it on and casually asked her, "does it look better *light* or *toose*?" She looked a bit befuddled and said, "I don't know what you mean." I became irritated and kept repeating, "*light* or *toose*" as I would pull the bracelet taut and then release it. When she finally realized what I was saying she began to laugh, and even though I didn't understand why she was laughing, I laughed right along with her. We laughed until we cried and she laughed even harder when I very seriously inquired, "Why are we laughing? Just tell me, *light* or *toose.*"

I recently learned that a speech disfluency is an interruption in speech that affects the flow of words. It is likely to happen when one is stressed or excited. There are people who rarely seem to notice that they have this speech disorder. Some of the most embarrassing moments in my adult life have occurred due to my inability to think before I speak. My words escape my mouth before my brain deciphers them. This usually does happen when I am excited.

In the 1970s, clogs were the shoe fad of the day. It was summer and I wanted a pair of white clogs. My friend, Barbara, and I went into an upscale shoe store and I spotted the display of the latest fashion style lined up on the floor. There were black and brown, tan and navy blue, even red, but nary a pair of white clogs. As I squatted down almost sitting on the floor, I heard a deep Lee Marvin tone of voice behind me. "May I help you, ma'am?" As I looked over my shoulder I saw an expensive pair of alligator shoes and sharply creased trousers. I slowly rose to see what I had sensed would be a very handsome man. I was not at all disappointed. He was the most attractive black man that I had ever seen. I had the shoe in my hand and a bit starry eyed as I held it up toward him and my shaky voice inquired, "Do you come in white?" Barbara headed for the door mumbling something under her breath and the good looking fellow in front of me burst into a laugh so hard that it was soundless. I thought that he was going to fall over as he headed toward the counter chuckling and repeating my unwittingly witty commentary. I was following him, trying to explain what I had meant, "Does this come in white?" He was too amused to even hear me and he had the other clerks wide-eyed and dissolving into laughter with him.

Over the years I had amassed a huge collection of Planters Peanut collectibles. Some of my most prized possessions were the large clear glass jars that adorned the country store counters in the 1930s and 40s. They contained individual bags of peanuts. These jars are rare and to find one in mint condition at a reasonable price is a collector's dream. I always looked forward to my weekend jaunts to garage sales and thrift shops hoping to find a prized addition to my collection. Arla Gay, my junkin' friend, was the daughter of a preacher and had also been married to a preacher. She was prim and proper and I was always careful to monitor my language when I was with her. One Saturday morning we stopped at a garage sale being held by an elderly couple. I immediately spotted a coveted jar with the glass peanut handle on the lid, one that I had only seen in pictures. I was so excited that I was trembling and bouncing from foot to foot. The gentleman approached me asking what it was that I was so excited about. Heading straight to the Planters Peanut jar, I squealed, "I collect *penis planters*." Arla Gay put her hands over her ears and made a mad dash to the car. The poor old man was looking down, pretending to have not heard me and unable to respond. I was so embarrassed when I realized what I had said. I could feel a flush creeping up my cheeks and my voice crackling as I tried to explain to him what I had meant to say, "I collect Planters Peanut memorabilia." I bought the jar, paid him and rushed away with my face, neck and ears burning, trying to laugh it off. Arla Gay was not at all amused.

On another of my collectible hunts I was looking for a wicker picnic basket. My friend, Linda, and I were in a quaint antique store in Missoula, Montana, when I found the perfect basket. It was out of the 50s, but had never been used. It had plastic dishes and utensils, plastic drinking glasses and adorable red and white checked napkins which matched the lining of the basket. Exactly what I wanted. The store had a second floor landing where I had made this discovery. Linda was on the main floor. I ran to the railing, so anxious to share my prized find. I called out to her, loud enough for the whole store to hear, "Look, look, a *wicker pecker backer.*" Another mortified friend and a room full of laughing customers. I guess I should shop alone and try to contain my excitement somewhat.

It seems that I was always embarrassing my friends. My friend, Alan, and I were walking through the Bellagio Hotel in Las Vegas and we stopped to admire the elegant gemstone world globes in the window of the gift shop. I was mesmerized, I had never seen anything quite that exquisite. "Let's go check them out," Alan suggested. The shop had the air of a museum with all of the beautiful art work. There were signs reading: 'DO NOT TOUCH.' As Alan was pointing out the different gems on the globe to me I recognized the aventurine, a form of quartz that has a shimmering or glistening look. The light from the window was shining on the globe and the aventurine looked almost like fine dust. Disregarding the 'DO NOT TOUCH' sign, I reached out to lightly brush the globe. Just as I did the salesman walked up to me... "May I help you, ma'am?" I was startled, feeling like a kid getting caught with my hand in the cookie jar. "Oh, no thank you. I just came in to dust your balls," I blurted out. I was instantly mortified hearing my own words. I had meant to say that we had come in to look at the globes. Another perfect example of my mouth overloading my brain. He and Alan were quite amused as I stuttered trying to correct my speech disfluency.

Oh, there are a few more embarrassing anastrophe (talking backwards) stories to tell and maybe someday I will, but for now I leave you all with this thought... *Trappy hails* to you until we meet again!

MARY FRANCES

"It must have been cold there in my shadow, to never have sunlight on your face. You were content to let me shine, that's your way. You always walked a step behind." The words from Bette Midler's song, "Wind Beneath My Wings," stabbed at my heart when one of my sister Mary Frances' friends sang it at her funeral in June of 2000. 'Sis,' the only name I ever knew her by, was born May 15th, 1932, to Mary and Francis Keane. She was eight years old when I was born and she loved her new baby sister. As a toddler I adored my "Sissy." She was a slow learner, but was always determined to keep up with the other children her age. Mother enrolled her in a dance class so that she might learn to be graceful. She loved the class and the interaction with the other kids, but she refused to do the dance steps as the teacher instructed. "No, you do it this way," she chided the dance instructor, shaking her finger for emphasis. She refused to return to the class after her first lesson. I think that her strong will is what carried her through a very unconventional life.

I was just six years old and alone with Sis when she experienced her first epileptic seizure. I was traumatized and in fear that she was dying. When the doctors confirmed that it was epilepsy, they also informed my mother that Sis suffered from severe developmental disorders which had been exacerbated by the physical abuse she had received from our father. I had witnessed his abuse to her and my brother, who was just seventeen months younger than Sis. He never laid a hand on me, but I vividly recall him, in a drunken stupor, pulling Sis and Jerry out of bed and beating them unmercifully. I stood crying in the hallway begging him, "Please don't hit Sissy." My mother was separated from him at the time and he had come to the house looking for her. I ran to the neighbor's house and they quickly called the police. By the time we got back to the house, he had left leaving all three of us sobbing. That was the last time I saw him for many years. My mother divorced him, but none too soon, as the emotional and physical damage had been done. Sis was very verbal all of her life as to her hate for him. She refused to be called

'Mary Frances,' or 'Mary Fran.' "My name is Mary," she would blatantly make known.

The doctors informed Mother that it would be best for Sis, and the family, to have her committed to the Montana Developmental Center, a state institution for people with developmental disabilities. The facility is in Boulder, Montana, just forty miles from Butte. At that time, and not owning a car, forty miles sounded like a world away. I remember how devastated my mother was, but to this day I do not understand why she agreed to it. Sis did receive an education that was based on her learning ability, rather than having to be held back or attend special education classes. She loved to read and always read the newspaper to keep up on current events. Her life, however, was deprived of all of the social and extracurricular activities that I was able to experience. I always felt guilty about that. We were not able to see her often, so I basically grew up not knowing her very well. I didn't like visiting the 'place,' as I called it. One visit in particular, when I was about ten years old, was a painful emotional experience for me. I was sitting in a large wooden rocking chair in the visiting room when Sis entered the room. She came directly toward me, so happy to see me. As she put her arm around me to hug me she was overtaken by a seizure and pulled me and the chair over with her. I was petrified. I carried that fear with me all through my childhood. As much as I wanted to see my sister I agonized about going to that 'place.' Sis did get to spend every Christmas at home with us and I always looked forward to that time with her. I loved buying her special presents. No matter how small or silly my gifts may have seemed, she was always so thrilled by them. As I got older I continued buying things for her. I always sent her Christmas and birthday gifts after I left home. Mother used to tell me not to buy her nice or expensive things because she gave everything away. That was her nature. She was so giving and always shared whatever little she had with those who had even less.

When she was with us at home I was not allowed to talk about my social life, my friends or movies I had seen. I could not share my accomplishments with her. *"So I was the one with all the glory, while you were the one with all the strength. A beautiful face without a name for so long. A beautiful smile to hide the pain."* Oh, she did have a beautiful smile, and the strength to endure the life she was forced to live. She never complained.

As Sis got older, the training school provided classes for her in practical nursing so that she would be able to get a job and perhaps learn to live independently. They arranged for her to take care of a retired school teacher, one Mrs. Margaret Henton. When Mrs. Henton's son, John, returned home in 1965 after serving in the Army, he won Sis's heart and they eventually married. To see my sister happy and living a normal life brought me so much joy. John worked for the Arco Smelter in Helena, Montana. He was a good provider. In 1968 they were blessed with a beautiful baby girl. They named her Anna Marie, which had always been my sister's favorite name. A year later they had a boy, who they named John, after his father. Sis and the kids never wanted for anything. Although it appeared to be a perfect family, there was one problem, John's drinking. I know that Sis would never have tolerated him being abusive to them. He was always meek and mild and very proud and caring of his family.

By the time John was fifty years old he was suffering with cirrhosis of the liver. He passed away at fifty-one, leaving Sis with two teen-aged children. It was a difficult time for her, as she had never been on her own. I know that the happiest years of her life were with John. She had good friends who helped her through the difficult times raising the kids. She was always over-protective of Anna, who had also been diagnosed with epilepsy and a learning disability. John, at an early age, became involved with less than desirable friends and in time was into drugs. My mother's fear was always - *what would become of the kids if anything happened to Sis?*

Many years of smoking took its toll on Sis's lungs. The last time I saw her was on her birthday in May of 2000. She was on oxygen, but still smoking. She probably weighed eighty-pounds. She told me in her determined tone of voice, exuding calm and focus, "I'm going to beat this, Honey." I was heart-broken, knowing that her days were numbered. She was sixty-eight years old when she passed away the following month. Her dear friend, Butch, looked after Anna until he passed away. Anna is living on her own now, and I am proud to say that she is doing well. John has been in and out of prison over the years due to his drug addiction.

Every time I hear, *"It might have appeared to go unnoticed, but I've got it all here in my heart. I want you to know I know the truth, of course I know it..."* I say, "Thank you, Sis, for showing me your strength." "Thank you, thank you, thank God for you, the wind beneath my wings"

MY LAST WEDDING

Remembering our wedding day is always special. Flowers, music, a beautiful wedding gown, a fabulous cake, family, and hopes for the future. These are just a few of the things that make for an unforgettable event of a lifetime. To experience this happiness and joy is every girl's dream.

Dreams don't always come true the way they should or the way we hope they will, but that is no reason to give up dreaming. I was lucky enough to have had two traditional church weddings. But, wait... isn't the third time supposed to be the charm?

A 1979 motorcycle ride to Reno from Seattle, and a proposal of, "Well, as long as we're here we may as well get married" came as a huge surprise. I had vowed, after two failed marriages to remain single for the rest of my life. Suddenly, the idea of security flashed through my mind and I boldly answered, "Will you put me on your car insurance?" I had spent my $50.00 insurance policy payment on a picture that I purchased as a gift for this man who was now proposing marriage.

We were married in a small chapel the next day, spent our wedding night in separate beds in Virginia City and headed back to Seattle on the bike in the pouring rain early the next morning. Our families and friends were all shocked. My boss said that it wouldn't last for six months.

Fast forward twenty-four years. I found myself single again, my choice. Larry was not one to give up easily, however. I moved to Fallon, Nevada, to be near my sister and transferred to a job in Reno with the company that I had been employed with for thirteen years. Larry persisted and said that he would sell our home and buy me a house in Nevada. After giving it much thought and concluding that I had, after all, given him the best years of my life, I decided to take him up on the offer. We bought a beautiful brand new house. I was happy. After a year I came to the conclusion that if something were to happen to Larry, I would have nothing but the house, no pension, no social security. As it was, I had no medical insurance and was still too young for Medicare. I announced to him out of the blue one day that if he intended to live in 'my' house he had better do something to assure me that I would be taken care of in the future. That's all I said. No demands, no threats, not even an ultimatum.

We both took great pride in our yard and had worked hard putting in our first garden. On May 25, 2004, I was in the garden, in my grubby garden cut-offs on my knees digging in the dirt when Larry appeared asking me, "Will you drive me to Reno." "No," was my quick reply. "I'll buy you a full tank of gas," he quickly added. "No, drive yourself to Reno. I am not going to go in and get cleaned up to drive to Reno." "Oh, you don't even have to change, just go like you are, no one will see you. You don't even have to get out of the car. It will only take an hour. Please." I've never been too good at saying no, so I slipped on my shower shoes, jumped in the car and with muddy knees, uncombed hair and a bit pissed off, I drove silently to Reno. I didn't ask any questions and he offered no explanation for the hurried trip.

"Just park at Fitzgerald's, I'll only be gone for a few minutes." When I parked the car he handed me a twenty-dollar bill and said, "You can go in and play the slots for a few minutes if you want." What? He hated me playing the slot machines. "I wouldn't even think of getting out of the car looking like this," I said. He left in a hurry and after about five minutes I decided, "What the heck, nobody in there knows me anyway." I brushed the dirt off of my knees, ran my fingers through my messy, sweaty hair and marched into Fitzgerald's. I found a nickel slot machine and made myself right at home. After about twenty minutes and being about twelve dollars ahead on the machine, I felt a tap on my shoulder and an almost frantic Larry saying, "Come on, hurry, we've got to go." He pushed the 'cash-out' button and nearly dragged me outside. *My God, did he rob a bank?* Parked at the curbside was a long black limousine with a smiling female chauffeur, his friend Cindy. "Get in," she chimed. Confused, I climbed in and away we went to the courthouse where the clerk was waiting with a certificate for me to sign. I couldn't decide whether to laugh or cry. I was amused but very angry. Cindy then drove us to the chapel where she was the licensed Justice of the Peace. "What kind of ceremony do you want, Larry?" she inquired. Guess I had no say in the matter. "You can skip the 'love, honor and obey until death do us part'," he jokingly replied. "Been there, done that, didn't work. Just say whatever it will take to make it legal so she can sleep at night." How romantic. So that's just what she did. Then to add insult to injury he took a Corona cigar out of his pocket, took the paper ring off of it and sweetly slipped it on my finger. I kind of wish now that I hadn't refused to have pictures taken. Such a truly memorable wedding.

      Over the years he has taken great pleasure in telling people that I married him the first time for car insurance and the second time for health insurance. I like to add, "And we lived happily ever after."

THE PIE
A FUNNY FOOD FOLLY

Who can tell me the difference between a cook and a baker? People cook food to provide sustenance, to nourish life. I learned to cook out of necessity. I felt an obligation to nurture my children as best I could, and if that meant feeding them nutritiously, then that was what I was going to do, and if I had to do it I made up my mind to do it well. Thus began my life as a cook. I didn't particularly enjoy cooking, but was determined to become what someday might be called a '*good*' cook. I became obsessed with cook books and would read them from cover to cover as if I were reading a novel. I experimented with new recipes, but still did not find much pleasure in cooking.

Standing in line at the supermarket one day I saw a series of cook books, one of which I couldn't take my eyes off. I grabbed it at the last minute, feeling guilty about spending a dollar on a paperback book. Just reading some of the recipes scared me. I couldn't remember my mother ever making a homemade pie. She had, however, passed on to me an amazing crust recipe that she used for the meat and potato pasties that she often made.

Perhaps I should have started my baking venture with a simple apple or berry pie, but a colorful glossy picture of a luscious lemon meringue pie caught my eye. "I can do that," I confidently told myself. I made a list of the ingredients, read the recipe over three or four times and headed to the store. My excitement elevated as I picked up the fresh lemons. Wow, I had never experienced this kind of excitement over a meat loaf or cooking breakfast. That, my friends, is when I realized what distinguishes a baker from a cook... JOY!

My first pie turned out almost as perfect as the picture in the book. I was so elated that I could hardly wait to make another pie. I must confess that I ate most of that first pie. My next attempt was to master the chocolate cream pie featured on the cover of the book. After that, as I turned the pages in my new treasured 'Book of Cakes and Pies' I discovered a Fresh Coconut Cream Pie recipe. That pie, in time, became my signature dessert. I made it for every special occasion or whenever I was asked to make something for a get-together. I used this pie to bribe my dad into visiting me when I lived in Hawaii. I promised him that I would make a coconut cream pie every day while he was there. I kept my promise and I am quite sure that after his month visit no one in the family cared to ever have another coconut cream pie. By the time his vacation was over I didn't even need to follow the recipe, I knew it by heart.

Many years passed and after we moved to Nevada my niece invited us to her son's birthday dinner. When I asked if I could take anything she quickly responded, "We would love to have your coconut cream pie." I decided to double the filling recipe so that it would amply fill a 10-inch crust. By then I was back to carefully reading the recipe. Following it carefully, I combined and stirred and boiled on low heat as directed. Boil five minutes the recipe said. *Why isn't this thickening?* I wondered. "Turn the heat up, add some more cornstarch," my husband suggested. After twenty minutes or so of boiling, stirring, and crying out loud, he suggested that I just start over. "Are you kidding, that is six eggs and six cups of milk. I only have two more eggs and no milk." The crust was already made and cooled, waiting for the filling. He offered to go to the store and get more milk and eggs. I did not want to disappoint my niece, so I agreed to just start over. "Maybe I should just make the single batch twice instead of doubling it." I had never, ever had this happen before.

When he arrived back from the store, having to drive a mile each way, I started over. I followed the recipe carefully. Mix, stir, and bring to a boil. "It's not thickening. I can't go to dinner without a pie. Will you go back to the store and buy four boxes of vanilla pudding and pie mix and more milk?" By then I was in tears. He came back with the pudding mix and it cooked up perfectly. I added coconut and some coconut flavoring and made him promise that he would not tell anyone that it wasn't my '*home made*' pie.

"Oh, Aunt Ruth, this is just as delicious as I remember it being," my niece said. That kind of hurt my feelings but I smiled and thanked her.

The following week I made cupcakes to take to work. When I went to the cupboard to get powdered sugar for the frosting, I realized that the container marked '*cornstarch*' was, in fact, full of powdered sugar. OMG!! This couldn't be! I had put powdered sugar in the cornstarch container. Needless to say, powdered sugar is NOT a very good thickener. I can't help but to laugh every time I make a coconut cream pie!

MY FAVORITE ENTERTAINER

Over the years I have had the opportunity to see many popular, even famous, people. To choose a favorite was not difficult for me. However, I tend to judge people not only for their talent and ability to entertain, but also for their overall persona and adeptness to relate to the people for whom they are performing. Making it personal and putting an audience at ease is in itself a talent that not all entertainers are capable of implementing into their performances. I've witnessed this many times, the first being when I saw my absolute idol at the time, Johnny Mathias, in Atlantic City in the early 1960s. He was young and very uneasy on the stage and even though his voice was clear and beautiful, the constant twitching of his fingers and his inability to relate to the audience was quite distracting. I did not enjoy the show and was so disappointed. But I still adore Johnny.

Sammy Davis Jr. was one who definitely not only knew how to relate to people but also enjoyed every single minute he was on stage. I saw him for the first time also in New Jersey and again in Honolulu in 1971. He was doing two shows a night at one of the hotels on Waikiki beach. We chose to go to the late show. Oh, what a show! He put his heart into not only dancing and singing but also relating to his fans on a very personal level. He told us that after the early show that night he had gone out of the back door to have a cigarette and when he saw the line waiting to get in for the second sold out show he could not even imagine anyone waiting in line and paying fifteen-dollars just to see him. "I'm going to see to it that you get your money's worth," he stated. And that he did. He was still singing and taking requests and talking to people at 2:30 AM. I thought he was going to sing all night. Now, that's an entertainer. Top notch, first class, but no, still not my favorite.

Don Ho picked me out of the audience to sing with him in Honolulu. When he asked me where I was from and I said "Montana," his next question, "Did you ever do '*it*' in the snow?" embarrassed me beyond words! How can you answer that in front of a room full of people? And then he serenaded me with "Tiny boobies on your chest, one points east, the other points west." No, he was far from my favorite.

I also had the honor of being serenaded on stage in Las Vegas by the Temptations singing "My Girl" to me. That was definitely my favorite event of the three years I lived in Las Vegas. Seeing Cher, who informed us that she had to rush to the hospital right after the show as she was awaiting the birth of her next boyfriend, and experiencing the magic of Siegfried and Roy, becoming personal friends with Marty Allen and his talented wife, Karen, and witnessing an impromptu performance by Santana in the middle of the afternoon in a little downtown club were only some of the benefits of living in Las Vegas

We had front row seats to see The Original Comets in Mesquite in 2002 performing what they called their "Viagra Tour," singing "We Ain't Dead Yet." When I closed my eyes they sounded exactly like they did in 1958. The youngest of them at that time was 78 years of age.

Before I divulge my favorite entertainer I would like to share some stories about my UN-favorites, and why they were. I was newly married and living on a Navy base in Norman, Oklahoma. I was so excited to hear that Lucille Ball was going to appear at a fund raising event that would be free to military personal and families. I would get to see her in person. When she walked on stage to what I guess wasn't enough applause for her ego, she took the microphone and said, "I didn't come all this way to entertain 50 people," and she walked off the stage. I could not even stand to look at her from that day on. It was supposed to be a charity event.

My next big disappointment was in the 1980s when I was doing trade shows. I had a ten-day show in Las Vegas. The show ran until 10:00 PM every night, which gave me time to catch the late shows on the strip. Bill Cosby was performing. This was at the time that his TV show, which I loved, was popular. I was thrilled to get discounted tickets to see him. He sauntered onto the stage and it was quite obvious that he had probably had one too many. He received a good ovation and began what seemed to be a very funny and entertaining narrative. He posed a question, and a young military man who was there with a group from Nellis Air Force Base jumped up and loudly answered, much to the amusement of the audience. Mr. Cosby was not at all amused, and very arrogantly told the guy, "This is MY show, Boy. You paid to see ME, now sit down and shut up, or leave!!" The whole group walked out and to this day I am sorry that I didn't join them. I was uncomfortable and disgusted with him for the rest of the show and never again watched his TV sitcom.

My personal encounter with one of my favorite movie stars when I was working at Rite-Aid in Las Vegas was extremely disturbing. I was the night shift supervisor and one evening a young man who was cashiering came to my office visibly upset, saying that there was a customer who demanded to see the manager. This lad was actually in tears trying to relate to me how rudely this man had talked to him. As I approached the gentleman I recognized him and I tried to contain my anxiety. When I calmly ask him what the problem was, he glared at me and with the voice that no one could deny, and said, "Do you know who I am?" Boy, that did it, and without even taking into consideration *who* he was, my answer came strong and clear, "I don't care who you are, you have no right to humiliate one of my employees to the point of tears." Without a word, he turned around and sauntered or staggered out. Why would Morgan Freeman be shopping in a Rite-Aid store in Las Vegas at ten o'clock at night? I guess some impersonators can be believable and I have always hoped that was the case. Oh, the controversy with the cashier was over the young man not being old enough to sell him wine.

I've been lucky enough to see some of my favorites, Barbara Streisand (seats so far away that you could hardly see her, in a stadium in Philadelphia in 1965), Neil Diamond, The Rolling Stones, Three Dog Night, Rod Stewart, John Denver, Tina Turner (Larry's favorite), Cindy Lauper, Charlie Pride and Waylon Jennings. We had tickets to see George "No Show Jones" in Seattle but he didn't show up. We also had tickets for Celine Dion's show in Las Vegas, only to be told when we got to Caesars Palace that the doctor wouldn't allow her to sing that night. It was the only night up to that point that she had ever missed a show. My biggest disappointment was an emergency transfer from Hawaii which had us leaving the day before I was planning to see Elvis' Christmas Show at the Honolulu International Center. We saw Alabama at a county fair in Utah, long before anyone had ever heard of them and my husband (ever the prophet) told me, "They are going to be famous someday." We spent New Year's Eve of 1992 with Kenny Rogers and Dolly Parton at the Tacoma Dome. My niece took me to see Willie Nelson at Lake Tahoe sometime in the '90s, and she and I got to see Donnie and Marie in 2019, just before their show in Las Vegas ended. My chance meeting with Meat Loaf at the airport in Reno is a whole story in itself.

In the early 80s, my brother took me, my mother and his neighbors to see his friend, who played the organ and sang at the ritzy

"Top of the Camlin Hotel" in Seattle. We were enjoying the show when all of a sudden I saw a horrified look on my mother's face. I turned to see a group of very grungy, utterly bedraggled, long haired fellows walking in. The waiter, seeing our shock, quickly came to the table and explained to us that this was The Motley Crue, who had done a concert at the Seattle Center that night and were staying at the Camlin. The evening ended up with them at our table, laughing and buying drinks for everyone. My mother was so impressed with their good manners and they were surely amused at her wit.

Having seen so many entertainers, you would think it would be hard to choose a favorite, but my choice is based not only on his velvet voice, but his gentlemanly demure and class. He was once called "The Funkiest Man Alive" and Frank Sinatra said that he had "the classiest singing and silkiest chops in the singing game." Mr. Lou Rawls, who sang gospel to blues, to jazz, to soul and pop. My friend, Gail, and I were given tickets to see his show at the Naval Base in Pearl Harbor in 1970. When we arrived at the Officers club where he was performing, he and his band were sitting in the cocktail lounge and my friend dared me to ask if we could take a picture. When I approached the table where they were sitting, all six of them stood up. He smiled, they were all so gracious. I snapped a few pictures of them and some with us. Then Lou asked if we could get a picture of him and the photographer (me) outside, beside the palm trees and tiki-torches. Having to wait a week to get the pictures developed was agonizing, but well worth the wait. Gail's husband was a good ol' redneck from Alabama and when he saw the pictures he became enraged and tore them up and destroyed the negatives. The picture of me and Lou Rawls was beautiful, probably the best picture ever taken of me. I can only see it in memory now, and when I hear, "Lady Love" and "You'll Never Find Another Love Like Mine", I fondly remember that glorious night in Hawaii.

Lou Rawls passed away from lung and brain cancer in 2006, but that velvet voice resounds in my memory and he will always be my favorite entertainer.

THE GIFT

    Is it true that what is worth having is worth waiting for? But how long must one wait? Growing up in a less than privileged environment tends to make you aware that some material things in life are limited to only the wealthy. I grew up thinking that only very rich people ever had fresh flowers in their homes. From an early age I was intrigued with jewelry. Neither my mother nor grandmother wore jewelry, with the exception of Grandma's tiny gold watch. I would sit in church on Sunday and stare at the gaudy rhinestone jewels that some of the better dressed women wore, and long for the day that I too could don such flashy stones. When I was about ten years of age someone told me that diamonds were the birthstone for April. From that day on I knew that if I never had anything else beautiful in life, I would someday have a magnificent diamond ring. When I was thirteen years old I saw Marilyn Monroe sing "Diamonds Are a Girl's Best Friend" in the movie "Gentlemen Prefer Blonds," and my wish became somewhat of an obsession.

    When my first husband proposed to me I was excited to learn that his father was best friends with the jeweler in town. I knew that I would have my dream come true when Pat told me that his dad was getting a good deal on our wedding rings. Oh, I would finally get my diamond... several to be exact. The wedding ring was sixty-eight dollars' worth of chip diamonds on a gold band. Not quite the one karat solitaire that I had envisioned. I tried not to show my disappointment.

    Seventeen years and four children later when my marriage ended, I tucked that ring away with plans to give it to my daughter someday. Life at that time was much too busy to even think about something as insignificant as jewelry. I had learned by then though that you don't have to be rich or famous to have fresh flowers in your home every day, and they seemed to bring me more joy than any diamond possibly could.

    I met Larry and we eloped to Reno on a motorcycle in 1979. He found a local pawn shop where he purchased a simple gold band. By that time in my life I had kind of given up on, or maybe just forgotten about my desire for the coveted *rock*. Several months into our marriage he commented, "You buy diamonds for someone you love." Oh, really? He bought me a diamond necklace for Christmas that year. It was ugly. It reminded me of an inexpensive Avon piece of jewelry. Knowing that I was disappointed he suggested that I return it and buy the camera that I had told him I wanted. I thought, "So much for ever expecting any more jewelry gifts."

Our marriage lasted twenty-three years and nine months to the day. We were only separated for a few months when he talked his way back into my life. He took me out to lunch one day and as we strolled past a jewelry store I hesitated and caught my breath when I saw the most gorgeous ring I had ever laid eyes on. "Let's go check it out," he suggested. "Oh, no, you could never afford something like that," I quipped back sarcastically with an arrogant laugh. He just stomped right past me into the store. The sales lady was quick to inform him that it was just a sample ring for the custom work they did. It wasn't even a real diamond but a Cubic Zirconium. The little chip diamonds and the sapphires that surrounded the large stone were real and it was eighteen-karat gold, but it was not for sale. "Good," I thought to myself. "A phony stone isn't what I want anyway." I walked out of the store and started window shopping my way up the street. After several minutes I realized that he wasn't behind me, so I sauntered back to the jewelry store and walked in just in time to see him hand the clerk his credit card. He never did learn to take '*no*' for an answer. I don't know how he convinced her to sell him the ring but he was sporting a smile that radiated winning. He presented the ring to me at lunch, almost as a persuasion tactic. I thus dubbed it my '*divorce*' ring. When we did re-marry several months later, it was not the Cubic Zirconium ring that he slipped on my finger, but a Corona cigar label.

Several years later we took a cruise which disembarked in Fort Lauderdale, Florida. During the cruise I had a tooth that was loose and when I bit down on something I felt it break. We found a dentist who could see me right away. After examining the tooth, he told me that it was abscessed and broken but that he didn't want to pull it without first putting me on antibiotics. He assured me that as long as it wasn't hurting and I didn't bite on it I would be okay until we got home. While he was telling me this and probing and poking around in my mouth the tooth fell out into his hand. I guess it really was loose.

I was so upset over losing a tooth. I left the dentist's office with tears in my eyes and my tooth in a tissue. I cried most of the day. "For God's sake, Ruth, I have seen women lose both breasts and not react the way you are over one tooth," were Larry's kind words of consolation. "Why don't you put it under your pillow and see what the Tooth Fairy will leave for you?" "What a jerk," I thought to myself. I was feeling better by bed time, having had a couple of glasses of wine, and I decided just being silly that I was going to put the tooth under my pillow. I awoke in the morning to find the tissue next to my pillow. I laughed and tossed it into the trash. "Well, what did the Tooth Fairy leave you, Dear?" Larry questioned in a kind of giddy tone of voice as he walked into the room. "Ha, ha, aren't you funny," I responded. "Didn't you look in the tissue?" he inquired. "No, I threw the damned tooth away." His face looked a little ashen as he made a mad dash toward the trash can. He pulled out the wadded tissue and handed it to me. "Open it." There in the crumbled folds of the tissue glistening in the light was a magnificent, brilliant, flawless one karat raw diamond stone. "That should make your ring the *real thing* and put a smile on your face," Larry proudly chimed. In a momentous instant, all of my childhood dreams had come true. I do believe that was the most precious material gift that I have ever received. My daughter's reaction was, "Wow, Mom, maybe you should have all of your teeth pulled."

TERRIFYING TURBULENCE

Having encountered several natural disasters in my life, I look back now on what seems to be not only the most life-threatening, but also the scariest event of my lifetime. I had experienced tornadoes in Oklahoma in 1958, a 7.3 magnitude earthquake in Montana in 1959, a typhoon that wiped out the island of Vieques, just off of the coast of Puerto Rico in 1959, and the eruption of Mount Saint Helens in 1980. It was reported to be the deadliest and most destructive volcano eruption in the history of the United States. Fifty-seven people perished that morning and even though it was over a hundred miles from our front door it rattled our windows and covered our trees with curtains of ash. None of this, however, compared to my fear and panic on the night of October 14th, 2007.

I am not a water person; I didn't ever learn to swim as a child because of my fear of the water. When in 1962 I had to sail from Puerto Rico to New York, just the thought of being on the ocean petrified me. After much anxiety and worry, I convinced myself that if anything were to happen to the ship I wouldn't drown because I would die of a heart attack before I hit the water. To my surprise, on the second day out I was actually enjoying the calm sea rocking me to sleep and the unexpected release of all of the tension I had built up worrying about the trip. Tears of joy and relief rolled down my cheeks the morning that we pulled into New York harbor and I got my first glimpse of the Statue of Liberty. I not only survived the trip, I had to admit that I enjoyed sailing.

During the 1980s and 90s we cruised several times to the Caribbean, and sailed up the Nile river in Egypt. In 1992 I took my then 83-year-old mother on a Mexican Cruise. This trip turned out to be one of my most memorable cruises ever. Perfect weather, beautiful calm sea, amazing food, great entertainment and company, I could hardly wait for my next cruise.

Flying to Italy to board the MS Westerdam in October of 2007 was like a dream come true. We spent three weeks visiting ports in Italy,

Monaco, France and Spain and were looking forward to our last port-of-call. We safely docked in Ponta Delgado on the island of San Miguel in the Azores. By this time, I had long forgotten my fear and anxiety of being on the water. After a delightful day exploring this enchanting village where the sidewalks are paved with beautiful inlay designs and scrubbed every morning, we boarded the ship and set sail for five exciting, fun-filled days crossing the Atlantic Ocean.

The sail-away party on deck was always one of my favorite shipboard events. The live music, fancy cocktails and everyone looking forward to the beautiful sunset quickly gave way to a huge, ominous cloud to the north and the captain announcing that he had received word of gale weather warnings. On his suggestion the party was quickly moved inside. At the dinner table all of the talk was about a monster extra-tropical storm, generating massive waves and severe winds that could develop into a deep North Atlantic depression between the Azores and Newfoundland. One fellow in particular who seemed quite knowledgeable was trying to explain to all of the wide-eyed guests at our table that a broad cold Arctic air mass spreading behind the low something, something, blah, blah, blah from Canada could cause… something. *What is he talking about? What does all that mean?* I pondered, thinking about the worst scenario. I could sense that I wasn't the only one at the table feeling uncomfortable, and by the time our dinner was served I was feeling too fearful to even eat. As we exited the dining room we were aware that the wind was steadily strengthening and the sun seemed to have faded into the heavy rain clouds that were advancing rapidly toward the ship.

Everyone seemed to be acting as normal as ever, preparing for the nightly entertainment and making their way to the piano bar and cocktail lounges. I, on the other hand, was feeling a bit panicky and attempting to mask my fear by forcing a watery smile and a joking tone. Then the captain announced that even though they expected the storm to intensify over night, he wanted to assure us that we were not in any imminent danger. I began to feel the queasiness of sea-sickness for the first time as the ship started to rock. As we were strolling on the fourth deck one of the ladies who was with us reached out and pulled the curtain open just as a gigantic wave went high over the window and slapped so hard that we all lost our balance. That was it for me! I was holding my breath – I could feel the adrenaline spike as images of what-could-be flashed through my mind. "I'm going to the cabin," I said, holding back a scream, but my voice cracking. Larry tried to assure me that everything was going to be OK and I would probably feel better staying up on the deck. The turbulence was getting to the point that it was difficult to keep your balance. When we got to the elevators they were hanging up the 'puke' bags, and many of the passengers quite obviously already needed them. As Larry steered me toward our cabin, I was thankful for the first time that we had an inside cabin. I told him to go back up to the Lido deck and enjoy the roller-coaster ride. By this time, I was feeling a bit sea-sick, but I was mostly just scared. Scenes from the movie 'Titanic' kept playing over in my mind. The rolling motion of the ship seemed to calm me down somewhat, but my prayers were still a bit frantic. "Dear God, please see me through this, please keep us all safe from this storm." I almost went so far as to say, "If I get out of this alive I will never get on another ship." Glad I didn't make that promise. When Larry returned to the cabin I was fast asleep. We awoke in the morning to sunshine, calm waters and smooth sailing.

Waiting at the elevator to go to breakfast we overheard the captain telling a group of people that he had been sailing the Atlantic Ocean for over twenty years and this was the worst storm he had ever encountered. Even he, he admitted, had gotten sea-sick. The atmosphere in the dining room was especially exuberant that morning. Everyone was sharing their stories, some even almost in tears, hugging and laughing, letting their relief sink in.

By the time we docked in Fort Lauderdale six days later we were already talking about our next cruise. We were not about to let one horrific storm ruin our travel plans. We crossed the Atlantic Ocean, without incident twice after that dreadful experience. We had booked a South Pacific cruise for March of 2021. It was, of course, canceled due to the COVID-19 pandemic. We were disappointed until on March 5th we saw on the news that a severe category five tropical cyclone, Niron, with winds up to 120 miles per hour was reported in the South Pacific. I am truly thankful that we missed that one, but looking forward to sailing again in the future.

NEVER TOO OLD
TO LEARN A NEW SPORT

I didn't have brothers and sisters to teach me to play ball, they were all older and mostly grown up when I came along. None of my family were ever sports fans. In the 1940s and 50s there was no televised coverage of sporting events. In fact, we didn't even have television in Montana until the mid-1950s. So when I started school I had never even thrown a ball. I was pretty good at hop-scotch and jacks and the only thing even close to a sport that I had ever attempted was playing marbles. I loved my marbles, and after my brother taught me to shoot them, I became very competitive. The biggest disappointment in my life, up to that time, was that the nuns would not let me spend recess on the boys' playground shooting marbles. I was just not interested in the dumb girls' playground, and none of the girls were about to play marbles with me.

In the seventh grade we were required to take Physical Education, which then was simply called 'gym.' This was my very first encounter with any kind of ball playing, and the first time I had ever even heard of volley-ball. I took my stance on one side of the net, not sure of what I was supposed to do. It didn't take me long, however, to realize that the object of the game was to duck before that speeding ball hit you in the face. Well, how about basketball? "What do you mean you have to bounce the ball and run at the same time?" This is when I learned how totally uncoordinated I was. Sister Scholastica was our gym coach and after watching me fumbling the ball and running the wrong way, she humiliated me by loudly proclaiming that I was supposed to be playing ball, not doing the Swan Lake Ballet. Gee, I must have been fumbling gracefully! It was really embarrassing to always be the last one chosen for any of the team games. I did discover, in the eighth grade, that I could outrun the entire track team (four boys total). We would race home from school every day and none of the guys could ever catch up with me. It got to be quite a challenge and on-going joke for the track team. I, of course, would egg them on, "you can't catch me, you can't catch me." None of them ever did. Too bad they didn't have girls track teams back then.

My oldest son loved baseball from the time he was a little guy. I would pitch the ball to him, but was still good at ducking when it was thrown back or if it was hit toward me. In spite of my athletic inability, I encouraged all of the boys to take part in sports. I was happy to just remain a bystander and cheer them on. That is until in their early teens when they became interested in archery. Their dad was an avid archer and he decided that it would be a great family sport. I was a little reluctant to even give it a try but the boys encouraged me, almost begged me to do it with them. After a couple of lessons, I realized that I had a good eye and a steady arm and I found something that perhaps I could do well and enjoy with my family. It became quite a family affair. We joined the Armed Forces Archery Association on Oahu and were spending week-ends and one night a week at the archery range. The kids loved it, and within a year I was teaching the Junior Olympic team. We all shot 'bare bow' which simply means that we did not use sights or compound bows. The kids' dad was shooting competitively and talked me into signing up for the state archery meet that he was taking part in. I was hesitant but he assured me that there was very little competition in the women's bare bow division, so on a whim I signed up. Much to everyone's surprise I took the title of "Women's Hawaii State Bare Bow Champion." I think the year was 1970. I also won the title the following year. Now, I have to confess… there was only one other woman in that division (both years) and she was really a lousy shooter. After four years in Hawaii we returned to the mainland. I have only shot a bow once since. My boys took me bow hunting in Washington and they were very disappointed

when at full draw I had a perfect shot at a deer only several feet away and I lifted the bow and shot in the air. I could never have shot any living thing, let alone Bambi, who was looking me straight in the eye. That was the end of my archery adventures.

While we were still living in Hawaii, my son, Patrick, was on the golf team and he talked me into taking golf lessons with him at the military golf course, which was free for military families at that time. Again I was unsure of my ability to hit that little ball, but I quickly learned that it didn't take as much coordination as it did concentration and determination, so with Pat's encouragement and patience, I took up golfing. I do not claim to be a golfer – I have never taken the sport seriously, but I do enjoy the game and have continued to play off and on, now and then over the years.

In my 30s I took up bowling. I bowled on a league for a few years and enjoyed it, but I never excelled. I had a 216 score game (my only game ever over 170) when I had an average of only 115. That was worth recognition and I even have a pin to prove it!

In 2009 we became 'snow-birds,' spending the winters in Arizona. It was then, at 70 years of age, that I discovered my sport of choice. Bocce Ball can be traced back as far as the Roman Empire. It is very popular in Italy and the word 'boccia' is Italian for 'bowl' in the sports sense. Finally, a sport in which I could excel, stand out in the crowd, outshine and above all NOT be the last chosen for the team. I loved the game, it was just like shooting over-sized marbles. I was anxious for our second year of playing when my right arm began to give out. I ended up having to have rotator cuff surgery in the fall of 2011, but I was not ready to give up the game. So, still in an arm sling, I played that season left-handed. I did so well with my left hand that all of the players teased me about "sand-bagging" when playing right-handed. I haven't played Bocce Ball since we quit going to Arizona a few years ago, but I am now a believer that YOU ARE NEVER TOO OLD TO LEARN A NEW SPORT.

RETURN OF THE STATE PATROL

Having survived my deplorable encounter with a Washington State patrolman in 1972, I became extremely aware of my driving habits and would become almost paranoid if I saw a patrol car behind, in front of, or next to me. My new found awareness paid off, as I went several years without a traffic ticket.

It was Halloween, 1983. As always, the employees where I worked dressed in costume. I was an amazing Raggedy-Ann. My husband had driven my car that day and left me with his truck. Driving home, my worst nightmare became a reality when I heard a siren behind me. Sure enough, it was a State Patrol car, with lights flashing! Forgetting that I was in costume I fumbled for my license and registration. When the patrolman got to the window he began laughing almost hysterically. My first reaction was fear, but then I realized why he was laughing. Obviously he had never stopped a live doll before. "I was not speeding," I blurted out before he had a chance to say a word. "No, ma'am, but your tabs expired eighteen months ago." What? That can't be. But it was. It seems Larry had been driving all that time on expired tabs. Luckily I didn't get a ticket, just a warning to have the registration updated within 24 hours.

Exactly three days later, I was on my way home on a county road at 11:00 PM. I had the radio blaring, and there was no traffic in sight when I saw the lights in my rear view mirror. As I began to slow down, I remembered hearing about someone who had been stopped by a would-be cop and beaten and raped. Here I was in the middle of nowhere all alone. My heart started to pound as my foot hit the gas petal. I was only about seven miles out of town and by the time I hit the city limits I had to have been going over ninety miles an hour with the flashing lights right on my tail. I drove directly to the police station on Main Street. That was dumb, as there was no one there at that time of night. The patrol car pulled right in behind me and as the officer exited the car I realized that I probably hadn't made a very wise decision by trying to out run the car pursuing me. "You scared the shit out of me," I screamed when he approached my door. "There is no way I was going to pull over and maybe be murdered." Poor guy didn't know what to say. "I'm sorry, ma'am, but you were driving over the speed limit." I was not even aware that I had been speeding. I knew for sure now that I would get a ticket, but he just asked where I was going. When I told him I was on my way home, and he realized that I was sober and really scared, he just gave me a verbal warning, told me to slow down and apologized for scaring me. Phew, another close call!

Before we moved to Nevada in 2000, I had acquired a couple more speeding tickets, which raised our auto insurance considerably. After five years these violations are erased, so when I got my Nevada drivers license I had a pristine driving record. That lasted for three years and then the bomb shell dropped. Oops! On a sunny Tuesday morning, headed to Fallon, those familiar lights again appeared in my rear-view window. I don't remember the fine on that ticket, but the one I got four months later in Fallon I know was considerably more. Before I left the house that morning Larry had given me the new insurance card to put in the car, as the one I was carrying had expired. I left it on the kitchen table. The fine in Nevada for not having proof of insurance is $700.00. That fine was taken off, of course, when I drove back to the court house later that day with my valid insurance card.

About six months later, I was detained in Reno on a cross-walk sting. I took the case to court, as I was already well into the cross-walk going thirty miles an hour when the officer stepped off the curb. I chose to proceed with caution. Had I stopped short in the cross-walk the driver behind me would have hit me. Well, the judge agreed but said that all she could do would be to commute the charge to a speeding offense to reduce the cost of the fine. So, again I had three speeding charges in less than a year. My insurance company was loving me, my husband not so much.

That fall my friend, Jan, came from Michigan to visit for a week. She and her sister would meet me and my sister in Las Vegas every year for a crazy bingo week. That particular year she chose to come to Reno. It was only after she returned home that I found out the reason for her decision. We spent a fun-filled weekend at Lake Tahoe. We gambled, ate at the finest restaurants and took in a couple of comedy shows. She was especially excited about our planned day trip to Virginia City. We had a great day and I decided it would be fun to take the Six Mile Canyon road back to Fernley. Cruising down the somewhat curvy road laughing and talking, I was all of a sudden aware that the big SUV that had been tail-gating me had suddenly slowed down. Then within minutes I realized why. When I pulled over for the State Patrol car two patrolmen stepped out, one coming on either side of my car. "Oh, God, no. I can't get another ticket." I handed him my drivers license and registration. Without even looking at them he asked me, "Do you know how fast you were going?" "No." "Well I thought you would slow down when you saw me." I was too embarrassed to tell him that I hadn't seen him, or I would have waved. "Do you drive this road often?" "No sir, this is only my second time." "Well, I'm not going to give you a ticket. I stopped you for two reasons. First to tell you this is a very narrow, dangerous road, and secondly, I am training my new partner on how to do a traffic stop. So if you don't mind taking the time to wait, we'll be right back." With my license and registration in hand, back to the patrol car they went. I was relieved that he said he wasn't going to give me a ticket, but when I realized that he would look up my driving record I began to panic. Poor Jan was on the verge of tears.

They were gone for what seemed like a long time, and then just the training patrolman returned. He didn't hand me back my license, but he did apologize for taking so long. "That's OK," I assured him. "Do you have a minute to spare? I have a story I'd like to tell you." He and Jan both looked perplexed as I proceeded with my tale: "A police officer pulled a little old gray haired lady over for speeding. When he asked for her drivers license she said, "Oh, I don't have a license." "Well, may I see your car registration, ma'am?" "It's not my car," she coyly answered. "Who's car is it?" "I don't know his name, but when I tried to steal the car he got so excited that I think he had a heart attack, so I threw him in the trunk." The officer slowly walked away from the car and called for back-up. In a very few minutes two police cars pulled up. One officer, with his hand on his holster walked up to the car. "Good afternoon, ma'am." The lady, without hesitation politely handed him her drivers license and registration. He checked them out and then said to her, "Officer Jones told me that you stole this car." She smiled sweetly and said, "And I suppose the lying bastard also told you that I was speeding." At that, the patrolman who had pulled me over, with my license still in his hand turned around and walked back to his patrol car. By this time Jan, never having heard my 'little old gray haired lady' story was about to bust a gut. "Now you probably *will* get a ticket for saying 'that lying bastard'," she cautioned me.

We looked up to see both officers getting out of the car again one coming on either side of the car. Oh, oh, maybe now I am in trouble. The patrolman looked at me very seriously and said, "Well, it looks now like we do have a problem." "What?" I stammered. "We're gonna have to get that body out of the trunk," he quipped as he handed me back my paper work, smiling. "Now promise me that you will slow down and drive carefully." I have often wondered how many times he has repeated my story.

Jan passed away shortly after returning home from our adventuresome week. Her niece called to tell me that of all of the wonderful memories she shared with her family our trip down Six Mile Canyon was, by far, her favorite.

By the way, I have not had a speeding ticket in over ten years.

DONNA MARIE

Being nineteen, unmarried and pregnant was definitely not as acceptable in 1928 as it is in today's society. My mother was still living at home with her mother and her mother's live-in 'boarder' when she found herself in such a situation. Her mother was a tiny, red-headed Welsh spitfire. Her boarder was a soft-spoken, kind gentleman who in later years we all referred to as 'Tappa Daley,' Tappa was my word for grandpa.

My mother gave birth to my sister on May 25th of 1929 knowing that she was not going to be able to keep her. She had no means to care for a baby and her mother had grudgingly made it clear to her that she could not bring this illegitimate infant into her home. It is hard for me to comprehend that at twenty years of age my mother was not able to make her own decision, and would abide by her mother's rules. I guess times really were different then and my mother must have felt that she had no say in the matter. She must have believed that she was a disgrace. Perhaps they had not even disclosed her pregnancy or the birth of the baby. I don't know if my mother was allowed to see the baby, but I do know that she gave her the name Donna Marie. Mother's maiden name, Young, was the legal name on the birth certificate. No one ever spoke of the father. The baby was whisked away to a Catholic orphanage in Helena, where she was nurtured by the nuns for the first year of her life.

Tappa Daley had a daughter, Margaret, who somehow learned that Donna had not been adopted, and after a year was calling the nuns "Mama." It broke her heart. She was, however, hesitant to bring the subject up to my grandmother. Meantime, my mother had found a job but was still living at home and mourning the loss of her baby girl every day. I don't know if my grandmother finally agreed to it, but Tappa Daley and Margaret traveled to Helena and brought Donna home. My grandmother was probably as upset as my mother was happy. Donna Marie finally had a home. Grandma was now 'Mama' and Tappa Daley was 'Daddy.' Those were the names Donna referred to them up until the day she died.

When my mother was in her 90s she and I were going through old pictures and I found a picture of a handsome young sailor. On the back of the picture was the name Ralph and it was dated 1930. "Who is Ralph?" I questioned my mother, wondering if this could be Donna's father. She then related to me a story that none of us had ever heard before. Ralph was the son of a family friend. My mother had met him when he was home on leave from the Navy. He proposed to her and she thought that if she married him she would be able to gain custody of her baby. That didn't happen. Whatever occurred the marriage was annulled when he left town to return to his Navy duty. When my mother met and married my father in 1931 her mother refused to let her take Donna. By then she and Tappa Daley had legal custody so my mother accepted their claim that there was nothing that she could do about it.

My sister, Mary Frances, was born in May of 1932. Donna was three years old. She called my mother "Mother," and she accepted that this was her new little sister, but she was being raised by her "Mama and Daddy." Seventeen months after Mary Frances was born my brother Jeremiah came into the world. Donna called her new siblings "my mother's kids."

Grandma and Donna moved to Reno in 1935 to be near grandma's sons. Donna, a tiny shy little girl, started school at the old St. Thomas of Aquinas parochial school. They returned to Butte in 1940, shortly after I was born. Donna was eleven years of age at that time. She used to love to tell the story of taking me out of my mother's arms when the train pulled into Butte. "You were my baby from the moment I laid eyes on you," she always told me. I adored her when I was growing up. She attended cosmetology school right out of high school and went to work as a hair stylist. I would walk up town every Saturday morning to have her wash and style my hair. If I dared to move my head she would crack me hard with the hair brush. I don't think that she treated her clients that way; they all loved her.

Donna didn't ever know who her father was, it was never discussed. There was a lady who went to the shop every week to have her hair styled. She tipped Donna well and one day questioned her about her birthday. When Donna told her May 25th she replied, "Oh, I have a niece who was born on the same day as you and her name is Donna also." This customer would always give her a gift on her birthday. It wasn't until years later that Donna learned that the lady was in fact, her aunt, her father's sister. Donna and my mother were having lunch one day and mother said to her, "Please don't turn around to look, but the man sitting behind you is your father." Of course she looked when she got up to leave. That was the only time she ever saw James Duggan.

Donna was very petite at four-foot-eleven, and she never weighed over one hundred pounds. There was a very up-scale shoe store next door to the beauty shop where she worked and they would use sample shoes for their window displays. These were in tiny sizes, so when the display was changed they would sell her the shoes for a dollar or two. She had over a dozen stylish high-heeled shoes and many expensive work and play shoes. By the time I was ten years old my foot was bigger than hers. I know that my love of shoes was inherited from her. I grew up envying her petite stature.

When I was eight or nine years old Donna married a sailor and moved to Washington State. I was totally devastated when she left Butte. The marriage lasted a short time and she moved back home. She told me never to speak of the man that she had married or the fact that she had ever been married. She even made me promise in later years that I would never let her children know that she had been married before she met their dad. She met Ronald at a dance at one of the local night clubs. He had moved to Butte to work in the copper mines. Donna loved to dance and he literally, at six-foot three and over two-hundred pounds, swept my tiny sister off her feet. They got married in 1951 and spent the next couple of years in Butte. After their first son, Jerry, was born in 1952, Ron took a job working in a mine in Absarokee, Montana. From there they traveled to California pulling a trailer that was to be their home on wheels for several years. If you have ever seen the Lucille Ball movie, "The Long, Long Trailer," you can appreciate pulling your home behind you. Donna loved that movie and laughed every time she saw it, remembering their early years. Their second son, Robert, was born in 1958 in California and she gave him the middle name 'James.' Was this after Tappa Daley or her biological father, whom she never knew? I didn't ever ask her.

Mining uranium in New Mexico was a financial windfall which allowed Ron to buy land and settle in Fallon, Nevada, where they would raise their family. Their daughter, Ronda, was born in Fallon in 1963. Donna was not a country girl and I still laugh picturing her chasing the cattle out of the front yard with a broom screaming, "Get out of here you sons-a-bitches." Ron had to submit three choices for their branding name. As a joke one of his three choices was 'YSB.' To Donna's delight that was the one that he was given.

My dad always called Ron "Midas" because he said that everything Ron ever touched turned to gold. Sometime in the 1960s Ron leased a turquoise mine in Austin, Nevada and, as luck would have it, he hit a vein of the highly sought after 'spider web' turquoise. His claim of fame was the beautiful squash blossom necklaces that Sonny and Cher wore on their then popular TV show, and the cover and article in a well-known collector book. I was visiting them one summer early in the 1970s and I was amazed at the gemologists and jewelers traveling daily from California seeking his stones. I had never in my life seen so much cash changing hands. On Ron's death bed at only fifty-one years of age, due to the uranium exposure, Ron asked me, "What does it profit a man to gain the world, and not be able to live to enjoy it?"

Donna was left a widow at age fifty. Her marriage had been on the rocks for several years, but she devotedly cared for Ron the last year of his life. She had spent her entire life feeling that she had been unwanted and unloved and she was very bitter, which kept her from letting people get too close to her. She was an ornery little dickens, and as cute as a button. She had the mouth of a drunken sailor. Her favorite word was 'shit' and she would get upset with me when I would tell her that she couldn't talk like that in public. "I can talk any God-damned way I want," she would snap back at me. She was asked to leave a restaurant in Oregon, while traveling with me and my husband, for cussing out the manager who told her that she

couldn't smoke in the restaurant. She sat out front on a bench and smoked while we had dinner and we had to stop and get her a sandwich when we left.

She and my husband were both Gemini and gave each other a hard time constantly. They sent the same birthday card back and forth to each other for years because she said that the 'damned bastard' was too cheap to buy her a new card. She called him more names that I can repeat, but it was him that she was calling for before she passed away. He would have done anything for her and she knew it. He phoned her one day and when he realized that she didn't recognize his voice he told he that it was so-and-so from Publisher's Clearing House. He told her to invite her friends and family over on Saturday so they could be there when she was presented with her grand prize. She did, and was she ever upset when he called her that morning to ask if everyone was there. She realized only then that it was him who had called her. "You son-of-a-bitch, I'll get even." She left us on February 25th, 2011, and I miss her more than I ever thought I could miss someone. She was loved by her children, her grand-children and many dear friends, and most of all by me. My prayer is that she left us knowing how much she was loved.

MY OVERACTIVE OLFACTORY NERVE

"So, what exactly is the olfactory nerve?" I questioned the doctor as he was carefully scanning my medical records. "It's a cranial nerve that controls the sense of smell," he explained in terms simple enough for me to understand. He had treated me the week before for a sinus infection and after several days of taking the antibiotic that he had prescribed I was back to tell him that I could neither taste nor smell.

The taste buds on the tongue are able to distinguish sour, sweet, bitter or salt, but it was impossible for me to determine any flavor of food beyond that. He shook his head, telling me that he didn't know if it was the infection or the medication that had caused the damage to the olfactory nerve. "It's probably not a permanent condition," he stated. "Probably not?" Was he trying to tell me that I may never be able to smell popcorn popping or coffee brewing? "The olfactory nerve can rejuvenate itself with the help of zinc, but we cannot determine a time frame for the healing," he warned me. He wrote me a prescription for a zinc supplement and sent me on my way.

To my dismay, coffee was so bitter, that even after adding sugar and cream I was not able to drink it. I decided that if a single dose of zinc a day was beneficial maybe I should just double the dose and it would work faster. Wrong! After a week I became extremely lethargic and my thinking was clouded with dizzy spells and confusion. When I called the doctor he told me to get to the hospital immediately. They did blood work and discovered that the zinc level in my blood was near lethal. The doctor took me off of the zinc until my blood level returned to normal and then prescribed a minimal dose of zinc. It was ten months before my sense of smell began to return. I was standing at a gas pump fueling my car when suddenly the gas fumes permeated my nostrils and I began screaming, "I smell gas! I smell gas!" I quickly realized that people were staring at me like I was some kind of a nut.

It was awesome to be able to smell and to taste things as they were supposed to taste. I became aware at that time of how I had totally taken for granted all of my life the ability to see, hear, smell and taste. I made a promise to myself that I would forever be thankful for the gift of these senses. Many years later, however, I broke that promise, cursing my sense of smell and my overactive olfactory nerve.

In the summer of 2004 we decided that it would be great to get out of the winter cold and become 'snowbirds,' migrating south every fall with our old crony friends who spent the winter months in Arizona. We had a mobile home set up on a private lot, had many friends, activities, and beautiful weather... this was the good life for sure.

After the first year in Arizona I learned all of the strategies for closing up the trailer for the long, hot Arizona summers. It was important to leave an open container of water in every room, at least a gallon, to keep moisture in the air, bay leaves in all of the drawers and cupboards to divert the ants, and coffee grounds to keep the air fresh. I would also wash everything down with bleach to make sure it was disinfected before we left. After cleaning the bathroom and having the water drained from the pipes, I would cover the toilet seat tightly with saran wrap to keep any fumes from getting into the trailer from the sewer lines.

It was always sad to see the season end. We held a farewell fiesta every year for all of our friends. It somehow seemed to grow bigger every year. One particular year we were anxious to get home as we had a summer cruise planned. I spent our last day there making sure all of my 'closing up' chores were completed. The car was packed and we were ready to hit the road. Larry had cleaned out all of the drain lines, and I had done all of my disinfecting and was preparing to cover the toilet. As I looked into the toilet I realized that there was still a little bit of water in the bottom of the bowl. I hollered out the door to Larry, "Shall I leave the water in the bowl or flush it?" "Flush it," came his prompt reply. I was looking directly into the toilet bowl as my foot hit the flush pedal. A geyser of sewerage, I swear with the power of Old Faithful, shot directly upward... Yup, right into my face! Raw sewerage was on the ceiling, the walls, all over the floor and I was standing in the middle of it all, with poop in my hair, and all over me. I was screaming to the top of my voice. I don't remember what I was screaming, but I am sure that it was not pleasant. Of course the water had already been turned off, so I couldn't do anything in the way of cleaning up the mess. Larry and the neighbor, Jerry, came running when they heard me scream, but all they could do when I came tearing out of the door was laugh. I was absolutely traumatized and hysterical and they were laughing! Jerry's wife, Peggy, came running across the yard, grabbed me and hauled me to her house where I stripped down and jumped into the shower. I had her throw my clothes away as well as the towels that I had thrown on the floor as I rushed out of the trailer. "I can wash them," she said as she was trying to calm me down. I must have spent half an hour in that shower. Larry unpacked clean clothes for me, but even after I was clean I couldn't seem to get that sickening smell to go away. To make matters even worse, when I got out of the shower and dressed, my dear husband said, "Well, I turned the water back on so that you can go in and clean up that mess before we leave." I did go back and clean it up and poured a whole half a gallon of bleach all over, even on me to try and rid myself of that horrible odor.

We finally got on the road. I was still upset and angry with him for laughing. I sure didn't see any humor in the situation. I called my daughter to tell her what had happened, and to my dismay, she too laughed hysterically. I was in tears. She said, "Oh, Mother, I can hardly wait to go to work and tell my co-workers that my mother doesn't even drink and she got shit-faced." Talk about adding insult to injury! When I finally calmed down I did see a little humor in her statement, but to this day I refuse to laugh about the incident itself.

When I returned to work and told the story, one of my customers dubbed me "shit-head." He still calls me that every time he sees me. When someone told him how rude that was, he and I both had to agree that I had rightly earned the nickname. I have to admit that I am now forever thankful to be able to smell the roses, my morning coffee brewing, and the fragrance of a vanilla candle. A bad odor will probably never affect me adversely again since I think that I experienced the worst of the worst as far as smells go. That should give me a right to curse my overactive olfactory nerve.

A FOREVER HOME

I have heard people say that, "home is where you hang your hat," or "home is where the heart is." By the time I was thirty-nine years of age I had lived in twenty-six houses. The longest that I had ever lived in one house at that time was five-years... off and on. That was the house that my husband and I bought while stationed in Bremerton, Washington. Being a Navy family we moved every four years or so as the orders dictated. From Oklahoma to Puerto Rico, Connecticut, Virginia, Pennsylvania, Hawaii and Washington, we could pack up and move, sometimes with very short notice. At one point my oldest son questioned me, "Mom, when someone asks me where I am from, do I tell them where I was born or the last place we lived?" I didn't ever give up hope that someday I would have a real home, a home to call my own, a forever home. I dreamed about the day that my husband would retire after twenty-years and we could settle in our cozy home in Bremerton. Dreams don't always come true, however, and as fate would have it, I found myself divorced and still on the move seven years after his retirement.

In 1976 I moved from Missouri back to Washington, promising my two youngest children, who were eleven and thirteen at that time, that we would be settled forever and that they would never have to change schools again. It was one promise that I intended to keep even though I had no idea at the time where we would be living. My children's father offered to let us move into his house until I could find a place to rent. I met a man who had just lost his dad and was looking for someone to clean and rent the house that he had inherited. When I inquired about the cost he asked me what I could afford. I explained that my child support was only three-hundred dollars a month and that I was only working a part-time job. He smiled, winked at his wife and said, "Three-hundred a month or whatever you can afford is fine with me." He really just wanted someone living in the house to take care of it. It was a fairly nice house, but it did need a lot of work. I was just thankful to have an affordable roof over our heads. I spent hours cleaning and fixing it up. There were only two bedrooms, so each of the kids had their own room and I bought a brand new hide-a-bed. It was just twenty dollars down and twenty dollars a month. I was fine with sleeping in the living room and sharing my daughter's closet. I really liked that little house.

Larry and I were married in August of 1979. It was now time to start making plans for the future. Since we were both renting it would only make sense to plan on buying a home. A home, a real home! This amazing man who agreed to pay my car insurance was now offering to make my life's dream come true. Besides, he wasn't looking forward to sleeping in my living room!

Starting over at forty isn't exactly easy. We set out almost immediately after getting married to look for property. Larry had a plot of land at a private camp ground, Gold Bar Nature Trails, located in the foothills of the Cascade Mountains. He had an Airstream trailer there where he and his kids enjoyed weekends and the summer months. He also had five acres of land on Whidbey Island where he planned to someday build his retirement home. He sold it all, along with his motorcycle and the mobile home that he was living in, to finance our future. Although his work was thirty-five miles from where I lived, he agreed to stay in the area because of my promise to my kids that they wouldn't have to change schools.

"This is the perfect spot," Larry squealed as the stooped, gravelly voiced gentleman showed us around the three acres that he had offered to sell us for eight thousand dollars. "And just how do we get to it? There is no access from the road," was my first response. I could only see woods, evergreen trees and wild blackberry bushes everywhere. There was no water, no power lines and it was on the top of a steep hill. Despite my objections and doubt, Larry was making a deal. What could I say, I had no investment in this venture. "Trust me, it will be awesome… you'll see," he assured me.

Getting a road into the property was the first major project. It was thirteen-hundred-feet, straight up a hill. Oh, yeah, what about power? And who ever heard of 'water witching'? A water witch is a person who claims the ability to detect water underground by means of using a divining rod, a forked branch or stick that is believed to indicate subterranean water by bending downward when held over a water source. We watched in awe as Charlie walked the property and eventually indicated to us the prime spot to have our well dug. Fifty-five feet down they hit water and it was so pure that after we had it tested my brother wanted us to go into the bottling business and sell it. With the septic tank installed and the drain fields completed we were ready for our new home. How long does it take to build a house? We decided to look at new mobile homes and found a top-of-the-line Fleetwood, three bedroom, two baths, upgraded appliances, ready to deliver and move into. I couldn't have been happier to call it our new home.

The day that the mobile home was to be delivered arrived. There was a huge problem, they couldn't get it up the hill. They had to hire a bulldozer to lift the front to get it in place. What a job! After it was skirted and decks built on both the front and back and a double garage put up on the side, it looked just like a stick house. It was the home that we had both dreamed of, our little heaven on earth. I told myself on the day that we moved in that it would be my home forever. Forever turned out to be just over twenty years. It was twenty glorious years of grandkids, holiday celebrations, Easter egg hunts, birthday parties and many memorable family get-togethers.

In 1999 Larry was diagnosed with COPD (chronic obstructive pulmonary disease.) The mold from the damp forest air was taking its toll on his lungs. The doctor told him that if he wanted to live a few more years he should move to a dry climate. He retired in 2000 and I was able to transfer to a Las Vegas Rite-Aid store. It broke my heart to leave our home. I cried for a week. It was the longest time that either one of us had lived in one place.

A young lady who I worked with and her husband, who was a contractor, bought our property and mobile home for $150,000 with plans of someday building a house. They had a six-year-old boy, Michael, who was autistic and very seldom spoke. When they came to finalize the papers, Krista called me to the living room window and there on the deck was Michael with our four-year-old Rottweiler. He was scratching the dogs belly and loudly singing, "My dog, Moses." "He makes up songs when he is happy," Krista told me. When her husband asked Larry if the riding mower was included in the deal his reply was, "only if you'll keep the dog." At that moment I was overcome with joy, not only from being able to share the home that we had cherished, but knowing that we wouldn't have to take Moses away from the only home he had ever known, and that he and Michael could share this new-found comradeship.

The mobile home served as their house while their new dwelling was being built. The long dusty dirt driveway is now a paved road, the mobile home is gone and an elegant two story, landscaped house sits surrounded by the beautiful natural background. When we visited Monroe in August of 2018 we heard that our old property was for sale. "Let's just go take a look," I pleaded with Larry. We did, and when we called to inquire about the sale price we were shocked to hear, $770,000.

We are now content to call our 888-square feet 'grandma and grandpa house' our 'forever home.' Home truly is where the heart is.

THE MOTHER ROAD

John Steinbeck's depression-era masterpiece, *The Grapes of Wrath*, was written the year before I was born. It was published in 1939 and was banned by some libraries, publicly burned and debated. In 1940 the movie won an Oscar award which lead to the intrigue of the iconic Route 66. The book was one of several on our high school required reading list, but I chose to pass it up for something less depressing. I did not want to read about the destitute migrants fighting their way through the dust storms hoping to find a better way of life in the West.

The 1960 TV series, 'Route 66,' starring Martin Milner tweaked my imagination about driving across the country. I learned some years later that most of the series' locations weren't even on Route 66.

Early in the 1980s I met a lady from Oregon who told me stories of her family fleeing the rain-starved Oklahoma in the early 1930s. They fought the dust storms of red dirt and worked for farmers in the fields along the way to achieve what they envisioned to be a better life. They would work for a dollar a day to buy food and enough gas to get them to the next farm. Sometimes they would have to go door-to-door and ask if they could work for food. They lived out of their car or in a chicken shack on the property where they were working. It all seemed to be right out of the pages of Steinbeck's novel to me. I became fascinated with the idea of experiencing this "Main Street of America" before it disappeared.

With much anticipation my husband and I planned to drive Route 66 from west to east. The old towns and attractions that have endured through the years were calling to me. It was not so much the idea of getting somewhere, but the journey itself that intrigued me. Seeing the first 'ROUTE 66' sign, which I had passed several times traveling east on Highway 40, sparked my enthusiasm. For years I had reminded myself *someday*... and now the day had arrived and I was as giddy as a child on Christmas Eve.

Our first Route 66 stop was Hackberry which is just an old, run-down gas station and country store. All of the vintage 'stuff' looks just

like it did in the 1930s and 40s. The road-signs were entertaining, especially the obsolete red and white 'BURMA SHAVE' signs that I remembered seeing as a kid. In Seligman the original Snow Cap Drive-Inn has a sign that boasts, "Sorry, we're open," and has two doorknobs, one which works and the other which makes you look foolish when you try to open it. Once inside you feel like you have left this era and are back in 1950-something. Another sign proudly states that they serve 'Dead Chicken' and a mustard bottle squirts yellow string, while the waitress inquires if you want new straws and napkins or used ones at a discount. "Do you want cheese on that cheeseburger?"

Continuing on our way, just before reaching Peach Springs, I noticed what looked to be little green apples along the side of the road. I know that they don't have apple orchards in Arizona. Maybe a truck had dropped a load of apples. A few miles farther down the road I saw another cluster and then another. I finally had to pull over to investigate. I reached down to pick one up, and low and behold, they were growing on a vine along the ground. *What the heck are they? Should I taste one?* They resembled a miniature summer squash but were a bright yellow/greenish. I decided to take one with me and inquire somewhere along the way as to what they were.

Our next stop was Williams. All of the buildings have been kept original and there are horse drawn carriages cruising the streets transporting tourists to the novel souvenir shops. From there on to Flagstaff for the night. When we checked in at the motel the young desk clerk inquired as to where we had started our trip. When I told her Nevada, and that we were driving Route 66 as far as Springfield, she looked at me in shock and said, "Wow, you are pretty old." Just what I needed to hear after driving all day. I felt kind of old, but didn't realize that it showed!

The next day I could hardly wait to get a picture of Larry standin' on the corner in Winslow, Arizona, but as I drove along happily singing about it he took a nap and I missed the exit. "That's OK," I told myself,

"I'll just take the next exit and go back." Thirty-five miles later Larry woke up with Winslow long behind us and me grumbling instead of singing. There was no *next* exit.

There are beautiful adobe fortresses in Gallup and old buildings and businesses that have all seen better days. Some of the finest Navajo rugs, pottery, and silver and turquoise jewelry are found in this "Land of Enchantment." The El Rancho Hotel opened in December of 1937. Autographed photos of many of the famous guests listed in the register line the walls of the magnificent two story open lobby with its circular staircase and heavy beams. Several of the 1940 and 50s western movies were filmed in Gallup and the likes of Ronald Reagan, Alan Ladd, Jane Wyman, Jackie Cooper, and William Bendix, to name a few, wined and dined at the El Rancho. It became known as "The home of the movie stars, with the charm of yesterday and the convenience of tomorrow."

On to Albuquerque where I found out that my 'little green apples' are hallucinogenic, sometimes fatal, wild squash-like forage. I still don't know if it is fruit or vegetable, nor did I ever learn if it had a name. I am just thankful that I didn't decide to taste it. We visited Old Albuquerque and the Cathedral Basilica of St. Francis of Assisi and some quaint open markets. Southwestern flair and colonial culture infuses this entire city. It boasts of the best Mexican food ever. Our last stop in New Mexico was Tucumcari, where the old gas station and motel look exactly

the same as they did fifty years ago. The only thing that has changed is the age of the people and the price of the gas.

Arriving in Amarillo, Texas, we learned that this is where real western hospitality begins. From Amarillo on to McClean where the first Phillips 66 station was built and leased to the Phillips corporation in 1929. It has been kept original, it even has the old Phillips 66 truck parked on the side of the building. In Shamrock, Texas, a small dusty town located at the intersection of Highway 66 and the Canada-to-Mexico Highway 83, there is a building that was built in 1936 with two tall towers sprouting out of the flat roofed building. The old gas pumps still stand in the front of the station but on the other side of the structure you will see several Tesla charging stations. This is an eye-opening mix of the old with the new. The restaurant is no longer operating but I got to sit in the booth where Elvis and the Colonel always ate when they traveled through Shamrock.

The minute I saw the "Welcome to Oklahoma" sign the nostalgia set in. We stopped for lunch in Clinton at a typical 1950s road house joint, the Del Rancho. Wow, they had *real* southern fried chicken. I had forgotten how hospitable those Okie folks are. I lived in Oklahoma in 1958. That is where my first son was born. This was my first time back. I had made reservations to stay at a Bed and Breakfast in Norman, where Patrick was born. It is just south of Oklahoma City. It was late in the evening when we arrived at Whispering Pines, which is several miles out of town, secluded in pine trees. It had the look and feel of an early twentieth century mansion, complete with a wrap-around porch, gazebo, and a grand staircase. It was Halloween night and there seemed to be an eerie feeling about the place. The dining room was closed and we didn't feel like driving back to town so we dined on pretzels and Coke. The room was amazing with a little dinette area. We were able to order our breakfast and tell the inn-keeper what time we wanted it served in the morning. It was delivered to the room right on time. The food was excellent as was the hospitality of the owners.

From Norman we drove east to Tulsa and then on to Joplin. Our hotel reservations in Joplin were for Days Inn at 3500 Rangeline Road on Highway I-44 and US 71. I put the address in our GPS, which Larry refers to as Emily. As I drove down Rangeline Road Larry told me, "There is the hotel." "No, Emily says that we have half a mile to go," I responded. I continued driving and as we approached the next intersection Emily directed us to take a left turn. As I turned her voice sweetly informed us, "You have arrived at your final destination." When we saw the sign

'FOREST PARK CEMETERY' I pulled over and we laughed for five minutes. I turned around and we drove back to the hotel that we had in fact passed. He was right, of course. Thanks for the laugh, Emily.

We spent two days in Joplin and then proceeded on to Springfield, Missouri, where Route 66 veers north to Chicago. We had cruised Route 66 as if it was 1950, and this is where our adventure ended. We were heading south to Branson, Missouri. The "Mother Road" had attached itself to my psyche. It was all that I had dreamed of and then some. I know that Route 66 will always be a part of the American culture, and for me it was a trip through the past that I will treasure forever.

We had three fun-filled days in Branson, attending the amusing stage shows, antique shopping and enjoying the down-home themed restaurants. It became obvious to me why people return time after time to Branson – it is unique and entertaining.

We continued on to Memphis, then to New Orleans where we boarded a ship to the Cayman Islands, Cozumel, Honduras, Belize, and Costa Maya and back to New Orleans. From there we drove to San Antonio, El Paso and on to Yuma in time to celebrate Thanksgiving with my daughter and her family. After driving over six thousand miles we were happy to be home and thankful for another safe, memorable trip. One more scratch off the bucket list. Go ahead, get your kicks on Route 66.

ETHICAL WILL
TO DONALD GEORGE

December 15, 2017
Happy Birthday!

My Dear Son Don,

Looking back on my life and reflecting on the things that were important to me, I find myself filled with regrets. Becoming a mother at an early age I was not prepared nor capable of understanding that the most important thing in life is not striving to make everything perfect. It was important to me to prove to the world that I was able to raise well-behaved, well-spoken, polite little puppets. I had no idea that being lenient, laughing and loving was much more crucial than clean shoelaces. Oh, I loved you and your brother, but I was determined to mold you into what I wanted you to be. I believed that tucking you into bed every night and listening to your prayers and reading to you was all that it took to be an ideal mother.

You were the most perfect baby, and you grew into an adorable little boy. People would stop me to admire you, saying you looked like Opie from the then popular Andy Griffith television show. You inherited my red hair and even though I did not want to admit it, you were also cursed with so many of my traits, good and bad. You were stubborn, determined, quick to anger, definitely your mother's son. You challenged me from the day you came into my life and over the years I have come to realize the value of that. I respect the fact that you were always true to yourself. You were a born leader, never having to follow or compromise.

You were your Grandma Mary's golden boy. She adored you and whenever you and I were at odds, which was definitely often, she would remind me how much you adored me. She predicted that you would be the one to take care of me someday. When you left me at thirteen to live with your dad, my heart was truly broken. I wanted you to be happy then, just as I do today. You knew that your dad needed you. You have always shown so much compassion.

I have every letter that you wrote to me in your adult life. I love reading them. It makes my heart happy to know that you could confide in me. I am thankful that I was there for you in your darkest days. I pray that you felt my love then and that no matter what happens in your life you will know that I have always and will always love you unconditionally.

So, for the mistakes I made I ask that you, after being a parent yourself, can forgive me. I pray that you will live the remainder of your life without regrets. We all make mistakes and hopefully learn from them. My hope is that when you remember me you will remember the good times, the smiles and the laughter, the joy of sharing the birth of your children.

I am so grateful for having had you in my life. I am proud of the man you are, the dad you have been to your kids and of the loving and caring you have always shown for the less fortunate. Always be grateful for every chance you have to bring joy into someone's life. Love with all your heart and know that in forgiving you will find peace.

My final prayer is that you will be delivered from the physical pain you have had to endure. So many times I have prayed that I could take your pain.

Stay strong, Son. Love and treasure your family, trust the Lord and always keep the faith.

Loving you always,

Mom

RIP Don   12/15/1959 – 8/5/2018

SHIP'S QUIPS

"I will not order naked." My husband is not a soft-spoken man, so his voice resounded across the entire Lido Deck, where the ship's guests were enjoying their leisure lunch. Heads turned and there were a few muffled gasps and giggles. I quickly explained to him that if he wanted his French fries without seasoned salt or cheese and chili, that he was going to have to order them the way they were listed on the reader board, "naked." We had the attention of several dozen people, a few of whom were laughing. This was just the beginning of what turned out to be my quest to make old, cranky people who seemed to have no joy in their lives, smile or better yet laugh out loud.

    The cruise that we had embarked on was our dream vacation, something that we had worked hard to make a reality. As I child I dreamed of someday going to Ireland, and Larry talked often of being able to visit his ancestor's homeland, Holland. This cruise however, even after the sixty-five percent discount we were offered, was still much more than we could afford. We had credit from a canceled cruise, so I decided to call our travel agent to see if we could use that credit as a down payment and make payments on the balance. It took us two years to pay for it. Most of the people who were booked for this thirty-eight-day Atlantic Ocean cruise appeared to be wealthy retired doctors, lawyers, college professors or business CEO's, none of whom seemed to be very happy. Larry was quick to remind me that money can't buy happiness, to which I replied, as the song goes, "Still I'd rather be rich."

    Three days after boarding the ship I started coughing. I made a trip to the ship's dispensary, where the 'too handsome for words' Danish doctor confirmed that I had a bronchial infection. He prescribed antibiotics and a heavy duty cough medicine and told me to stay in bed for two or three days. "This is just not fair. I never get sick at home," I whined. I didn't want to stay in the cabin all day and night but I was coughing so hard that I thought it best not to be around people. The cough medicine he gave me was thicker than maple syrup and tasted like two of my least favorite things – rutabagas and scotch. It is made in Austria and the label said it was all natural, marshmallow root and thyme. "Take every four hours," the instructions read. I wondered if it was alcohol-based because I slept like a drunken sailor and was all but well in forty-eight hours. I don't know if there is a comparable product available in this country but I did google 'marshmallow root' and learned that it is an ancient herbal curative that was used for phlegm two thousand years ago.

When I watch musical movies I always wonder if anyone actually breaks out in song and dance in an everyday normal setting. I always wanted to do it, and I finally got my chance when I smiled at a grumpy old fart in a wheel chair early one morning while strolling the deck. He mumbled something gruffly and made a God-awful face. Without hesitation I bent down to eye level with him and started to sing, "It isn't any trouble just to S-M-I-L-E." As I sang the whole song some of the onlookers began clapping and tapping their feet and singing along. He finally broke down and gave me a huge grin which I returned with a hug.

On a ship with almost two thousand people you don't always see the same folks on a daily basis. The last day of the cruise we were on the elevator and when it stopped and the door opened a man inquired, "Are you going up?" I began singing "Up, up and away" and a lady in the back of the elevator squealed, "Oh, my gosh, she's still singing."

While on the subject of elevators, I was waiting for the elevator early one morning and when one stopped I inquired if it was going up. "Read the light," a not so friendly gentleman snapped at me. Before the door had closed completely I pushed the button again. The door opened. Oh my, if looks could kill. I hadn't done it intentionally. "Lay off that damned button," the man growled. "I'm so sorry sir, are you going down?" Before he could answer and as the door was closing someone else walked up and pushed the 'up' button. By now this guy was hot and really thought that I was messing with him. "I hope I never see him again," I thought out loud as the door closed. The very next day as I was walking along the deck, who should I encounter heading straight toward me? I didn't know whether to turn around and walk the other way or just pass him by and act like I didn't recognize him. But before I could make a move he approached me, tapped me on the shoulder and said, "You know lady, you made my day yesterday in the elevator." He was actually laughing and sharing the incident with his comrades.

You might think that thirty-eight days on a ship would get a little hum-drum, but with all of the fabulous food and nightly entertainment and the ports of call every few days there is never a dull moment. Meeting people and making new friends is also an added benefit. We now have invitations to visit people in Georgia, South Carolina, Arizona and New York.

A lovely eighty-five-year-old lady invited herself to join us at breakfast one morning. Her reason was that she had heard we were from Reno and she wanted to know if I would please take her to the casino and *teach* her how to do 'scratch-offs.' We seldom frequent the casinos on the ships but for her I would make an exception. She ended up winning sixty dollars and it cost me twenty-five dollars for her lesson. On the day we left the ship she gifted me with a little patchwork pocket purse that she had made. She said it was my lucky 'wonder wallet' for all of my winnings in the Reno casinos.

Larry makes it a point to get to know all of the galley hands, waiters, hostesses and cooks, and before the first week of the cruise was over even the head chef was having coffee with him every morning. He would be up on the Lido Deck at 5:30 or 6:00 a.m. every day. The servers and floor supervisors in the dining room all knew him by name and when they would greet us personally for dinner and seat us at a private table. The other guests would look at us like, "who the heck are they?" On our anniversary we were served a magnificent and delicious decorated cake.

One evening we were dining at the buffet and as I approached the dessert section I hesitated, trying to make up my mind if I should have carrot cake or cheese cake. How about one of each? A dignified gentleman who was waiting patiently for me to decide, backed up a step or two and I realized that he was giving me the once over, looking very disapprovingly at me. I smiled and graciously told him, "I'm a recovering anorexic and I'm doing quite well, thank you." He didn't know how to react and I couldn't keep a straight face.

Another evening in the dining room when a slender, stylish lady at our table turned down dessert I reminded her of all of the people on the Titanic who had refused dessert on that cold April night. The next evening, she was the first at the table to order cheesecake, reminding me with a sweet smile, "You are right, my dear, life is too short to deprive oneself."

My crusade to make people smile or laugh, maybe just for a day, was in my mind a success even at the cost of making a fool of myself now and then. I will always have fond memories not only of the phenomenal places that we visited but of all of the awesome people we met along the way. Hopefully, some of them will remember me and smile.

MY BEST FRIEND

"Doffy doesn't talk right. She calls me Boofie," I informed my mother on the day that I met my first best friend, Dorothy. We were inseparable the summer that we were four years of age. We sang and danced and laughed, and even tried to learn to play hopscotch. In the fall of 1944 new neighbors moved in next door to Dorothy's family. They had a little girl who was frail and shy and for whatever reason she became my best friend's best friend. Dorothy no longer wanted to play doll house with me. I would see her and Ruby Ann romping on the playground and when I tried to join them they would run away or laugh and taunt me. My heart was broken. I had no one else to play with and even at that early age I thought that best friends would be forever.

The following spring the O'Donnell family moved in just across the complex from us. A family with six kids – I couldn't have been happier. Margaret was my age and Kathleen was just a year older. I didn't need Dorothy any longer. Margaret and I started school together and in our eighth grade graduation picture there we were side-by-side. Best friends *are* forever I assured myself.

In 1953, we moved from the east side of town to a brand new housing development on the upper west side. I was unhappy about the move and leaving my grade school pals, but I quickly made friends with a new neighbor who was the same age as me. Donna's grandma, Goldie, and my mother were friends and belonged to the same bridge club. Donna and I bonded, almost as sisters, from the first day we met. She had what my mother called, "the voice of an angel." Donna was much more quiet and reserved than I was, and shy about singing in front of anyone. With her grandma's prodding, I talked her (or maybe bribed her) into entering a talent show that was being held by our local TV station. I promised her that if she would sing I would tap dance. I was more excited than she was when she won the contest. The chorus director of the high school, having seen the show, called Donna to his office on Monday morning, encouraging her to join the school chorus class. She

Donna S

appeared in many musical presentations throughout the years. When she graduated from high school, she and her brother enlisted in the Army to escape from what had been a horrendous home life. She secured a spot singing with the U.S. Army Band and had a career traveling and doing what she loved. We lost contact, but I thought of her often over the years. One day in 2002 my phone rang, "Ruthie Keane?" OMG!! After all those years I actually recognized her voice. We arranged to meet for our fiftieth class reunion. We visited and laughed for three days. On our way to the reunion banquet we sang, "Playmate, come out and play with me, and bring your dollies three… climb up my apple tree…" Wonderful memories from our childhood friendship. Donna, my longest and dearest friend.

When I started high school I met Maureen. Never before had I had someone with whom I could share my innermost thoughts and feelings. Now I knew that I had truly met my best friend.

I got married and left home the summer that I turned seventeen and Maureen went away to college. She became a registered nurse and eventually a physician's assistant while I was busy raising my children. We stayed in touch and saw each other every five years at our high school reunions and we always exchanged Christmas cards to stay updated on our lives. My daughter is named after her, after all she was my best friend.

Being a military family we traveled and moved often and I made friends wherever we lived. It seems that I always referred to each of them as my '*best*' friend. There was Evelyn, Ethel, Eleanor, Elsie, Nancy, Linda, Betty and Betty, and oh, yes! Another Betty!

Who is the one who has always been there for me? Who was with me during all of my labors, through divorces and losing my loved ones? Who cries with me, laughs at my jokes even when they aren't so funny? Who is it who never judges me when I do stupid things? Who tolerates my horrible singing? Who assures me daily that I am going to make it, that I can fulfill my dreams, find peace in my heart and survive this adventure called life? Let's face it... I am my own best friend! I always have been and I always will be because best friends are *forever*, right?

Me and Donna S

JEREMIAH JOSEPH

"Jerry Joe broke his toe climbing up the steeple. He rang the bell to go to hell to see the Chinese people." My mother made up nonsensical rhymes for all of her children. Jeremiah Joseph was her only son, born on October 19th, 1933. He walked before he was a year old and having two older sisters he learned to talk at a very early age. He was a bright, curly-headed bundle of energy. When he started school, the teachers were amazed by his photographic memory. He had the ability to vividly recall images from memory after only a few instances of exposure. This enabled him to learn very quickly. He knew every nursery rhyme after seeing the story just once, and after he learned to read he could read a poem, close the book and recite it word for word. My mother told the story of when he was in the second grade and was told to learn a poem to share with the class. Near our home there was a construction crew working on a building. Jerry arrived home excited one day, telling my mother that the guys on the job had taught him a good poem. Mother just smiled and went on about her business, not asking him to recite the poem for her. Late the next afternoon she received a phone call from Jerry's teacher, Sister Mary Catherine. "Mrs. Keane, I am calling to inform you that Jeremiah shared a poem with the class today that was quite inappropriate for a seven-year-old. I think that you should have a talk with him." When Jerry arrived home, Mother questioned him as to what he had recited in class that day. He very proudly told her, "The mountaineers, they have no fears. They screw their wives with rusty knives."

Jerry was seven years old when I was born. He was, for as long as I can remember, always there for me. He teased me unmercifully but he was the one who scooped me up when I fell from the top of the monkey bars, the one who carried me home after I was hit by a milk truck, and comforted me when I was bitten by a dog. He was also the one who told me to put my tongue on the frozen teeter-totter bar, made me eat sardines and scared the wits out of me taking me to see "Scar Face" instead of "Bambi."

Jerry joined the Navy right out of high school. When he was discharged, he returned home to Butte. He married his sweetheart, Barbara, and in 1962 he moved his growing family to Seattle. Having worked in our grandfather's bakery in Butte, he was hired by Gai's Bakery in Seattle. He worked diligently to support his wife and seven children but always made time to coach the kids' ball teams and to be there to teach them, by example, the importance of being honest and dependable. For all of my adult life he was my counselor, my advisor, my sounding board, the one steadfast entity in my life. I never made an important decision without consulting with him first. Although he had no formal education beyond high school, he was one of the most well-read, knowledgeable and worldly-wise people that I had ever known. I would call him often for silly trivia questions. He always had an answer for anything that I asked. It was amazing to watch 'Jeopardy' with him. I could not imagine my life without him. I made him promise me at one time that he would never die. "They say no one lives forever," he

jokingly answered me, "But they haven't met me yet."

He was proud of his Irish heritage and was a typical Irishman – witty, determined and remarkably devoted to his family. He talked of someday visiting Ireland, but he never did. He and his wife, Barbara, traveled to Branson, Missouri, to see the Irish tenor Daniel O'Donnell perform. He loved the old Irish ballads and Irish dancing. The day he passed away in March of 2018, I received a Facebook message of Daniel O'Donnell singing "Gallway Bay." I felt a warm glow as I recalled the last time that I was with my brother and we sang together. "If you ever go across the sea to Ireland, then maybe at the closing of your day, you will go and see the moon rise over Claddagh or see the sun go down on Gallway Bay." I wasn't able to be with him at the end, but he knew that I was there in spirit and I whispered the last words of the song we both loved, "Tis all the heaven I'll ask of God upon my dying day, my soul to soar forever more above you, Gallway Bay."

At his request his ashes were spread on Ennis Lake, in Montana on July 1st, 2018, 72 years after a boating accident there that took the life of our cousin, Bobby.

I wrote this poem for his 82nd birthday:

MY BROTHER

From the day I was born you've been by my side,
You laughed with me and cried when I cried.
All through the years, through the good and the bad
You were always there for me, happy or sad.

You teased me and bugged me, most of my life,
But you were my confidant, you walked me through strife.
Always witty, smart and funny, dependable and fair,
When all my world was caving in, you were there to care.

So, here we are now, old and gray,
There's not much more that I can say.
Except to let you know, my first and longest friend,
My love and thanks for all you've done will never,
ever end.

A FAVORITE PLACE

Recalling all of the places that I have been and recently sorting through pictures, I have become extremely aware of the countless blessings that I have experienced in my life. It is difficult for me to choose any one place as my 'favorite.' Having traveled the world over, I have many amazing memories. I have seen four of the seven original wonders of the world and two of the new wonders: The Great Pyramids of Giza, The Colossus of Rhodes, The Temple of Artemis at Ephesus, The Hanging Gardens of Babylon, Christ the Redeemer Statue in Rio de Janeiro, and the Roman Colosseum. Visiting the Vatican, attending mass at St. Peter's Basilica and being blessed by Pope John Paul II were some of the greatest highlights of my life. Seeing the Sistine Chapel and visiting Pompeii were like dreams come true for me. I have experienced the unbalanced feeling of standing next to the Leaning Tower of Pisa and the wonder of hearing the bells toll at the Notre Dame Cathedral. What a sight to see, the storekeepers in Spain and Portugal scrubbing the beautiful inlaid sidewalks outside of their places of business every morning before opening their shops. Walking through the Pablo Picasso Museum in Barcelona gave me an eerie feeling that he was right there with us. Watching the original 'Girl from Ipanema' stroll the beach on her last walk (as an old lady in the 1980s), one could not help but to hum the tune. The extravagant casinos in Monte Carlo are as elegant as the people who frequent them. I had the honor of attending the changing of the guard at Monaco, it was very impressive. I like to believe that the handsome gentleman waving to me from the balcony was Prince Rainier.

I have sailed the Nile, the French Riviera, the South Pacific, the Mexican Riviera, both the Eastern and Western Caribbean and traveled through the Panama Canal. After taking in the wonders of Athens and Delphi, Greece, we sailed the Mediterranean Sea into the Aegean Sea to tour the Greek islands of Mykonos, Santorini, Crete and Rhodes. While in Kusadasi, Turkey, we traveled to Ephesus and visited the home of the Blessed Virgin Mary.

I have marveled at the Northern Lights and the glaciers in Alaska, and was in awe of the Fjords in Norway. All of my dreams seemed to come true when I was able to visit the homeland of my ancestors, Ireland. We discovered the beauty of Larry's parentage, Holland. I was expecting windmills and tulips but Amsterdam seemed to be a mass of bicycles and marijuana. Rotterdam was beautiful. England, Scotland, Iceland, Greenland and Newfoundland were also included in that once-in-a-lifetime cruise which crossed the Arctic Circle, not once but twice.

I have been in all but one state in our beautiful country. Somehow, traveling through the New England States, even living in Connecticut in the early 1960s, I managed to miss visiting Vermont. Sailing on the Mississippi River I became aware that I would like to see more of the United States. I have learned to love the South and the wonderful, warm, welcoming people who inhabit it and above all the food! Georgia and South Carolina are so rich in history. Traveling Route 66 from Arizona to St. Louis and then heading south to Branson, Missouri, was one of the greatest road trips ever. As a child I yearned to see Niagara Falls and attend the Kentucky Derby. Sometimes dreams do come true. I felt the thrill of standing directly under the falls at Niagara and was able to view the beauty of it from both the American and Canadian sides. I did make it to Churchill Downs, but I didn't get to see the Derby. I had to settle for the Derby Museum, which was amazing. I got to watch the video of the 1958 race and see 'Tim-Tam' (after whom I named my first son) trot to victory. Visiting New Orleans at any time is an adventure but being able to be there for Mardi Gras is beyond exciting. I could never have imagined standing on the stage at the Grand Ole Opry, but there I was, being serenaded by none other than that famous country singer Larry VanDyke. A better thrill yet was sitting in Elvis' private plane at Graceland. My bucket list is shrinking every year. After seeing the Grand Canyon, Sedona and Zion and Bryce Canyon National Parks, I now hope to be able to visit as many of our National Parks as time allows.

How could I ever choose a favorite place? I will admit that I do have a favorite city to visit. When I hear Tony Bennett croon, "I left my heart in San Francisco," I tend to find myself in some state of euphoria, thoughts scattering, recalling all of the memorable days that I have spent in that beautiful city by the bay.

My first trip to 'Frisco' as my dad referred to it, was in 1972. I had never in my adult life been anywhere without my children. My dear friend Ethel, who was from Pennsylvania was living in San Diego. She had purchased a thirty-day Greyhound bus pass to travel back east to visit her mother. When she returned after only ten days she called me with the brilliant idea that I could use her pass with her identification to ride the bus from Seattle to San Diego. She assured me that it didn't matter that she was five-years younger, five-inches taller and a brunette. She said that no one had even asked her for identification when she presented her ticket. I was more than a little skeptical to even give it a try. San Diego and a vacation did sound inviting though. When my childrens' dad offered to stay at the house with the kids, I decided why not? I had never had a vacation.

I had a great time visiting my friends in San Diego, and taking an exciting day trip to Tijuana. When I told my niece, Sheri, about my trip she suggested that I make a stop in San Francisco on my way back home. She had taken a job in San Francisco as a key punch operator and her work schedule allowed her to set her own hours. She would be able to arrange to work some night shifts so that she could show me the city. It sounded like a pretty good idea to me, I had no reason to hurry home.

I think that I fell in love with San Francisco the first time I saw the skyline, the impressive Coit Tower and the Transamerica building, a touch of the old and the new. Looking out across the bay to Alcatraz and seeing the sunrise over the Golden Gate Bridge literally took my breath away. From the Presidio to Fisherman's Warf, the open air market at the Embarcadero and Ghirardelli Square, Sheri and I became tourists for a week. I was anxious to ride the cable car. It proved to be an  exciting adventure as I lost my shoe half way up the hill. We stopped at the famous Buena Vista Café at the end of the cable car line on Hyde Street to enjoy their much-touted Irish Coffee. It was the first time that I had ever tasted Irish whiskey.

On Sheri's day off we decided to attend a hippie concert at Golden Gate Park after which we headed to Lombard Street, the most crooked street in the world. Sheri's little green 1972 Datsun wound its way down the famous landmark in record time with me hanging on for dear life. "Oh, that was fun," I squealed as we came to a stop. "Wanna do it again?" she asked. "Sure!" I wasn't prepared for what was about to take place. She shoved the car in reverse and up the hill we went, backward! Luckily it was 3:00 AM and there were no other cars, nor cops in sight... thank heavens.

A visit to San Francisco isn't complete without visiting China Town. The Dragon's Gate welcomes you to one of the oldest China towns in North America. Walking down the unique, busy neighborhood decorated with historic street lights, hanging lanterns and pagoda shaped roofs, Sheri suddenly turned into a narrow hole-in-the-wall doorway. As I followed her into what I would never have guessed to be a restaurant, a very rude waiter handed her a large bowl of noodles and pointing to the stairway barked, "Second floor, table two," and abruptly disappeared into the kitchen. This was Sam Wo's legendary Chinese restaurant, built shortly after the 1906 earthquake. The food was good, the prices reasonable and it was always busy, despite the rude waiter and the overly friendly, touchy, feely owner, Sam. Sam's was closed in 2012 due to health and fire codes. The new Sam Wo's restaurant opened in 2015 on Clay Street.

San Francisco has always been noted for the entertainment. The Broadway production of the popular musical 'Hair' was playing at one of the local theaters and Sheri was able to get tickets. The music, the costumes and the dancing were phenomenal. It was my first live musical experience and I was in awe... that is until the curtain opened on the finale and everyone on the stage was bare-ass naked. We were both in absolute shock!

That exciting vacation was only the beginning of my San Francisco adventures. The year after Larry and I were married, 1980, he and I took our first trip to San Francisco. He had been stationed at Fort Ord when he was in the Army in the late 1950s, and San Francisco had been his off-duty recreation spot. His cousin owned the Hyland Hotel in the Tenderloin District and he knew the city inside out and upside down. On our first day there I wore the soles out on my brand new leather sandals. I had to buy a pair of walking shoes, and walk we did, from the Mission District to Haight Ashbury and back to #9 Fisherman's Grotto which was Larry's favorite restaurant on the Warf. We covered every block of China Town. He introduced me to North Beach with all of the quaint Italian sidewalk cafes and magnificent pastry shops, Gino and Carlos's, the local hangout, and the Club Fugazi, home of the legendary 'Beach Blanket

Babylon,' an outrageous musical revue. It was the longest running musical review in live theater history, entertaining six and a half million people over the years. Sadly, after forty-five years the final show was on New Year's Eve of 2019.

Finocchio's was a nightclub that opened as a speakeasy in 1929. It was flaunted as "The Carnegie Hall of cross-dressing, where all the most beautiful women are men." The performers were expected to dress as men as they arrived and left the club. "We are illusionists, not transvestites," one of the show's stars stated. The master-of-ceremonies, who impersonated Sophie Tucker, worked for the postal system by day and was the father of six. He starred at the club for twenty-seven years. It was amazing entertainment. It closed in 1999, as have many of our favorite spots over the years. Lefty O'Doul's, with all of the sports memorabilia and great home-style food, and the old Gold Dust Lounge with the beautiful cherub murals on the ceiling have moved from Union Square. It is not quite the same as the old city we knew and loved. John's Grill, known to the locals as the home of the 'Maltese Falcon' was built in 1908 and is still in business.

Legend has it that Dashiell Hammett wrote his famous novel in booth twenty-one of John's Grill.

When we started going to San Francisco to see the Giants baseball team play in the early 1980s, the games were held in the acclaimed Candlestick Park. The team played there until 2000 when they moved to PacBell Park, now known as Oracle Park. Candlestick Park was demolished in 2015.

Over the years we have taken several of our grandchildren to see the Giants play baseball and to introduce them to our favorite city. Even with the changing times and the obvious decline of the welcoming atmosphere, due to a large population of homeless, we still enjoy taking the train over Donner Pass at Christmas time. The ride itself is fantastic, especially if there is fresh falling snow. We delight in taking part in the

San Francisco traditions of having Chinese food on Christmas day, shopping at Macy's the day after Christmas and hopefully getting to watch the sun set from the top of Russian Hill.

So, when Tony Bennett croons, "The loveliness of Paris seems somehow sadly grey… The glory that was Rome is of another day," I can vividly imagine the little cable cars climbing half-way to the stars, and I can feel the morning fog chill the air and *I don't care.* A little bit of my heart remains there… in San Francisco.

RETURNING TO NEW ORLEANS

There is an old song from the 1940s - "If I Had My Life to Live Over." Doris Day sang it, so did Eddy Arnold. Even as a little girl I loved that song. But thinking about it as an adult, I'm not so sure that, as the lyrics go, "I'd do the same things again." There are many time periods in my life that I would not want to have to repeat. However, traveling isn't one of them. I have been blessed to see a lot of our wonderful world, and I have many priceless memories of my travels. And yes, there are places I have been that I would love to return to, maybe even again and again.

Fat Tuesday, translated to French, is 'Mardi Gras.' The name "Fat Tuesday" refers to the last day of eating rich foods before the Lenten season begins on Ash Wednesday. Mardi Gras is all about music, parades, floats, partying and excitement. It is celebrated in a big way in New Orleans. The parades go on for a week. The floats are spectacular creations, each one trying to outdo the others. Beads and trinkets are thrown to the crowds who rush to claim the treasures. The young and old alike are all adorned in lavish costumes. The colors purple (for justice), green (for faith), and gold (for power) are seen everywhere. Beads are thrown from the decorated balconies of the tall brick apartment houses in the French Quarter, and the million dollar homes in the Garden District are adorned with extravagant decorations. There are jazz musicians on every corner, some as professional as concert hall virtuosos. Music fills the air as the crowds sing, dance and some brazenly flash their breasts to have beads flung to them from the passing floats along the parade route.

The first time we visited New Orleans was in 2006. It was just a year after the category five hurricane Katrina had devastated the city. Signs of the storm were still evident. Eighty percent of the city had been flooded after a levee broke, leaving parts of the city in shambles with no power, no drinking water and some homes completely washed away.

Fifty thousand people scrambled, waiting to be evacuated. Thousands sought shelter at the Super Dome, and were left for days with no food or water. As we toured the ruins of the city we were told that the numbers marked on the demolished homes indicated how many people had perished there. In the downtown area windows in the high rise buildings were yet to be replaced. Our tour guide had lost a brother and a nephew in the deluge, and did not know where her son was for a week. They didn't even have cell phone service. I cried as I took pictures of the aftermath of the horrendous storm which claimed over 1800 people and left millions along the Gulf Coast homeless. This was not the New Orleans that I had looked forward to seeing.

Fast forward nine years. In 2015 we were able to revisit New Orleans. The spirit of the people there had pulled them through the worst of times, and the city was back to what I had hoped to see on our first trip. There can't be a better time to be in New Orleans than the week of Mardi Gras. Where else can you find *'ashes to go'* on the street corners on Ash Wednesday. I couldn't believe my eyes! "Apartment for Rent –

Not Haunted," was another sign that you most likely would never see anywhere else. Squeezing into Cafe Du Monde in the French Quarter to enjoy beignets (fried squares of pastry sprinkled with mounds of powdered sugar) is the perfect way to start the day. Strolling through the French Market Place, visiting Saint Louis Cathedral, the old United States Mint which was built in 1838 and closed in 1909, and seeing Fats Domino's piano at the Music Museum, which is located in the old mint building, can take up most of the morning. After a quick lunch at Pirate's Alley, a ride on the trolley car to the Garden District is a great way to spend the afternoon.

Touring the cemeteries is a must for many tourists. The graves are all above ground in the Spanish custom of vaults because of the high water table. If they were to bury the caskets they would fill with water and literally float to the surface. Each family has its own private vault. After 364 days the remains of the deceased are swept with a ten-foot pole with a broom on the end through an opening in the back of the vault to make room for the next family member who passes. We were told that this is where the old saying, "I wouldn't touch that with a ten-foot pole," originated.

We returned to New Orleans again in 2019 and many things had changed. The historical old hotel with the red tile bathrooms and nude ceiling paintings where we had stayed in Lee Square had been converted into an upscale Holiday Inn. It was directly across the street from the seventy-six-foot tall monument to the "Hero of the South," Confederate General Robert E. Lee. It was erected in 1884. In 2015 we watched from our 6th story window in horror as the angry crowds protested the presidential election, defacing the monument and breaking windows in the ground floors beneath us. Police sirens and gun shots ensued all night. This was the first riot I had ever encountered. For many New Orleans residents, this monument, as well as several others in the city, glorified slavery, racism, white supremacy and oppression. After a six-to-one vote by the city council later that year, it was removed on May 19, 2017.

During the COVID-19 pandemic in 2020 all of the Mardi Gras hoopla in the city was canceled, but the die-hard locals set up huge replicas of the floats in their front yards, and tossed beads to the people who passed by, attempting to keep the spirit of the grand celebration alive. They pegged it: "Yardi Gras."

So, is there somewhere I would like to go again, some experience I would love to relive? Maybe next year. Meantime, we will celebrate with our homemade beignets, a bit of jazz music and our wonderful pictures and memories of glorious New Orleans.

PS: We will be returning in December of 2022 to board the American Queen for a voyage on the Mississippi River.

TEACHING MOMENTS

Doesn't every little girl at some time or another want to grow up to be a teacher? From the first grade in parochial school I was in awe of every nun who taught me. I believed that someday I would grow up and fulfill my dream of being just like them. I was convinced by age nine that my vocation was to enter the convent and become an exceptional educator. I would make all of the younger kids in the neighborhood play school with me. I had them sit in lines and I would make up absurd questions to ask them, feeling so superior when they couldn't answer correctly. By golly, I was going to be the best teacher ever!

By the time I was in the eighth grade I had decided that the convent was probably not my calling after all. I didn't give up on the idea of pursuing a teaching career, however. When I was in high school I worked every Saturday morning at the local dance studio teaching a 'baby ballet' class. It was for kids three to five years old. I took the job to pay for my private dancing lessons. I loved working with the little ones, which made me realize even more that I wanted to teach – maybe dancing. Life seems to have a way of sidetracking plans, and I found myself married at eighteen with my education put on hold. I learned over the next few years (and four children) that the title "Mother" encompasses every aspect of being a teacher. These curious little beings that I brought into the world had so much to learn. I was their teacher and how I loved seeing each new step they took, word they learned, everything they discovered. This was my real vocation.

When my oldest boys were ages three and one, we were living on a Naval Base in Puerto Rico. Special Services was putting together a program of activities for the children on the base. My husband told them that I could teach dancing. "No," I told him. "I'm not certified to teach." I ended up with three tap dancing classes for kids, ages ranging from six to sixteen, two private ballet students and a teen jazz class. When I happened to mention to someone that I had been a majorette for my high school band, the head of the program asked me to teach a baton twirling class. The girls were all so eager to learn and Special Services provided all of the batons. I was enjoying my new found teaching job. The mother of one of my students approached me one day at a jazz class wanting to know where the teacher was. I was just twenty-one and in my pony tail and leotards I guess I looked about fifteen. The director of Special Services and several of the mothers helped me to arrange a recital at the end of the first year. It was such a success that the number of my students almost doubled by the second year. When my husband was transferred back to the states I was sad to leave after three years of being called "teacher."

When the boys were old enough to join cub scouts I volunteered to be a den mother. I loved working with the boys, teaching them new skills and encouraging them to work toward earning their badges. I even taught my den to tap dance for a scout rally performance. I was learning new skills along with them. I was given the opportunity to attend classes to learn to instruct scout leaders. I had the honor of being the first female scout trainer in the state of Washington.

Our kids were in public school so I saw to it that they attended CCD (Confraternity of Christian Doctrine) classes every week as they had all been baptized Catholic. The parish priest, who knew me through scouting, approached me one Sunday after mass and asked me if I could teach a catechism class. When I hesitated he told me that I would be trained and the classes would actually be planned out for me weekly. I have been ever thankful for that opportunity. It not only gave me a better understanding of my religion, but prompted me to later study theology through an extension program. When we moved to Hawaii the diocese on Oahu was more than happy to have me join their CCD program. I taught middle school children whose parents were all amazed that the kids were actually enjoying their weekly classes. We met at my home and of course I always had snacks for them and even though we had an assigned lesson each week, I would take the time to let each of them talk about their week and question them as to how they could relate it to the subject we were studying. I was amazed and delighted at how they were so anxious to open up and participate. When the musical "Jesus Christ Superstar" came to the Honolulu International Center I sent letters to the parents asking if they would attend the show with their children. We went as a group, and I paid for some whose parents couldn't afford it. It was so amazing to see their reactions to this fantastic show. For our church's Advent procession my class made beautiful "Jesus Christ Superstar" banners. For Christmas that year they gifted me with the sound track album from the musical. I treasured it for many years and still sing the songs.

While stationed in Hawaii my husband was affiliated with the Armed Forces Archery Association. By now the older boys were in junior high and high school and involved in shooting archery. After much coaxing I agreed to learn to shoot also. I like to brag about being the 1971 Women's Bare Bow Champion, but the truth of the matter is there was only one other woman on the island of Oahu who shot bare bow, and she just happened to be a little bit lousier shooter than I was. When I was asked to teach the junior archers at the base I couldn't say no. Some of them ended up shooting in the local Junior Olympics. I was pretty proud of that. Wow! They were *my* students, that made *me* a teacher.

In the 1980s I was working a part time job in direct sales and the company sent me to their Career College in Kansas City, Missouri, every year for training to train the trainers. I don't know exactly what my title was, but again I enjoyed teaching and finally was certified to claim the title 'instructor.' That was close enough to teacher for me! My granddaughter, Michelle, has gone back to school at thirty-five years of age to attain her teaching degree. I could not be more proud of her.

BATHTUB TALES

My brother was eight years older than me, and for as long as I can remember I always believed everything he ever told me. One of the earliest things I remember him telling me, when I was perhaps two years old, was that if he pulled the plug in the bathtub I would go right down the drain with the water. I had no reason to doubt him. From that day on I was fearful of any holes. I became hysterical over an empty hole where a rung was missing from a wooden chair. My mother had to cover it with tape to assure me that I wasn't going to be sucked up into that dark hole. I recall being petrified when my brother poked a hole in my hallow chocolate rabbit on Easter. Of course it was his way of getting the treat away from me. As I got older I realized that I was not going to go down the drain, but for some reason I still always got out of the tub before I pulled the plug. Come to think of it, up until and including my very last bath, the water was always drained from the tub *after* I got out.

I loved soaking in a hot bubbly bath as an adult. That seemed to be my reward after tucking the kids into bed at night and a perfect relaxing way to end my hectic days. Remember the old "Calgon, Take Me Away" commercials? That became my anthem. I also liked to read in the bathtub, and as the water cooled I would just add more hot water. I spoiled myself with extravagant bath soaks and bubble-bath when I could afford it, and when I couldn't afford it, I settled for the cheap ones like Calgon and Epsom salts. I always said that I couldn't take a 'naked' (meaning a no foo-foo) bath. Once I discovered Vita Bath, I would never settle for anything else.

One of the greatest joys of my life was when Larry and I bought our house with a garden tub. Shortly after we moved into our new home my mother came to visit. Larry and I had only been married a short time and Mother had not yet met him. I must explain that my mother was a very prim and proper lady, I never heard a bad word come out of her mouth. She was one of the most humorous people I have ever met, and her quick wit was at times a little off color. Of course, Larry, having never been around her, was not aware of that side of her personality. One day he and my daughter were having a heated exchange of words. Becoming quite frustrated with them, taking a deep breath, I picked up the Reader's Digest and announced that I was going to go take a bath. "It seems like the tub is the only place I ever get any peace in this house," I gruffly exclaimed. It got very quiet for a minute, and then my mother, with her index finger placed lightly on her cheekbone and looking a little perplexed, very gingerly replied, "Hmmm, I can't recall if I ever had a piece in the tub." The look on Larry's face as my daughter and I doubled over in laughter was much more side-splitting funny than Mother's salty quip. You could almost hear his jaw hit the floor in shock. It surely broke the ice between them, and he learned in time what we always knew, that you could never be too sure of what would come out of Mother's mouth.

In 1959 my mother and dad bought a two-story, four-unit apartment house, known as a 'flat' in Butte. It was built in 1900. All four apartments had the large old clawfoot bathtubs and the toilets with the water box on the wall and the pull chain as a flush. Over the years the toilets were all replaced but the bathtubs remained. After my dad passed, Mother sold the building on the condition that she could live there for the remainder of her life. After the new owner remodeled all of the units, we moved Mother to one of the downstairs apartments. The old tubs had all been discarded and walk-in showers installed. My mother had never taken a shower and was scared of being burned. I had to teach her how to adjust the water temperature before she stepped into the shower. Amazingly she had climbed into that high-sided, huge tub until she was eighty-three years of age never having any fear of falling. She was very disappointed not to be able to, as she put it, "bathe properly."

I can now relate to her discontent in having to give up her bathtub, as we have had to replace our deep tub with a walk-in shower. After my radiation I developed a condition known as lymphedema, and am not able to have my legs in hot water for any length of time. I also think showers are much safer for older folks. This, however, also meant that I could no longer enjoy the hot tub that had been my 'comfort-zone' for the past twenty years. Now I can only reminisce about the joy and tranquility of a long soak in a hot bath. On the positive side, I no longer have to fear being washed down the drain with the bath water.

FLOWERS

Somehow, as a very young child I believed that only rich people could have 'real' flowers, live flowers that is, in their homes. I have no idea where that thought originated. Maybe it was because we were poor and didn't ever have fresh flowers in our house. Even at a very early age I detested plastic or paper or any artificial flower. I remember telling my mother that fake flowers were like plastic candy. How disappointed would you be if someone gave you candy and you realized that it wasn't real? I envied the neighbors who grew flowers in their yard. At about eight years of age my mother bought me a package of sweet-pea seeds and made a spot by the back step banister for me to plant them. As I write this now, I can almost smell the sweet fragrance of those beautiful, delicate little blossoms. I was so sad to learn that they wouldn't last forever.

I loved visiting my aunt's house in the summer and smelling the fragrant roses that she grew in the back yard. I was excited when she let me cut some roses to make a bouquet to take to my mother. I savored the aroma that permeated the air in the house, and refused to throw them away until every petal had fallen from the stems.

Memories of my first prom are mostly of the corsage my date brought for me. It was a beautiful white flower and I was thrilled, until I opened the box and got a whiff of it. I almost gagged when he lifted it out of the box. It was a gardenia, which might be a pleasant fragrance to some, but to me was nauseating. I tried to smile as I thanked him, but I was so repulsed by the smell that I had to excuse myself and leave the room until I could regain my composure. My mother followed me out of the room, concerned with my odd behavior. When I explained to her how I couldn't stand the smell of that flower and didn't want to have it pinned to my dress, she suggested that we tie it to my wrist, so as not to hurt Freddy's feelings. When I think about it now I wonder if that is how the wearing of a corsage on your wrist fad started. It was many years later, after I was married, that we were painting a house, and I suddenly became aware of an unpleasant odor under the bedroom window. Low and behold, a beautiful gardenia bush! It was a bitch to dig out, but there was no way I wanted that aroma finding its way into my bedroom. The neighbor was delighted when I gave it to her.

Who doesn't love lilacs? Lilac seems to be another fragrance that I cannot stand. I do not like the smell of lilies either. I don't think they have much of an aroma, but for some reason, for as long as I can remember, lilies remind me of a funeral parlor. Which brings to mind a funny flower story. When my third son was born, my husband, Pat, and one of his Navy buddies whose wife had given birth the same day, were on their way to the hospital and as they passed the cemetery they decided to stop and get some flowers. He brought me the most beautiful rose arrangement that I had ever seen. It was several months later that I heard them laughing about it. As I recall they were white roses, which have always been my favorite. When Pat passed away a few years ago I had my daughter put a white rose in his coffin for me.

I have always thought that flowers were the most thoughtful, loving gift you could give someone. When my daughter was about three years old she presented my mother with a sweet bouquet of colorful irises. "I picked floudoos for you, Grandma," she smiled. The neighbors, whose yard she had picked them from, were not nearly as thrilled as grandma. I always made it a point to buy my mother an orchid for Mother's Day. My sister on the contrary, couldn't imagine why I would buy flowers for her. "Why do you spend money on flowers? They just die," she would scold me when I would take her flowers for her birthday. It's difficult for me, but now I buy an artificial flower arrangement for my sister's grave every year, knowing that she is smiling down on me.

Larry, from the first time I met him, won my heart by seeing to it that I always had fresh flowers in the house. We had beautiful azalea and rhododendron bushes in our yard when we lived in Washington. I now enjoy the rose bushes and an array of seasonal flowers that adorn our little yard. How dull the world would be without the beauty of flowers. According to Luther Burbank, "Flowers always make people better, happier and more helpful; they are the sunshine, food and medicine for the soul."

THE CHANGING TIMES

Do you remember when 2022 sounded like a world away? I have always looked forward to the future but I didn't expect the year 2022 to creep up on us so quickly. We have all made it this far in a world so full of change. Some people insist that change is a good thing. They believe that with all of the advances in science, industry, technology and education the world as we know it today is better than the one in which we grew up. I believe this to some degree. I also believe that with modern day expertise in all fields, and people endeavoring to advance, we have somehow lost sight of the importance of people caring for their fellow man and striving to make this world a better place for everyone. Seeing simple acts of kindness from time to time leads me to believe that there is still hope.

Just how have times changed over the past few decades? As an example, I was in an elevator in a hotel in San Francisco on Christmas day after attending mass, and someone happened to mention how people go to church so shabbily dressed in this day and age. I had to agree. Remember how we donned our 'Sunday best' when we went to church? No one would have ever dreamed of wearing blue jeans or shorts and flip-flops to church in the last century. A woman in the elevator spoke up to say that her husband wore shorts to church and *her* God didn't care how you dressed, just so you went to church. I was taken back because I didn't understand what she meant by *her* God. I was raised to believe in *one* God, the Father almighty. He would never judge us by how we were dressed, with that statement I agree. I think that people today have changed to the point that they have no idea or understanding of what it means to be respectful to others by dressing appropriately for any given occasion, be it church, school, a public gathering or a restaurant. To me it is not a matter of what others think, it's a matter of self-respect. Where has it gone?

Speaking of respect, I would have never allowed my children to speak to me the way kids speak to their parents and elders today. I have said many times that if respect grows out of fear, so be it. I am sure that my kids were afraid to talk back to me. They grew up knowing how to be respectful to everyone because that was what they were taught from a very early age. What are they teaching the kids today? To 'express' themselves. If one of my kids had ever said, "F_ _ _ off, Mom" to me, as I heard a young man scream at his mother at the mall, I probably would have led him out of the building by the ear and grounded him for a month. Not to mention the verbal beating he would have had to endure and an ongoing lecture about respect. I think that my kids just knew that they dare not talk to me or to any adult that way.

My niece was at the Auto Museum this past week with her grandson and there was a family there with a boy who she said appeared to be about nine or ten years old. He wanted something and when his mother told him no he proceeded to throw a screaming fit. When the mother threatened him that his dad would take care of him when they got home he looked at her grimly and replied, "Oh, yeah?... I'll kill him!!" So, tell me, has the change we have seen in child rearing enhanced our society? Since when can't you tell your kid *no* without fear of retaliation?

We didn't have much when I was growing up, just the basic necessities. We lived in low income housing and because my grandfather owned a bakery we never went hungry. He also saw to it that we always had shoes. I grew up not knowing that we were poor. Christmas for us was mostly gifts from grandparents and aunts and uncles. Can you imagine giving a child today a Christmas stocking with an orange, some nuts and sticky ribbon candy in it? We were always happy to get that. Try to convince me that things haven't changed. For the better? I think not. We may have all of the material necessities and then some, but where is the joy and appreciation for the little things. Making presents out of next to nothing for our siblings and parents was always a loving effort and so very much appreciated. Today the kids expect the high-tech, high-cost gifts given with little thought or love on either the giving or receiving end. "He wants it, we had better buy it whether or not we can afford it," speaks for the mentality of the adults. How crazy is this, to buy things that you cannot afford just to please a child who shows no appreciation or even cares about the financial burden it might cause? In our day you didn't buy anything that you couldn't afford to pay for with cash. You saved up to buy a special present or in some cases even a necessity. The 'now' generation doesn't seem to understand that you will never get ahead in life unless you are willing to sacrifice or do without.

This is definitely a change that I find hard to accept. The kids want for more, they want it now, and hardly appreciate what they have. Is this greed or is it ignorance? And who is to blame?

Is this attitude or way of thinking ever going to change? Is there anything that can be done to make the younger generation aware that without a drastic change in the way they live today there will not be a very bright future for them or their descendants? Sadly, very few people today really seem to care.

I hear people talk about bringing Home Economics, Wood Shop, Mechanics and Social Studies back to the school curriculum. Why were they ever eliminated? Was that a change for the better? Maybe for someone's financial benefit. Without these basic life skills how can anyone profit? If every child growing up today becomes a technological genius who's going to do the cooking? Oh, that's not a problem, that's why fast food chains stay in business. Which brings up the subject of food. Remember when we all sat down and enjoyed dinner together as a family? Remember the basic food charts, and mom preparing nutritious preservative and additive-free meals? Many families even found time to grow a garden and raise their own food. Mom would can fruits and vegetables, make homemade jams and preserves, bake bread and home-made cookies. Oh, yeah, mom was home then to keep the laundry done, know where the kids were after school, to help with the homework or at least make sure that it was done. She always found time to read to the kids too.

No, I don't like change. I am sad to see the world as it is today. Remember when we, as kids, could go to the Saturday matinee at the movie theater with our friends, or even alone. When I was young I used to ride the train from Butte to Reno all by myself in the summer. Did anyone ever worry about me getting there safely? Nope! Was I afraid? I had no reason to be. Would we even think of letting a kid get on a city bus alone today? We even have to worry about the safety of the school buses. Sad, but true, our society has become non-trustworthy, uncaring, unloving, and disrespectful. The human race seems to be out to destroy itself. The God-fearing faithful seem to be the minority in this day and age. Now, I ask, what can we do to change our state of being? I wish that I had the answer to that question. I wish that I had the power to make our world a more desirable, safer place for future generations. I would like to know that my grandkids could worship in their church or shop at the mall or attend school without the fear of being shot.

I wrote a poem a few years ago entitled "The Inevitability of Change." In it I state that a change of attitude is maybe all it would take for me to accept change. It would be great if it were that easy. Sometimes it is difficult to maintain a positive attitude because of the changes that we have seen over the past few decades. My prayer is that people will somehow come to realize that nothing will change until we can eliminate greed and all learn to work together with love, respect and concern for a better life for all mankind.

Hopefully the future will bring some positive changes, starting with the little things that you and I can do to make every day better in some small way.

THE INEVITABILITY OF CHANGE

Change is all around us, I see it every day.
If I don't learn to accept it, there might be a price to pay.

I have to face the fact that **change** is just a part of life.
Change is never easy, but it sure can settle strife.

Wake up every morning with a smile upon your face,
Knowing that a **change** may make the world a better place.

The fact is that we all have **changes**, every single day.
We **change** our minds, we **change** our plans, and we **change** the things we say.

Bad behavior, **change** that too. That **change** could make your dreams come true!
Just slow down, **change** your pace. **Change** that frown upon your face.

Change your shoes and **change** your hair, don't forget your underwear.
Change the light bulb, **change** the sheet, **change** the way you cook your meat.

Change of life can't be denied, but you can **change** the mood applied.
Now, knowing this I must admit, I'll have to learn to **change** a bit.

A **change** of attitude is probably all that I need,
To help me to accept the fact that **change** is here to stay, indeed.

PANDEMIC 2020

    The new year of 2020 arrived with hope and plans for a year of travel and adventure. How quickly our lives and our world would change in a few short weeks.
    On January 9th the World Health Organization issued a warning about a severe acute respiratory syndrome that was spreading rampantly in Wuhan, China. It was identified as a new strain of the Coronavirus, labeled COVID-19. The symptoms included: fever, cough, shortness of breath, aches, sore throat and vomiting. These symptoms would appear two to fourteen days after being exposed to someone infected with the virus. The White House was notified of this virus on November 24th, 2019, and nothing was done to try to prevent the spread of the disease into our country by limiting the influx of people flying into the United States. It was the third week in January when COVID-19 was detected on American shores. On Sunday, January 19th, a man in Everett, Washington, sought treatment for a cough and fever. He became the first person in the United States diagnosed with the virus. One day later, a woman in Chicago was hospitalized for pneumonia. She became the second. Orange County, California, reported the third case on Wednesday of that week. All three had been in Wuhan, China, shortly before falling ill. All three would survive.
    On January 26th President Trump assured the public that the virus was under control, then on January 29th he admitted that he knew how bad the COVID-19 virus was but still neglected to enforce any travel bans. By February 2nd we had three million passengers arriving in our country from China, Great Britain, Italy and Spain. Fifty full flights of possibly infected people flew to the west coast from China.
    On February 1st the Holland America cruise ship Westerdam departed from Hong Kong on a fourteen-day cruise. The ship was forced to dock on February 13th in Cambodia and the American passengers were flown back home. Then on February 16th it was reported that forty

American passengers on the cruise ship, Diamond Princess, were infected with the virus. A later report was issued saying that six of them had died.

As of February 16th there were 600 deaths reported in mainland China and over 32,000 cases confirmed across the world with 638 reported deaths. President Trump was still claiming, "It will disappear like a miracle." (His televised quote on February 27th, 2020).

At this time all of our travel plans for the year had been booked and paid for, beginning with a Bingo Bash trip to Las Vegas on Palm Sunday, April 5th. Two full days of bingo with the hopes of winning the big one – $25,000! From there we would drive to Mesquite for a couple of relaxing nights and more bingo on our way to St. George, Utah, where we would visit Zion National Park and vacation until my birthday on April 16th.

On March 11th my niece, Sheri, called to tell me that her sister, Mary Ellen and her family were flying into San Francisco from Hawaii on March the 15th. They had rented a house for a week in Truckee, California, which is just an hour over Donner Pass from Reno. Mary was bringing her grandkids to see snow for the first time, and according to the weather report there was a snow storm predicted for the weekend. I hadn't seen Mary in over ten years and was excited when Sheri invited us to join them. Not wanting to drive over Donner Pass in the snow we decided that it would be a great one-day train trip. I called and made reservations with Amtrak. We would leave Reno in the morning and return late in the afternoon on Tues, March 17th, St. Patrick's Day.

On the very same day that we made our plans, the World Health Organization declared that COVID-19 was characterized as a pandemic. They rang the alarm bell loud and clear, stating that all countries should activate and scale up emergency mechanisms, communicate with everyone about the risks and how they could protect themselves. Meantime, President Trump was downplaying the exponential spread of the Coronavirus, comparing the death toll to the number of Americans killed in car crashes and the seasonal flu.

It was at that point that we began discussing the danger of people flying into the United States from the Far East. Shouldn't something be done to stop people from coming into our country possibly carrying the virus? Then I began to wonder if they would let Mary and her family fly out of Hawaii. Larry and I decided that even the train, which would be coming from the East Coast, may not be safe for us to ride as the news on the 12th of March reported that the number of cases in New York was tripling every day. I sadly canceled our train reservation and let Sheri know that we wouldn't be traveling at all, anywhere. She informed me the next day that Mary's doctor had discouraged them from flying, due to her husband's lung condition. People with lung problems or other medical problems, and the elderly are more susceptible to the virus. I decided that it was time for me to isolate myself and try to convince Larry that he too should stay at home. After a shopping trip to Costco, where they still had toilet paper, on the 12th of March, we enjoyed what was to be our last meal out for a long time. Some people thought that we were over reacting by putting ourselves on quarantine but I kept insisting that I would rather be safe than sorry, or dead.

I had an appointment to have my driver's license renewed on the 19th of March, but considered canceling it. I wasn't able to do it on-line because of an age restriction. After seventy years of age, you have to renew in person or have a physical evaluation form from the doctor and a vision test. The problem was solved for me when the DMV canceled all appointments and issued an extension on expiring licenses. I called and made an appointment with my doctor for April 7th to have him approve the form and make it possible for me to renew by mail.

Our daughter, Julie, is an agent for Alaska Airlines at Sea-Tac International Airport. Seattle, by this time, was being labeled as the epicenter for the spread of the virus. She was calling us every day literally begging us not to leave the house, while she herself was in grave danger of being exposed to this quickly spreading disease. My anxiety and irrational fear for her welfare gave way to a total meltdown talking to her on the phone. She finally requested a leave of absence for fourteen days. Her husband, Joey, works at the Boeing plant in Everett, Washington. I hadn't considered his being exposed until we got word that two of his co-workers had died from COVID-19. After the third death, Boeing closed the plant and Joey was given a fourteen-day leave of absence also. Now I could breathe a little easier for a while.

On March 17th Nevada Governor, Steve Sisolak, ordered an immediate closure of all non-essential businesses statewide, including hotels and casinos, for thirty days. Pharmacies and grocery stores were allowed to remain open. Restaurants were required to transition to curbside or home delivery. The order was also intended to discourage public gatherings. "You are being told NOT to go out," the Governor repeated twice. "My ultimate goal is to come together as Nevadans, to save lives," he added. All Nevada schools were ordered closed until at least April 6th. As of March 17th, the state of Nevada had reported forty-two confirmed cases of COVID-19, and one person in Nevada had died as a result of the virus.

Within just a week, on March 24th, there were more than 46,000 confirmed cases and 539 deaths in the United States. New York City's cases were doubling every day, with the most affected being ages eighteen to sixty-five. In Italy there were 700 deaths in one day. We watched daily as states were added to the list of statistics. Irrational fear and anger seem to dominate the newscasts. On the other hand, we saw and heard of people reaching out to each other as they never had before. I had three phone calls in a week from people just checking to see that we were safe and staying in, and inquiring if there was anything we needed. How nice to know that people really do care.

On the 25th of March the news reported that the virus was spreading faster in New Orleans than anywhere in the world, as of that date eighty-three people were reported dead, the youngest being a seventeen-year old. This was probably due to the crowds celebrating Mardi Gras, the last week of February. I was thinking about having been in New Orleans in 2019 for all of the fun and festivities. Who would ever have imagined that it could be a possible death threat for those planning to celebrate the beginning of Lent.

By the end of May there were 6,800 deaths in Italy reported, 683 in 24 hours. Spain's toll now topped the cases reported in China, and there were, as of that date, 5,000 new cases reported world-wide in twenty-four hours. Thirteen patients in one New York hospital died <u>in one day</u>. Prince Charles was diagnosed with the virus and was being quarantined. It is so hard to hear these statistics daily, and being told that the worst is yet to come is almost unbelievable. It seems that the world as we knew it is now unpredictable. Most of the states were now on "Stay at Home" orders, yet President Trump announced that we should all be able to congregate in Church for Easter. He is so worried about the economy and the drop in the stock market, which is lower than it has been since the last recession, that he doesn't seem to care about the welfare of the people. Dr. Anthony Fauci, who is the head of the National Institute of Allergy and Infectious Diseases, was quick to publicly oppose Trump's claim that we should not adhere to the isolation that we had been instructed to practice. Within a day or two Trump was humbly backtracking on his statement.

Thursday, March 26, 2020. I had to leave the house to pick up a prescription, so we decided that we would do whatever shopping had to be done. Armed with our spray antiseptic and antiseptic wipes in baggies in my pocket, we headed for Walmart and Costco. We had been told that they would have early shopping for seniors at Costco on Tuesdays and Thursdays, so we were there earlier than the opening time on Tuesday. The parking lot was full and there were at least three hundred people waiting in line all the way around the building. We just drove right on by. When we went back on Thursday after lunch there wasn't even a line; we walked right on in. Whoever thought people would be fighting over toilet paper? People were buying all of the toilet paper off of the shelves. I would think they would have been a little more concerned about what they were going to eat. There was no toilet paper at Costco, but we had stocked up with two thirty-roll packs the week before. It was limited to one pack per customer even then. We purchased our vitamin supplements, laundry soap, coffee and a few other necessities. We were pretty well set for probably at least a month.

We wore gloves to shop and when we left the store Larry sprayed everything that we had in the basket with a Lysol disinfectant spray before we put it in the car. A lady at Costco walked by while we were loading our purchases and looked at us like we were crazy... oh, well. When we got home we had a table set up in the garage that we put everything on, sprayed the back of the car and then sprayed all of the product again and left everything, except what had to be refrigerated or frozen in the garage. I washed all of the fresh fruit and veggies before I put them away. Maybe we *were* being a little paranoid.

We canceled all of our travel plans through October. It was hard to imagine the state of Nevada with every casino, bar and restaurant closed. We also had reservations in Palm Springs for the last week of April. I had planned to meet my son, Raymond, who lives in Alaska, in Yuma and go with him to Algadones, Mexico... cancel. From Palm Springs we had planned to go to Anaheim for five days... cancel. We had a fall trip planned to the Smokey Mountains and then onto Branson, Missouri, for a week and a Hawaiian cruise booked for March of 2021. I canceled it all.

Basketball 'March Madness' was canceled, as was baseball Spring Training and the Olympic Games. All of the professional sport events were postponed. No professional golf, no NASCAR, and they even canceled the Kentucky Derby. Both Disneyland and Disney World were closed, as were all of the National Park sites. Life as we knew it a year ago has been altered in a way that we could have never expected. The schools will now be closed for the remainder of the year in most states, and public church gatherings are being halted.

The US Navy Medical Ship "Comfort" docked in New York to take on a thousand non-COVID-19 patients due to the overload in the area hospitals. Governor Cuomo was pleading for 30,000 ventilators. Two hundred New York Police Department personnel were reported infected with the virus, and the warning was that the peak of the pandemic was still weeks off. New York was at that time considered the 'epicenter' of the Coronavirus, with 365 deaths in one day, thirteen people dying in a twenty-four-hour period in one hospital. The news showed a refrigerated truck backed up to the hospital removing bodies.

By the last day of March, Washoe county reported the first Coronavirus death, a man (not sure of his age) who had returned from visiting family in New York on March 17th. Nevada's positive COVID-19 cases had jumped to a 1,038 statewide. Thirty-two had died. There were 121 cases in Washoe County. Washoe County Commissioner, Bob Lucy, pleaded to the public on the evening news, "STAY HOME FOR NEVADA," and extended the social distancing order to April 30th. Thirty-nine states were on 'stay at home' directives.

The US Navy Aircraft Carrier Theodore Roosevelt was on deployment in the Pacific, when on March 31st over a hundred sailors tested positive for the Coronavirus. The ship's Captain, Brett Crozier, sent an unclassified email to multiple Navy officials explaining the situation and two days later was relieved of his command for not going through the 'chain of command' with his report. His crew cheered for him as he disembarked from the ship. He will remain in the Navy and will retain his rank. Navy Secretary Thomas Modly who relieved Crozier criticized him, saying he was "too naive" or "too stupid" to be a commanding officer. Modly's speech was leaked to the media and after apologizing, he resigned his position.

April Fools' Day. Our day started out with Larry sneezing and pulling a ligament or a muscle or a tendon, or who knows what, in his groin. He could hardly walk and it was almost impossible for him to get onto the bed without me lifting his left leg. Could this be Mother Nature's way of slowing him down? Luckily the toilet is only seven steps from his side of the bed, so he was able to make it to the bathroom and back. The heating pad, ice pack and ibuprofen became his best friends.

It was reported that Boris Johnson, the British Prime Minister, was taken to the hospital suffering from COVID-19 and was in the intensive care unit. The Holland America ships Zaandam and Rotterdam were given permission to disembark passengers in Fort Lauderdale,

Florida. About 250 people had reported flu-like symptoms, and were denied port entry into Florida. Four deaths were reported, with another nine critical cases. Buses took passengers directly from the ship to the airport to board two chartered planes waiting on the tarmac. Those who were too sick to travel were required to remain on the ship under quarantine for at least seventy-two hours.

The second week of April brought us bad news. Our son-in-law, Joey, fell sixteen feet from a tree that he was pruning and broke his ankle. The break was bad enough to require surgery. We were thankful that it wasn't worse. Because of the virus quarantine neither Julie nor their son, Joseph, were able to be at the hospital for the surgery. The day after Joey's accident Larry received a call that his friend, Marvin, was in the hospital in Phoenix on a respirator after being diagnosed with COVID-19. Marv and Larry had worked together in the 1960s and remained friends for over sixty years. Marv's wife, Betty, was not able to be with him at the hospital, so he passed away all alone. We were hearing everyday about the deaths from COVID-19, but it seemed much more real when it was someone we knew. I felt so badly for the nurse who had to sit him up in his hospital bed to hear his wife tell him good-by. He was probably already gone and it was her way to make it easier for Betty. To think that these medical workers were facing these horrible events daily is heart wrenching.

Governor Sisolak announced that there will be no public religious services allowed for Easter or Passover. On Easter Sunday, April 12th, I posted on Face Book, "Get up, Dress up, Think up, Look up!" Taking my own advice, I actually broke out my 'Sunday best' and got all dolled up, styled my hair and put on make-up. Surprised the hell out of Larry! It really made me feel good. Larry had bought a little Hormel Cure 81 ham, so I made our traditional Easter dinner; ham, scalloped potatoes, and my ever popular Hawaiian salad that I only make on Easter Sunday. I just made half of the recipe and we still ended up eating it for the rest of the week! This was an Easter that we won't soon forget. Just trying to make it special took the edge off of the newscast that there are a thousand Americans a day dying in the United States and that this pandemic is "far worse than we ever imagined." The United States cases reported to be over 240,000 with at least 6,000 deaths. Our statistics in Nevada were by this time over 2,000 cases with 81 reported deaths. New York City reported 800 deaths in twenty-four hours.

April 16th – my 80th birthday. How did I get this old so quickly? Seems like only last year I was fifty-seven. It was a very uneventful birthday. Larry ordered me several CD's to replace the ones that I had lost a few years ago in a car trade-in deal. Rod Stewart, Neil Diamond, Tony Bennett and Lady Gaga, and Barbara Streisand, what a great gift! He also took me to the nursery and bought me a white rose bush. It actually turned out to be red when it finally bloomed. By my birthday the statistics for the virus had risen to 530 in Washoe County with thirteen deaths, and there were 3,144 cases state wide. New York City reported that cases were doubling every day, and they had lost twenty-three of their police officers.

By the 28th of April the United States had surpassed one million cases of the virus, with 60,000 reported deaths. Nevada had 4,734 cases and 226 deaths. In spite of these horrific numbers, the mayor of North Las Vegas, Carolyn Goodman, was urging the casinos in Las Vegas to open by the first of May, against Governor Sisolak's lock down order. Thank goodness that she didn't have any jurisdiction over the Las Vegas Strip. The media showed a picture of her driving down the strip in a convertible with Tide-Pod earrings and a champagne glass, and quoted her as saying, "Assume everyone is a carrier. Let them gather and gamble, smoke in confined spaces, touch slot machines all day – and let the chips, and apparently the infections, fall where they may." When Anderson Cooper displayed a graphic showing how the virus had spread in a restaurant in China, Goodman rudely interjected, "This isn't China, this is Las Vegas, Nevada." "Wow! that's really ignorant!" was Coopers response.

Cinco de Mayo. It looks like we will be having tacos at home this year! To add to the worry over the rampantly spreading virus, we now have a report of killer bees, Asian Giant Hornets, swarming the Pacific Northwest. The New York Times forecasts a rise in deaths from COVID-19. Every day since April 2nd, there were 2,200 new cases and 1,000 deaths reported in the United States. There have been over six million unemployment claims filed in the United States, with seventeen million jobs lost in three weeks.

Meat plants in several states had been closed due to the number of virus outbreaks in the slaughterhouses. One plant, in South Dakota, reported over seven-hundred employees were infected with the virus. This was, of course, affecting the availability of meat in stores. Costco limited their meat sales and all of the markets were looking sparse in the meat departments. One thousand Wendy's franchises sold out of beef, which brings to mind the old 1980s Wendy's commercial, "Where's the Beef?"

In spite of all of this, Trump planned to disband the Coronavirus Task Force. He described himself as a 'war-time' president, describing citizens as 'warriors' suggesting that some fighters might have to die. "We can't keep our country closed down for years," he said. Ashish Jha, the director of the Harvard Global Health Institute put this into perspective saying, "There is no valor in sacrificing peoples' lives to fight the pandemic. People who are dying of this virus are not dying to protect the American way of life. They're dying because their government has had a completely ineffective response to this infectious disease." (Los Angeles Times 5-7-2020). This sure seems to reiterate the Columbia University study which reported that if the United States had enacted social-distancing measures a week earlier than it did – in early March rather than mid-March - about 36,000 fewer Americans would have died. That would have been more than one-third of the current death toll.

By the first week of May there were over 81,000 deaths reported nationwide. Our county, Washoe County, Nevada, claimed 1,116 cases with 40 deaths by May 13th. Governor Sisolack declared Nevada to be in a state of fiscal emergency with thousands of people having filed for unemployment.

There were two cases of COVID-19 reported in the White House in May. The president's press secretary tested positive, but Donald Trump was still refusing to wear a mask. Dr. Fauci put himself on a "modified quarantine" after coming in contact with one of the infected staff members.

On May 12th, The Senate held a Coronavirus hearing and Dr. Fauci testified, warning of 'needless death.' "The United States is not out of the woods," he stated and warned against the reopening of businesses too soon.

A mysterious inflammatory childhood illness was reported to be associated with the COVID-19 virus. Sixty-four children were hospitalized in New York with symptoms ranging from fever, abdominal pain, diarrhea and vomiting, trouble breathing, chest pain, lethargy, irritability and confusion. On the 14th of May a national warning was sent out to all of the states to be aware of this condition, which seems to be affecting children and young adults.

I can't imagine sleeping through a 6.5 magnitude earthquake, but that is exactly what we did on the night of May 15th. The quake epicenter was near Tonopah, about two hundred and thirty miles from our home in Reno. We heard about it on the morning news. There were no deaths or serious injuries reported. The area is out in the middle of nowhere in the desert. There was, however, extensive damage to US Highway 95.

By the middle of May more than one million people were infected with the COVID-19 virus and over 88,000 deaths were reported. Two-thirds of the states had relaxed restrictions on how Americans could move about, which lead experts to predict a resurgence of the disease. Only about 3% of the population had been tested, leaving its true scale and path unknown according to the New York times.

Graduations around the country were canceled. What a sad thing for the classes of 2020. These kids had worked hard to get where they were, and undoubtedly had looked forward to and anticipated the excitement of the celebration of their achievements. It seems like just a short time ago we were celebrating my great-nephew's high school graduation and now he was looking forward to his graduation from the University of Nevada. What a disappointment for him and his family. The family arranged a 'drive-by' celebration for him, so we made a big poster, "CONGRATS SHON," "BRAVO," "HOORAY," "CLASS OF 2020!" Colorful ribbons and balloons adorned the sign and we drove by honking and waving along with about 30 other cars. They planned to have a real ceremony for the class in December.

Former president Obama gave two virtual commencement speeches to the 2020 graduates, touching on leadership, respect and community. He also criticized the current administration's handling of the pandemic. Meanwhile, President Trump is lashing out more and more with distractions and disinformation and refusing to wear a mask. He also claims that he has been taking hydroxychloroquine (the anti-malaria drug) for a week and a half. To quote the Los Angeles Times, "It seems that our POTUS has turned the most powerful and influential office into a megaphone for wholesale fabrications and bizarre claims in an effort to confuse voters and salvage his own political future." He also threatened to withhold federal funds for Nevada and Michigan, two election battlegrounds states that were trying to make it easier and safer to vote by mail. It's unclear, however, what funds he could withhold. He didn't threaten Republican-run states taking the same or similar measures.

The good news at this point was that a vaccine developer, Moderna, Inc., announced promising results after early stage test results proved promising. An actual vaccine was still a long way away. This news was both exciting and frustrating. One of the pharmaceutical reports said that a vaccine had to be proven to not have side-effects that cause more damage than the virus itself.

My sister, Donna's birthday was on Memorial Day, the 25th of May. We drove to Fallon to the cemetery, where I left a bright, daisy windmill on her grave. Other than two doctor visits and a trip to the post-office, this was my first *'outing'* since March 12th. It was a pleasant drive. I still had not received my drivers license, but there was a ninety-days grace period due to the Coronavirus.

Because of the Memorial Day holiday, health officials had advised people to resist the urge to visit friends or family, even from a distance of six feet. The best way to protect ourselves is by remaining physically isolated from one another. Well, I guess my visit to my sister was pretty safe!

The evening news reported that a forty-six-year-old black man, George Floyd, was arrested in Minneapolis on suspicion of passing a counterfeit twenty-dollar bill. He did not resist arrest or in any way pose a threat to the arresting officers. He was reported to stay calm and even said "thank you" at one point. He was handcuffed and when he fell to the ground one of the officers knelt on his neck, another applying pressure to his torso and yet another holding his legs. In the video taken by a by-stander, you can hear Floyd repeatedly saying "I can't breathe, I can't breathe," and "Mama." He repeated that he could not breathe at least sixteen times. For eight minutes and forty-six seconds the officer held his knee on George Floyd's neck. He was unresponsive when the ambulance arrived, the three officers looking on did not attempt to provide medical assistance. He was pronounced dead at the hospital. All four officers involved were fired and one charged with second degree murder and the other three charged with aiding and abetting second degree murder.

Outrage over the death of George Floyd incited a wave of demonstrations and unrest across the country. The demonstrations and protests were initially peaceful, but quickly escalated into riots and vandalism. Windows were broken, fires set, rocks and other items thrown at the police. This led to the police using tear gas and rubber bullets. It was shocking to see rioting in downtown Reno. We watched the local news coverage as someone broke the front door of City Hall with a skateboard and set fire to the main floor. I could not believe this was happening in our peaceful "Biggest Little City in the World." The protests continued in cities all over America for several days with twelve states calling up the National Guard. Curfews were imposed on at least twelve major cities. Reno declared a curfew which lasted for several nights.

President Trump publicly announced, "When the looting starts, the shooting starts." Twitter said the message violated the company's rules against glorifying violence. Twitter has also placed 'fact-checking' links alongside two of Trump's tweets that contained false claims about voter fraud. The loss of lives due to the Coronavirus put Trump's re-election at risk, as numerous polls showed widespread belief among voters that he had mismanaged the crisis, from his early denials of a problem and promise of zero deaths to his erratic response to the reports once the death count began to rise.

With reports that Las Vegas Casinos will be opening on June 4th, state and company officials promised that every precaution would be taken to protect the public. In his statement on Tuesday, the 26th of May, Governor Sisolak said, "I don't think you're going to find a safer place to come than Las Vegas." Good luck with that folks! We were anxious to get back to our favorite bingo spots in Las Vegas, but it won't be before there is a proven vaccine available. The governor canceled his scheduled live broadcast on the 27th, conferring with reporters by phone. He was self-isolating at home after possibly being exposed to the virus.

By the end of May, United States deaths officially surpassed 100,000. This is twenty-eight percent of global deaths, despite the United States having only four percent of the world population. In less than four months the virus killed almost twice the number of Americans lost during the entire Vietnam war.

On the 8th of June, while George Floyd was being immortalized in Houston, Texas, where he grew up, Bonnie Pointer, Grammy winner and founder of the 1970s R&B group, The Pointer Sisters, died at her home in Los Angeles. When I heard of her death, all I could think of was the song, "We Are Family" by the Sisters Sledge, made popular in the early 80s by the Pointer Sisters. As I listened to George Floyd's eulogy and saw his family's grief, the words of the song echoed in my mind. We are all family, and the pain that I was feeling for his family was the pain of a mother, a sister, a sibling.

Thousands of people continued to protest across the country, carrying 'BLACK LIVES MATTER' signs and posters and demanding the officers involved in George Floyd's death be brought to justice. Their call was for sweeping police reforms to prevent the use of excessive force that activists say are predominantly targeted toward Blacks and Hispanics.

In Washington DC they painted giant yellow BLM letters the width of the street on the road to the White House. This was commissioned by the mayor, who officially deemed the section of 16th Street bearing the mural, "BLACK LIVES MATTER PLAZA" complete with a new street sign. St John's church, the site of Trump's criticized photo-op holding a bible, sits along that road.

On the 9th of June hundreds of protesters marched to Seattle's City Hall calling for Mayor Durkan to step down, after the police continued to use gas to disperse crowds, despite the thirty-day ban on tear gas that she had announced on the previous Friday. A city council member led protesters from Capitol Hill to City Hall where she allowed them to enter the building. No arrests were made.

After days of demonstrations and clashes with the police, protesters claimed several blocks around the Seattle Police Department East Precinct in the Capitol Hill area. How long can it last? Is it a distraction from the larger movement for police accountability and racial justice? A new Black-led group, says protesters will decide how long CHOP (Capitol Hill Occupation Protest) will last, despite the mayor's urging that it is time to go home. Trump threatened to take federal action to control protests, mocking local officials for not doing so. Jay Inslee, the governor of Washington State, returned the scorn saying that Trump was 'incapable' of governing. The mayor of Seattle, Jenny Durham, told Trump, "Go back to your bunker and make us all safe." It is obvious that the rioting and the spread of the virus had killed the tourism business in Seattle. With conventions and cruises being canceled, the small business owners were struggling to stay afloat in a very tough climate.

In light of the racial unrest, NASCAR prohibited Confederate flags from its events. Trump rejected a Pentagon proposal to consider renaming military bases named after confederate officers, and taking down statues of confederate war heroes, which were being defaced by the protesters. Warner Media pulled "Gone with the Wind" from its HBO programming.

By June 11th the number of COVID-19 cases in the United States had reached the two million mark. This as Trump was announcing his plans to schedule his first political rally in Tulsa, Oklahoma, on June 19th the date that is known as Juneteenth, commemorating the day in 1865 when the last remaining enslaved people in Galveston, Texas, finally learned of their freedom, established by the Emancipation Proclamation over two years earlier. The Tulsa newspaper and local officials called for Trump to reconsider hosting campaigning in their city, since the

Coronavirus is still posing a serious health challenge. "This is the wrong time and the wrong place for the rally," the editorial added. Oklahoma was marking a new high in reported cases, reporting 225 new cases in twenty-four hours. As of June 14th the state had reported over 8,000 COVID-19 cases and 359 deaths from the virus. Trump included a disclaimer for the event. Registered attendees for the rally would have to agree not to sue if they contracted the virus. He was fully aware that the transmission of COVID-19 was dangerous and spiking. He also included 'injured' in the disclosure because he was aware of the possibility of violence. One of the reporters stated, "And let's not forget his racial motivations – shameful, irresponsible, deplorable." Trump retaliated by calling the journalists scum bags who should be executed.

By the middle of June there were more than eight and a half million cases of Coronavirus confirmed worldwide. Arizona, Florida, and Texas all reported their largest one-day increase. Cases in Texas had doubled, supposedly due to the ongoing protests, the willy-nilly reopening of bars and restaurants and beauty salons after pressure from the small businesses and the people who were frustrated by the lockdown and being out of work.

Doctor Anthony Fauci reported to CBS news that the intensifying anti-science sentiments had led people to ignore public health guidelines during the pandemic. "This is disturbing and disappointing," he said, adding, "The best way to protect yourself and prevent the spread of infection is to avoid crowds."

Due to the rise in cases and hospitalizations, we decided to call Branson and cancel our reservations for November. We were told that all of the hotels, show houses and restaurants were closed, and that after two beauty shops had reopened both of the owners and some other hairdressers had contracted the virus and there were a 129 cases confirmed.

The question on June 28th was, "So, when will we have a vaccine?" On the eleventh of July, the Los Angeles Times reported that scientists had devised a way to use antibody-rich blood plasma of COVID-19 survivors to inoculate people against the virus for months. By the third week of July, there were four million cases of the virus with over 140,000 deaths. Doctor Fauci announced at this time that he was "cautiously optimistic" about a vaccine. 30,000 volunteers would be needed to test a vaccine.

July brought the country a bit of a feeling of normalcy when Major League Baseball returned. The games were played in front of cardboard cut-outs, but it was better than nothing.

As if 2020 wasn't already hard enough, two category Hurricanes, Laura and Marco slammed into the Gulf Coast in August with 150 mile-an-hour winds. A million people were ordered to evacuate and almost 400,000 people were left without power in Louisiana and Texas. Meanwhile, the West Coast had fires raging through five counties in California, growing to more than 124,000 acres, destroying more than one hundred structures and threatening 25,000 others. The largest blaze, a series of Preserve Desert fires ravaged the heart of one of the world's largest Joshua tree forests. What was once a trip through a magical landscape will be a tour of the world's largest Joshua tree grave yard. More than a million beloved 1000 year-old trees, and one of my favorite places, can never be replaced.

September marked six months of quarantine. I woke up every morning hoping that it was all just a bad dream, but the news media was reporting that the death toll would probably reach two million. With most of the states on "Stay at Home" orders, and the news that several companies had announced promising results after early stage testing of vaccines, there seemed to be a glimmer of hope for the future.

The fires continued to rage into September as did the surge of the pandemic. By the first day of fall, September 22nd, there were two million confirmed deaths from COVID-19 in the United States. In October President Trump was admitted to the hospital for three days after testing positive. He again attempted to downplay the severity of the pandemic. "Don't be afraid of COVID," he tweeted. "Don't let it dominate your life." This rang alarms among health professionals, who pointed out that the disease remained deadly and was spiking in numerous states. On October 30th, Doctor Fauci said that we may not start to feel anything like 'normal' until 2022, and that's only if the United States gets a significant share of the population vaccinated by mid -2021.

On November 11th Nevada governor Sisolak urged Nevadans to stay home for two weeks to combat the Coronavirus surge. The following week Washington State was put back on close-down amid the worsening virus crisis. By the middle of November more than 245,000 people had died in the United States from COVID-19. This was more than any other country. According to the New York Times the pace was likely to accelerate in the coming weeks. There were more than 1,000 deaths every day, with three people in the United States dying every minute. California had six straight days with at least 10,000 newly confirmed Coronavirus cases, and the highest death rate since May. One epidemiologist summed up the crisis in stark terms, "The months ahead are looking quite horrifying." Public Health officials urged Americans to avoid travel over the Thanksgiving holiday and to celebrate only with members of their immediate household. Pfizer's vaccine was being reviewed by the FDA for emergency use. It was announced that the first Americans could possibly get a vaccine by the middle of December. Doctor Fauci predicted "surge upon surge' and said that he does not expect that the recommendations for social distancing will be followed before Christmas. He added, "We're all hoping, however, that with a vaccine on the way, there's light at the end of the tunnel."

On Sunday, December the 6th, the New York Times reported one of the most devastating weeks in the United States since the Coronavirus began nine months ago. Hospitalizations topped a 100,000, more than double at the beginning of November. The most vulnerable were nursing home residents, people with underlying conditions, and lower-income communities. Mass vaccination campaigns were preparing for the release of a vaccine. Health care workers and the elderly would most certainly get the first shots. Who goes next seems to be debatable. Ultimately, states will determine who will be included in the first inoculations. Front-line workers and essential workers who cannot work away from home and are at a greater risk, due to interacting face to face with others will no doubt also be in line for the first release of the vaccine.

After Britain started vaccinations on December the 8th, a New York Times editorial described the vaccine to be like a fire hose. At ninety-five percent effective as it appears to be, it is powerful, but the size of the fire is still a bigger determinant of how much destruction occurs. At the current level of infection in the United States a vaccine that is ninety-five percent effective, distributed at the expected pace, would still leave a terrible toll six months after it was introduced. Almost ten million or so Americans would contract the virus, and more than 160,000 would die. No vaccine can eliminate a pandemic immediately, just as no fire hose can put out a forest fire. While the vaccine is being distributed, the virus would continue to do damage. A positive way to reduce the virus' spread is to wear a mask, and practice social distancing. These safety measures can have profound consequences to saving more lives in the coming months.

December 12th, the FDA, after promising results in the testing of a vaccine, announced that the Phizer vaccine had been approved. This was followed by the announcement on the 19th that the Moderna Vaccine was also being made available. After nine long months of waking up every morning hoping that this pandemic was all just a bad dream and wondering if the world, as we knew it, would ever be the same, there was finally a glimmer of hope. Doctor Fauci predicted that people with no underlying conditions will get the vaccine by the beginning of April, 2021. He added that by the fall of 2021 life may start to look normal again. I hope so. I considered 2020 as a time of not being 'stuck' at home, instead I thought of it as our time of being 'safe' at home. That was one positive way of dealing with it. I heard Wayne Brady say, "God has given us all a time out."

The following analogy was sent to me anonymously during the pandemic.

"SUDDENLY"

Suddenly, we slept in one world and woke up in another.
Disney has no more magic and Paris is no longer romantic.
Suddenly, in New York everyone sleeps.
And the Great Wall of China is no longer a fortress.

Suddenly, hugs and kisses become weapons.
Holding hands and walking in the parks become outlawed.
Suddenly, not visiting aging parents and grandparents becomes an "act of love."
Suddenly, our bombs and machine guns, our tanks and artilleries begin to gather dust.

Suddenly, we realized that power is with God alone.
And that money has no value when it can't even buy you toilet paper.
Suddenly, we have been put back in our place by the hands of the universe.
And we've been made aware how vulnerably "human" we truly are,
when faced with a microbe so powerfully inhumane.

ATOMIC STRONG

Traveling east from Portland, Oregon, on Highway 26, you will discover the bustling, busy city of Gresham. Although Gresham was founded as a farming settlement in the mid-1800s it is now the fourth largest city in Oregon. The residents of Gresham, along with cities all over America, were in January of 2020 made aware of a severe acute respiratory syndrome that was spreading rampantly in China. By the middle of February more than 32,000 cases of COVID-19 were confirmed across the world.

When word of a volunteer quarantine due to this Coronavirus was announced in most of the western states in March, a young couple in Gresham realized that they wanted to step up and help people who would be isolated in their homes. They designed and promoted a program for people of all ages to improve physical strength and promote their quality of life.

Jeremiah Hammon and Brooke Braga decided that by offering their 'ATOMIC STRONG' plan on social media they could empower people individually through self-education. ATOMIC STRONG is not just about working out and physical strength, but includes mental and emotional aspects which can enable one to lead a life of fulfillment. The personal touch that Jeremiah and Brooke had woven into this program, from mapping your fitness plan with you, to sharing recipes and nutritional information, gives you all of the encouragement that you need to succeed in reaching your goals. They don't just preach, they practice! When the Coronavirus began, they knew that everyone needed to stay ahead of more than one curve. There was a mental, emotional and physical health curve to deal with. With the local gyms closing their doors they did not want to see family, friends and others neglecting their health and well-being. They remained diligent in keeping their social media network strong with encouragement, interaction and positivism as well as home workouts, daily inspirational posts, tips on handling home office life and home schooling, maintaining good nutrition and suggestions on managing stress and thriving during those trying times.

Another major aspect to add to this was the music that they integrated into their program. Jeremiah and Brooke are both talented music artists, composers and performers. Their band, 'ATOMIC 45' had been performing in local clubs in the Portland area. The shows were canceled, due to the pandemic, which derailed their path for a time. They ultimately began a suicide awareness campaign from their home, helping to educate people on suicide prevention with verified sources. Their song 'Delicate' from their third album "G.O.D." was a step in promoting their Suicide Awareness campaign. "No better outlet and connection tool than music!" says Jeremiah.

A personal message from Jeremiah and Brooke:
"Atomic Strong is about learning the 'Art of Self Mastery' realigning and designing a life that gets you excited to get up and conquer each day with the same amount of passion! We strive to help you create the schematic to a better you, to live fulfilled and stop chasing the next fad that brings you only instant gratification. We give you the tools that are sustainable to be physically, mentally, and emotionally fit. Our intentions always come back to one thing; we believe that human potential is limitless. Sometimes we just need help tapping into it."

ATOMIC STRONG and the work that Jeremiah and Brooke have done to provide people inspiration and motivation to carry on during this troubled, uncertain time was a great reminder to all of us that we truly are *'all in this together.'*

MY HAPPY PLACE

As I began to write for a class assignment, I was contemplating the subject, "My Happy Place," and I found myself singing, "Happiness is, happiness is... different things to different people, that's what happiness is." This is a tune from a Ray Conniff album that was popular in 1966. "To a golfer it's a hole in one, to a father it's a brand new son. To a banker lots and lots of dough, to the racer it's a GTO"... on and on about what happiness is.

I grew up in a house where music was the background of life. Not a day went by that someone in the house was not singing. "You've got your problems, I've got mine," was the tune we'd hear if we were complaining. "Forget your troubles and just get happy," if we were sulking or worrying about something. I would wake up in the morning to the tune of, "Zip-a-dee-doo-dah, zip-a-dee-ay, my, oh my, what a wonderful day."

In my youth there was a marvelous, magical place at the foot of the Rocky Mountains. I think of it now as the precursor to Disneyland. Columbia Gardens was built in 1899 as a gift to the people of Butte by William A. Clark, the famous "Copper King." It was acres of beautiful flower gardens and the most wonderful amusement park imaginable. To this day I can close my eyes and remember going through the turnstile at the gate, and the smell of the popcorn as we walked up the boardwalk, past the concessions and games, toward the old rickety wooden roller coaster and the flying biplanes. I can so clearly hear the "Carousel Waltz" streaming from the magnificent, ornate merry-go-round. I would rush to my favorite horse, and as the music accelerated, my heart would pound and the joy and laughter around me would blend in with the tempo of the music. This was, without a doubt, my happy place. Happy, carefree days, never to be forgotten.

As a child I also loved going to church because of the music. Even though I didn't know the words to the hymns, I would sing along and when the choir quit singing, you could clearly hear me belting my heart out, "Don't fence me in." Or I would loudly make my own request, "Play 'My Melancholy Baby' for me." The congregation loved that one!

    I sang and danced my way through high school in fabulous musical productions, having major roles in "Finian's Rainbow" and "Oklahoma." For my sixteenth birthday my mom bought me the sound track album from "Oklahoma." I still sing those songs that I so loved, and I'm magically transported back to the happy place of my youth.

    My kids grew up surrounded by music. I am a firm believer that happiness isn't a place or a thing, happiness is a state of mind, and music can definitely influence your state of mind. Singing "Swinging on a Star" to my boys when they were very young seemed to convince them that they should rather 'swing on a star' than to grow up to be a fish. They really believed that if they'd 'hate to go to school,' they may grow up to be a mule. And they knew for sure that if they 'wished upon a star,' anything their hearts desired would come their way. We sang a lot, we laughed a lot, it was truly my happy place.

    As the kids grew older I learned to love their rock and roll, and the wonderful music of Elvis and the Beatles. In the mid-70s one of my boys hid my Jim Croce eight-track tape, "Time in a Bottle," because they were so tired of hearing it. Now when I think of the words, "we never seem have enough time to do the things we want to do," it seems so relevant to our life today. The music of the 80s brings back treasured memories. My grandkids love that I enjoy rap, well *some* rap. The beat of rap music reminds me of the old minstrel music, and who can hear minstrel music without tapping to the beat and smiling.

    Just last week an old friend called me feeling down and kind of depressed about the pandemic and having to stay home and not seeing her family. I, without hesitation, started singing "When you're down and out, lift up your head and shout… it's gonna be a great day." She laughed, or I guess maybe if I could have seen her face it was a smirk and a sigh. After talking for a while and trying to cheer her up a little, we ended our conversation with me suggesting that she turn on some music and dance. About an hour later my phone rang and I answered it to hear, very loudly, Donna Fargo singing, "I'm the happiest girl in the whole USA." My friend thanked me and told me that her over-all attitude had improved. Of course I spent the rest of the day singing that darn song – I couldn't get it out of my mind.

    So after meditating and giving thanks every night before I go to bed, I calm my mind and soul with music. My husband always tells me, "Sweet dreams." The other night when I started humming, "Sweet dreams till sunbeams find you, sweet dreams that leave all worries behind you," he rolled over, gently kissed my cheek and softly whispered in my ear, "Please don't sing."

I drifted off to sleep knowing that music has always and will always be my happy place.

PET PEEVES

There are a lot of things going on in today's crazy world that can be particularly irritating. Everyone seemed to be annoyed and frustrated by having to stay quarantined during the COVID-19 pandemic and being told to wear a mask if we dared to go out in public. It was disappointing not being able to visit family and friends, and having to cancel our travel plans. Although this seems to be a personal vexation, I can't at this time refer to it as a pet peeve. It is only now a minor ordeal that I keep telling myself will eventually be eliminated. A pet peeve, on the other hand, is a form of constant irritation that you feel will never disappear. It is something that will bug you to the point of driving you nuts forever… or for as long as you let it.

I was raised with a firm belief in promptness. Being late for anything was never acceptable to me. I can remember arriving at the church just after Mass had started and refusing to enter. I waited in the vestibule until time for communion so that I could quietly sneak in to receive communion. I did not want anyone to ever see me arriving late. I considered it irresponsible, whereas some people think nothing of being 'stylishly' late. I cannot not tolerate tardiness. In all the years that I worked retail and had to punch a time clock, I never once punched in a minute late.

So, it sounds like people who are always late, or have no concern about the importance of being on time, would be one of my pet peeves, but on the contrary. I loathe being early, or anyone who doesn't respect a given set time of arrival. Nothing irritates me more. The sad fact is that I live with a man who thinks that being 'on time' means fifteen minutes to a half-an-hour early. This really drives me bonkers!

I should have known after our first date that it was in Larry's nature to be early. He arrived an hour before our set time. That was just plain RUDE! I had not showered and was sitting in front of a burned oven, trying to clean up the mess I had made baking an apple pie to impress him. His cheery greeting, "Oh, you're not ready yet?" certainly didn't make matters any better.

Shortly after we were married I invited Larry's parents to dinner. I, of course, wanted everything to be perfect. I planned to have the meal prepared and the table set before they arrived, not only to impress his somewhat snobbish mother, but also to allow time to visit. Although I planned dinner for six o'clock, I told her that we would eat at five-thirty. Well, surprise! They showed up at four o'clock. Again, I was not even dressed, had barely started cooking and was furious when they drove up. This happened several times over the years and each time I became even more irritated. I finally decided that I would tell her that dinner was an hour later than I actually planned it, hoping that would solve the problem. It was so frustrating for me to try to get things done with her following me around the kitchen and breathing down my neck. I hate anyone in the kitchen when I am cooking, that being my second pet peeve. I am sure she knew how upset it made me and I swear she did it intentionally.

Easter was our biggest celebration every year. With seven grown kids and quite a few grandkids, plus cousins, aunts and uncles and close friends, there was a lot of preparation for the event. One year I sent out Easter invitations to the whole family stating, "The Easter Bunny requests that you do not arrive before noon." My mother-in-law showed up at eleven o'clock.

For several years I did a home party plan sales job for Christmas Around the World. I would book parties for a given time and arrange with the hostess to arrive a half an hour early to set up for the party. Because I didn't ever want to be late, and not having GPS at that time, I would usually drive to my destination earlier than the scheduled time, find the location and then drive a block or so away and wait, so as not to be early. I could not bring myself to ring a doorbell one minute earlier than the time I said I would be there, knowing how irritating it would be to me if I were the hostess.

Well, it seems that time does not change people's ways, and over the years I have had to learn to tolerate my early bird husband's compulsion to be the first to arrive at any event. It has become quite a joke and really laughable between us. I have learned that when he tells me we have to be somewhere by four o'clock, that whatever the given occasion, it is more than likely scheduled for five o'clock. I now ask him what time we are going to leave the house. When given a specific time I plan accordingly. With half an hour or so to go, he begins to watch me carefully, because of course he has been ready for an hour. When I get to the point of combing my hair and applying lipstick, he rushes outside and starts the car. Now this can sometimes be fifteen minutes before the designated time agreed on, so I just let him sit with the engine running. When he gets upset I tell him that I thought he was just giving me time to call my friends!

What is the sense of arriving any place early? I can only think of the things I could be doing in that given time. So, that seems to be my biggest pet peeve. If the early bird gets the worm, good for him!

APRIL FOOLS' DAY

Because I wasn't quite sure of the meaning or origin of April Fools' Day, I had to do a little research. It turns out that this crazy day for nonsense has been observed for hundreds of years, but its origin still remains unknown. Some say that it was originally a celebration of the beginning of spring. The first day of April... a day set aside for practical jokes, hoaxes, pranks and belly laughs. A day to embrace all of the benefits of laughter, including stress relief. On the other hand, we might observe the negative view of this day, some describing it as 'creepy and manipulative,' 'rude' and a little bit 'nasty.' Some even say 'deceitful.' Sometimes stories intended as jokes are taken seriously. I, personally, do not like being teased or lead to believe that some false information is true. So, of course, April Fools' Day isn't one of my favorite days. With this being said, I have to admit that I have a few memories that do make me smile.

Growing up, my boys were always trying to come up with jokes or pranks to play on April 1st. My oldest son put ping-pong balls in the egg holder in the refrigerator when he was only about eight years old. I'm sure someone had to have given him the idea. I realized when I picked one up what it was, but watching the look of anticipation to my reaction on his face I had to pretend to be fooled as I tried to crack it. He squealed with joy, sharing the moment with his siblings. A couple of years later the boys decided it would be fun to put salt in the sugar bowl. Their dad drank his morning coffee with two teaspoons of sugar. They waited eagerly, with eyes wide, for him to take that first drink of coffee. As he spat all the way across the room they all, in unison, shouted, "April Fool." Thank goodness he was a man of good nature. As they were hooting and jumping up and down in sheer delight, he was trying as hard as he could to contain the grin on his face. He promised he'd get even... I don't know that he ever did.

When we were living in Hawaii my son Don and his friend, Joe, decided it would be a great prank to put a whole bottle of dish detergent in the fountain at Waikiki Beach. I probably wouldn't have ever known about it if it hadn't made the evening news. They were really proud of their madcap adventure, and could hardly wait to brag about their "Best April Fools' Day joke ever." I was just thankful that they didn't get caught.

My favorite April Fools' Day memory goes back to 1986. It happened to be a year when Easter was early. Easter is always the first Sunday after the first full moon of spring, so sometimes it falls in late March. My first granddaughter was born on Easter Sunday, March 26th, 1978. In the year 1986, Easter Sunday was on March 30th. I remember this well as I make candy every year for Easter and my co-workers always looked forward to the treat. I had leftover chocolate so I dreamed up what I thought would be a great April Fools' joke. My boss was always so impressed with my hand-dipped chocolates. Why not make him a special batch of his own? Knowing that he didn't like dill pickles I cut the ends off of several pickles, shook them in cornstarch and dipped them in chocolate. I made up a plate of light and dark chocolate and beautiful pastel colors to take to him on April 1st. My co-workers were all aware of what I had done. It was really too funny not to share with them. I left the gift on his desk when I got to work, and went about my day. An hour passed and we were all sharing the excitement and giggling about what his reaction would be to my devious prank. And then, loud and clear over the PA system, we heard his stern voice, "Ruth, may I see you in the break room?" I felt a little flutter in my stomach, imagining what was about to happen, but nothing could have prepared me for his retaliation. As I flung open the swinging door leading to the back room of the store, a blast of cold water hit me straight on. He had hooked a hose up to the sink and put a sprinkler nozzle on it and had it aimed directly at the door as I came through. As I shuffled backwards, squealing, I could hear the bark of laughter and loud "April Fool" behind me. I was stuttering, speechless, as I realized the joke was on me! Once the initial shock had passed and I stood dripping wet, I mustered up a stiff smile in an effort not to lose my composure completely. John had a really good belly laugh, shared with all of the employees, and then sent me home to change clothes. I had to promise him that I would never make 'special' candy for him again. This event was jovially recounted every year for as long as I worked there. I retired from Rite-Aid in 2003.

April Fools' Day was canceled for the first time ever in 2020 because everything after March of that year was a prank. April 1st... just like any other day, believe in nothing and trust no one.

2020 REVISITED

I had hopes that 2020 would be the year that I got everything I wanted. Now I know that 2020 was the year that I learned to appreciate everything that I have.

We had exciting travel plans arranged for the whole year, beginning with a train trip to Truckee in March to meet with my niece and her family who were coming from Hawaii. We planned to attend a huge bingo blow-out in Las Vegas in April, followed by a week in Utah to visit Zion, Arches, and Bryce Canyon National Parks. The last week of April would find us in Palm Springs, where I would meet my son for a trip to Mexico by way of Yuma, Arizona, to visit my daughter, granddaughter and great-grandson. In September we had planned a train trip to Chicago, then on to Charlottesville, Knoxville and a week in the great Smokey Mountains. After a stop-over in Dollywood, we would rent a car and drive to Georgia and Alabama, to visit friends, and then on to Branson, Missouri, for a week of flea markets, antiquing and great entertainment. What's the old saying, "The best laid plans of mice and men...?" As disappointing as all of the cancellations were, I could say that we begrudgingly survived, but the truth is that we actually enjoyed taking a break from all the hassle of packing, rushing from train to hotel, finding a decent restaurant and paying too much for a meal we didn't really enjoy, and then wishing that we were home in our own bed at the end of the day. I guess you might say our nine-month 'stay-cation' proved to be not only enjoyable, but relaxing and very soul searching. Oh, sure, the Hawaiian Cruise that we had planned for a year would be great, but it takes us right back to telling each other, "been there, done that, let's put that money toward feeding a needy family, or two." We have found so much satisfaction in doing just that.

Bored? Depressed? Cabin Fever? For some reason none of that applied in our case. I realize that not being alone helps considerably, and I am thankful every day to have someone to share the frustration and loneliness that comes with quarantine. Even though we hadn't eaten out in over a year we were not feeling deprived. In fact, we were enjoying trying new recipes and taking turns cooking. To our surprise the time passed quickly. Guess that happens when you get old! We laughed a lot. For some reason things that might have aggravated one of us back in the 'normal' good ol' days took on humor. Misplacing things, dropping eggs, leaving the bathroom water running, forgetting names, all of these things that would have left us frustrated, seemed to be laughable. Our daily morning therapy seemed to set the pace of our day. Our therapy consists of the best two out of three games each of dominoes, Farkle and Yammy Slam. Playing for a nickel a point doesn't seem like much of a gamble, but I lost $206.00 in a year. Thank goodness we're not playing for a quarter a point! No, I'm not ready to quit yet, with a little luck I might just catch up… ha, ha! I never give up hope!

    We are thankful every day that we stayed healthy throughout the pandemic and that our family was not adversely affected. It is heartwarming to see families become closer due to the fact that they had to spend so much time together, getting to know each other. I have seen and heard stories of how children are learning the meaning of compassion. A little eight-year-old girl, named Haley, in Chicago, asked her mother if she could sell the bracelets that she was making for two-dollars each to buy food for some of the kids in her school. Her mother put it on social media and Haley raised over $25,000 for their local food-bank. It is amazing to me that one child can make such a difference in these trying times and be such a role model for other kids.

    As in any bad situation, we do have the choice to complain, bitch and moan or to look at some positive aspect, as hard as that may seem. The little things that we have always seemed to take for granted; a beautiful sunset, the smell of freshly baked bread, a walk in the park, a drive to the lake, all of these and more, seemed to take on new meaning during quarantine. Why had I never noticed that you can actually see a smile in someone's eyes, even though their face is masked? How had I not realized that every word of appreciation I ever spoke was a simple prayer? When did I admit to myself that without the grace of God, I could not know this peace of mind during such a tumultuous time? I have always prayed. I pray for peace, I pray daily for my family and friends, I pray for patience and good health, but my prayers seemed to have more of an ongoing, personal conversation with my higher power. "Are you talking to yourself?" would come a voice from the other room. "No, just searching for an answer, or guidance." I noticed that I was more thankful every day for the little things that I have always taken for granted. Meditation seemed to come easier for some reason and I gained a peace of mind that I had not known in my busy day to day life.

So, in looking at the bright side of 2020, I realized that I could no longer ignore the fear and horror that we all face daily. It was devastating to watch the death toll rise every day, every hour, knowing that each person who passed could have possibly had a longer, healthy life if not for the horrific pandemic. Knowing that every one of those fatalities was someone's mother, father, grandparent, sibling, spouse or child brought me to tears almost every day. It was difficult to watch the shootings and rioting and the fires and tropical storms that claimed peoples' homes and lives. Being aware that people had lost their jobs, businesses had to close and kids could not attend school all added to the disparagement. The political unrest in our country tore us apart and divided our nation.

Something that I read shortly after the outbreak of COVID-19 seemed to help me cope through all of the trying times. I don't know who wrote it, but I think it's worth repeating: "On this road called life… you have to take the good with the bad, smile when you're sad, love what you have, and remember what you had. Always forgive, but never forget, learn from your mistakes. People change. Things go wrong. But just remember, the ride goes on."

So, having made it through the worst of the pandemic, let's try to just be kind to each other, laugh at the confusion, smile through the tears and keep reminding ourselves what Charlie Brown said: "Keep looking up… that's the secret of life."

MY OBITUARY

PROLOGUE:

As the bells of St. Mary's church in Butte, Montana, chimed the Angeles at 7:00 AM on Tuesday, April 16, 1940, Ruth Agnes Keane made her grand debut onto the stage of life. Let the show begin.

ACT 1:

Being the youngest of four children of Mary Phoebe Young and John Francis Keane, Ruth was welcomed joyously by her older sisters, Donna Marie and Mary Frances, and her only brother and dearest life-long friend, Jeremiah Joseph. Growing up in Butte, Ruth danced her way onto local stages, appearing in dance recitals, musicals, talent shows, and an Irish dance troupe, which entertained throughout the state every year in March to celebrate St. Patrick's Day. She loved to dance and dreamed of someday being on Broadway. She was devastated to learn, at age twelve, that you have to be five foot six inches tall to qualify for the Radio City Music Hall Rockettes.

Set the Scene for ACT 2:

Ruth met and married Patrick O'Neill when he was home on leave from the Navy in August of 1957. Now the world would be her stage, as her gypsy soul was given the opportunity to travel. July of 1958 brought joy when first son, Patrick Timothy, was born in Norman, Oklahoma. Seventeen months later, Donald George joined the troupe, making his debut in San Juan, Puerto Rico, in December of 1959. In August of 1963 a new cast member was added when Raymond Russell arrived on board in Portsmouth, Virginia. The prima-donna, Maureen Therese, was the final cast member, appearing on stage in November of 1965 in Philadelphia, Pennsylvania.

ACT 2 – SCENE 1:

The show was on the road, literally. After traveling from the East Coast to Washington State and doing a three-year stint in Hawaii, Ruth found herself not only the director of the family show, but the producer, the choreographer, the promoter and the financier when her co-star decided this was just not his gig, and bowed out. But, the show must go on. Ruth seemed to find humor in even the most serious situations and always found something to laugh about. Her smile was sometimes her only salvation and she always told her children, "If you see someone without a smile, give him yours." Her theme song was, "Smile, though your heart is aching, smile even though it's breaking"… and she did.

ACT 2 – SCENE 2:

Cub Scouts, baseball, swimming lessons, working full time and raising four kids, with her sidekick niece, Sheri, being her only supporting actor, kept her not only busy, but constantly striving to make life better for all of them. Keep smiling she reminded herself often, your audience deserves an award winning performance. The critics were much easier on her than she was on herself.

ACT 3 – SCENE 1:

Enter stage left, Larry VanDyke, a new leading man, along with his troupe of three, Larry Jay, Alan and Julie. As Anne Murray sang, "You Needed Me," Larry held Ruth up and gave her strength to carry on again. A new lease on life, a new home, stability, a new chapter, so many new adventures to look forward to. There was fun and laughter, along with much pain and heartache. Watching the children grow into adults, the wonderful joy of becoming grandparents and the opportunity to travel the world, made for a story-book life.

ACT 3 – SCENE 2: THE TRAGEDY

The plot of this scene was difficult and very sad, something that the heroine was never able to get over. Losing a child is, as any parent who has been through this knows, the most devastating thing life can hand you. Losing her grandson, Bryan, and sons, Alan, Patrick, and Donald, was unbearable, but life had to go on. And, so it did. A long, happy and healthy life.

Ruth took her final curtain call on this stage of life on _____,… leaving this closing monologue.

MONOLOGUE:

To my soul-mate, my children, grandchildren, nephews and nieces,
And all of my wonderful friends,
I leave you with a legacy
I hope will never end.
My love and thanks to all of you,
The good and the bad you saw me through.
May the memories of the smiles and laughter
Live in your hearts forever after.

FINAL CURTAIN

ABOUT THE AUTHOR

Ruth VanDyke is a published poet and the author of an autobiographical cook book, "Memories With Recipes". This heartwarming collection of true short stories of her life, simply entitled "Memories", is sprinkled with humor and tears and filled with exciting adventures from her travels over six decades. Her style of writing has been compared to the late Erma Bombeck. You can join her daily as she posts recipes, short stories and poetry on her popular BLOG, "Ruth's Food for Thought".

www.ingramcontent.com/pod-product-compliance
Lightning Source LLC
Chambersburg PA
CBHW071958110526
44592CB00012B/1128